The Daily Telegraph

BEST
FLOWERS

TO GROW AND CUT

DAVID JOYCE

The Daily Telegraph

BEST
FLOWERS
TO GROW AND CUT

FRANCES LINCOLN

CONTENTS

Frances Lincoln Ltd
4 Torriano Mews
Torriano Avenue
London NW5 2RZ

A catalogue record for this book is available from the British Library.

ISBN 0 7112 2366 1
Printed and bound in Singapore

1 2 3 4 5 6 7 8 9

To the memory of Frances Lincoln,
with admiration and gratitude

HALF-TITLE PAGE
Magnolia × loebneri 'Leonard Messel'

OPPOSITE TITLE PAGE
Tulipa 'Groenland'

INTRODUCTION

Fascination with the mysterious and enormously varied beauty of flowers is one of the great constants in the sometimes brutal relationship between human beings and the natural world. How soon after the development of the first human settlements plants were cultivated for their ornamental rather than their practical value is not quite clear, but certainly at a very distant period gardens were being made using plants chosen for the sensuous and aesthetic qualities of their flowers. In continuing the activity of garden-making today we are faced with an astonishing range of plants. The aim of this book is to help gardeners make choices by presenting a selection of outstanding plants in a way that reveals their defining ornamental qualities.

To Charles Darwin, the great nineteenth-century naturalist, the origin of flowering plants was 'an abominable mystery'. Although much has been learned about their evolution in the last 150 years, gaps in the fossil evidence still leave many questions unanswered. There is broad agreement, however, that early flowering plants appeared in the Cretaceous period, about 100 million years ago, and that by the end of the Cretaceous period, some 45 million years ago, they dominated the earth's vegetation. Flowering plants have proved so remarkably adaptable that today they are to be found in almost every corner of the world, pushing even into the fringes of the harshest deserts of rock and sand or ice and snow.

In their appearance flowering plants are enormously varied, ranging from tall trees, such as some of the finest magnolias, to mere hummocks and mats, among them tiny perennials and shrubs that have adapted to life in alpine conditions. Their flowers – the feature that distinguishes them from other plants such as ferns and conifers – are even more remarkable in their variety than the general appearance of the plants; so much so, in fact, that it is difficult to believe that the function of all flowers is essentially the same. Their consistent role in the life of

◀ Sumptuous Oriental poppies (*Papaver orientale*) are set against flowers of markedly different character and ample foliage to make a garden of lasting appeal.

plants is to present their sexual organs in such a way that pollination will occur, leading to the production of seed that will perpetuate the species. To succeed in this purpose, the vast majority of flowers rely on an intimate association with a range of pollinators, usually insects, or even with one pollinator quite specific to the plant. This intimacy, honed by the evolutionary crafting of both flowers and pollinators, sees that the pollinator, be it insect, bird or even bat, responds to the flowers' signals and triggers what in many cases is an exquisite mechanism of pollination, and is rewarded with food, mainly in the form of pollen and nectar.

Flowers and their pollinators are bound together by biological imperatives. The intimacy between humans and flowers that is such a striking and deep-rooted feature of almost all cultures is quite different. At a prosaic level it arises from the medicinal and culinary value attributed to certain flowers. Saffron (*Crocus sativus*) is a case in point. Today, as in ancient times, the dried stigmas of this autumn-flowering crocus are valued as a flavouring and colouring. More elevated are the religious and symbolic dimensions to our relationship with flowers. Now, as in the past, flowers are widely used as offerings in religious ceremonies and as tokens of respect, friendship and love. The desire to create living collections of flowers, in the form of gardens, is an expression of the most genial relationship human beings have forged with the natural world. Reverence and sentiment may play a part in our attachment to flowers but it is through their astonishingly varied sensual and aesthetic qualities that they have a hold on the affection of gardeners. It is these qualities that are the particular focus of this book and my aim is to present them in a way that avoids reliance on the technical vocabulary of botany.

HOW THIS BOOK IS ORGANIZED

There are 250 entries in the book, led by a key plant that is a well-established classic or promises to become a classic of the future because of the quality of its flowers. Some, such as as the elegant perennial from China, Korea and Siberia known among other names as bleeding heart (*Dicentra spectabilis*), are species that are as beautiful in the garden as they are in the wild. Some are plants that have been raised and selected in cultivation. Falling into this category are the various cultivated varieties or cultivars of the popular spring-flowering hyacinth (*Hyacinthus orientalis*). Many are hybrids,

mainly the result of crosses made intentionally or by chance between closely related plants growing in cultivation. For example, of the many roses in cultivation, most are hybrids; this is true even of those that have been in cultivation for centuries. As one would expect of good garden plants, the majority of those included are widely available from garden centres and large nurseries. The few that are relatively uncommon are worth seeking out from specialist growers. These are people who really do know about the plants they are selling and their advice on new introductions and alternatives is always worth taking on board.

Conventional encyclopedias or directories often group plants according to their life cycle (annuals and biennials, perennials and so on) or pattern of growth (trees, climbers, ground cover). Here, in order to underline the hallmark quality of their flowers, the plants are grouped according to well-defined characteristics of shape, texture, colour, conspicuous markings, scent and the arrangement of flowers on the plant. Headings referring to the structure of flowers take account of simple and elaborated shapes and also conspicuous details of form. There are also headings for textures, colours, conspicuous markings and scents. Sections within the main groupings pick up features that make an immediate impact on the non-specialist. As well as a description of the key plant, most entries contain information about close relatives of the key plant that share the highlighted feature. In addition, each section includes a short list of other good garden plants with flowers that display the specified characteristic or characteristics.

The organization of entries by easily appreciated characteristics reveals my own take on the ornamental quality of flowers. Much more importantly, it also allows me to share my enthusiasm for their qualities as good garden plants and, in many cases, excellent material for cutting.

THE FLOWER GARDEN

No single way provides the ultimate solution to assembling plants in a garden so that their flowers are seen to best effect. Cultural, aesthetic, social and economic factors all influence the way gardens are conceived. Location, climate and soil impose limitations. The choice of plants that can be readily obtained is another factor. In casting the spotlight on new plants and new trends in gardening, the extensive coverage of gardening in the media may provide the dithering gardener with a clinching inspiration. But it is as well to keep an independent mind: an original and interesting garden stands above fashion, a modest version of paradise to which any gardener can aspire.

Gardens of the past provide modern gardeners with many stimulating ideas but it is neither desirable nor practicable to follow historical models to the letter. In the nineteenth century the introduction of new plants and the large-scale development of glasshouses gave an impetus to formal gardening using massed planting to produce blocks or distinctive patterns of colour. Certain kinds of plants lend themselves to scaled-down versions of grand bedding, notably tulips in spring and, in summer, various long-flowering half-hardy annuals and even roses, the most suitable being the Floribundas; and the bold effects of these broad-brush schemes can be highly effective, especially in an architectural framework. But the downside is that the individual qualities of plants are subordinated to the overall effect.

One of the classic expressions of flower gardening is the herbaceous border. This is traditionally a large rectangular plot, frequently one of a pair, in which mainly perennial plants are to some extent graded by height, the tallest at the back, and often also arranged according to various colour themes. A well-planned and well-maintained herbaceous border presents a magnificent and varied spectacle at its summer peak. It is not, however, a way of assembling plants that can be recommended for a small garden or even one of moderate size planted and managed by a single person or couple in their spare time. It was, after all, a form of gardening perfected during the early twentieth century in large country properties with many gardeners. It requires a certain scale, it needs a setting in which there are other areas of interest for the many months when the herbaceous border is flowerless, and there are periods when it is very labour intensive.

In Britain, the cottage garden is a recurrent theme and as both myth and reality has itself been an important influence on the herbaceous border. In the commonly accepted version the garden is laid out in beds but the emphasis is on plants rather than the way they are organized. The selection of ornamentals is on the conservative side, old roses, common shrubs, perennials and annuals – many, such as pinks, to which gardeners have long been sentimentally attached – vying for space with herbs, vegetables, fruit trees and bushes. The concentration on a particular repertoire of plants gives the cottage garden its character but is also a limitation.

For many gardeners with medium-sized plots planting a catholic collection of plants in mixed borders has proved the best way of creating a garden that is relatively easy to maintain and interesting throughout the year. Such plantings are not labour free but gardeners can so plan them that they can enjoy the work involved without becoming their garden's slave. The mature garden usually has one or two trees and a good clothing of climbers trained on vertical surfaces but the dominant plants in borders, which may be formal or informal in shape, are shrubs and perennials, with bulbs, annuals, grasses and ferns playing lesser but important roles. In the early stages more weight may be given to annuals and bulbs, which are useful fillers, as are fast-growing shrubs, while slower-growing plants develop. In such borders foliage, stems and fruit count for more than they do in the herbaceous border, not just because of their ornamental value but also because good leafy cover inhibits the growth of weeds. Gardeners sometimes fear that a generous use of foliage will dilute the effect of flowers, but if it does, it is generally for the better.

Mixed borders can be colour themed but in general it is more important to concentrate on establishing a rhythm of plant growth and flower production that runs throughout the year. Where the climate allows, start with winter-flowering shrubs such as *Viburnum × bodnantense* and the earliest bulbs. Extend summer into autumn with late perennials, such as many of the asters. In between, contrive climaxes that result from the happy coincidence of neighbouring plants in flower, even if the combination is as common as tulips and forget-me-nots. The case for choosing plants with a long flowering season is strong, especially when the aim is to keep a small garden colourful for many months. So too is that for including plants that repeat, whose season can in many cases be extended by the regular removal of spent flowers. However in some instances outstanding qualities may fully justify choosing plants that have a very short flowering season. For example, some of the crocuses are at their peak for a short period only but they are worth planting because they are so early. Although their display is fugitive, the globular flowers of *Paeonia mlokosewitschii* are of such rare beauty and the whole plant so distinctive that it deserves to be widely grown.

Choose woody shrubs that will not need frequent cutting back in order to be contained in the space available. Many shrubs and trees, including magnolias, require only minimal pruning to establish and maintain a well-balanced specimen. The flower production of other shrubs can be enhanced by the way they are pruned. Two broad generalizations cover a wide range of shrubs. Those that flower in spring and early summer usually do so on wood produced in the previous year. Cutting out a proportion of the old wood immediately after flowering will encourage the production of new wood that will bear flowers the following year. Shrubs where this is appropriate include deutzias and mock oranges (*Philadelphus*). Shrubs that flower in late summer and early autumn usually do so on wood produced in the current season. Removal of a proportion of the old wood in early spring will encourage new growth that will flower later. Cultivars of *Buddleja davidii*, for example, are best cut right back to a low framework.

For annuals and perennials think big before thinking small. Excessive use of compact and dwarf cultivars, disproportionately numerous in garden centres and nurseries, can create a grotesque toyland effect. However, it is best to avoid the tallest of the perennials and annuals, such as many of the delphiniums, which are prone to wind damage, particularly in an exposed garden, as staking is a laborious chore.

In a large garden it is worth devoting an area to ornamentals for cutting, with the plants in lines so that they are easy to reach. Although it will be plundered regularly, such an area need not be unattractive. Planting a few bushy plants for foliage, including – where the climate is mild enough – coppiced eucalypts, helps to give substance to a cutting garden. If your garden is small or medium-sized and cutting material is part of your display you will need to collect carefully, taking blooms from several plants rather than a single plant to make up a bunch and wherever possible choosing flowers from the back or sides rather than the front. With a limited number of plants from which to cut you will probably find that you have to make up mixed arrangements. A casual medley can be hugely successful – close inspection usually reveals that a deliberate or unconscious process of selection has modified the apparent randomness. It may be that there is a good proportion of foliage,

offsetting or enhancing difficult colours. Intermediate shades may help to bridge warring colours. And sometimes the shock of the unexpected is enough to make acceptable a daring association of colours that goes beyond crude confrontation.

WORKING WITH THE GRAIN

For plants to grow well and flower generously they need to be growing in conditions that suit them. Even easy-going plants have optimum conditions. In this book the information given at the head of each entry gives a quick guide to the conditions in which the key plant will perform well and the approximate dimensions of mature specimens. Speed of growth and ultimate size will depend in part on the growing conditions. In addition, all the plants are given a hardiness rating. (For a key to hardiness zones, see p.175.)

The hardiness of a plant limits where it can be grown year-round out-of-doors. Many plants that are tropical or subtropical or come from areas with a Mediterranean climate are half-hardy or tender. These are likely to be killed or seriously damaged by frost. Even in parts of the world that have harsh winters numerous half-hardy or tender plants are grown outdoors in the summer. They can be treated as annuals and thrown away after one season, or else overwintered under glass, either as fully grown plants or as rooted cuttings. Many who garden in temperate regions find the challenge of growing plants of borderline hardiness irresistible. If planted in particularly favourable conditions, for example in the microclimate that exists at the base of or near a warm wall, relatively tender plants may come through a winter successfully. With these borderline cases there is, however, always a risk of loss and it generally pays to back up by overwintering rooted cuttings under glass.

All green plants must have light. It is the source of energy which, through photosynthesis, is fundamental to plants' growth and to almost all life. However, the light requirements of plants vary considerably (for garden hybrids and cultivars as well as species) and in their natural habitat plants' adaptations to specific light levels are very clear. Plants that demand an open position and full light include quick-growing annuals and compact alpine plants. In a temperate climate relatively few flowering plants tolerate deep shade but a large number are well adapted to

▲ The coneflowers (*Echinacea*) and many sea hollies (*Eryngium*) are sun-loving plants well suited to free-draining soil.

the dappled shade of the woodland edge or glade and some, such as snowdrops (*Galanthus*) and primroses (*Primula vulgaris*), which develop and flower before the canopy is in full leaf, will tolerate quite dense shade in late spring and summer. Sun-loving plants grown in shade are likely to be lank and flower poorly. Shade-tolerant plants are generally more versatile and can often be grown successfully in open positions provided they get adequate moisture.

Water plays a vital role in the life of plants. It provides hydrogen, essential for photosynthesis, it transports soluble nutrients within the plant and it helps to give a plant rigidity. It accounts for up to 95 per cent of a plant's weight. Water is lost through transpiration and has to be replaced by what is absorbed by the roots. Windy conditions greatly speed up the rate at which water is lost. Plants are adapted in varying degrees to dry conditions or to a

superabundance of water. At one extreme there are plants that grow in deserts where in many years the rainfall may be negligible. At the other are plants that relish permanently wet boggy conditions or those, such as the waterlilies (*Nymphaea*), that flourish even in a fair depth of water. The supply of moisture available to plants is partly determined by rainfall but also strongly influenced by the structure of the soil. Water is not retained by sandy and gravelly soils but is slow to drain away on clay soils. All soils can be improved, particularly by the addition of well-rotted organic matter (most cheaply available by recycling garden and kitchen waste through a compost heap), which will also maintain the structure; but the underlying structure will remain a factor to be reckoned with. My selection of plants covers a good range of plants for dry and moist conditions. To say that a plant needs moist but well-drained soil may at first sight seem contradictory. In fact a large number of plants require a regular supply of moisture but also need air at the roots and will not thrive or even survive if the ground water is stagnant.

For plants to make strong growth they need mineral nutrients as well as water. The ornamental garden does not require the force-feeding that may be necessary in the kitchen garden. The regular addition of well-rotted organic matter will top up the nutrients taken out by plant growth. Balanced organic and inorganic fertilizers are useful for boosting nutrient levels in the container garden and to a lesser extent in the open garden. In standard formulations of fertilizer the proportions of nitrogen, phosphate and potassium are usually the same, seven parts per hundred of each. In formulations designed to encourage the production of flowers the phosphate level is slightly higher.

Successful plant growth is also determined by another aspect of soil chemistry. Some soils are extremely acidic, others markedly alkaline and most fall somewhere between. The acidity or alkalinity of a soil is measured in pH degrees. A pH value of 7 is neutral. Above that the soil is alkaline, below it acidic. Most plants do well in a neutral to slightly acidic soil (pH 6), a number tolerate both markedly acidic and alkaline conditions, and several important groups of ornamentals are lime-hating – that is, intolerant of alkaline soils. Ericaceous plants, including heaths, heathers and rhododendrons, are a major group of lime-hating plants. By far the most straightforward approach if your soil is alkaline, as it will be if you garden on chalk, is to accept its limitations and enjoy the wonderful plants that are tolerant of lime. If you are determined to work against the grain the best solution is to grow lime-haters in raised beds or containers using an ericaceous compost.

Thorough preparation of the ground, including the removal of perennial weeds, provides the essential conditions for vigorous plant growth. Many flowering plants, such as alliums and sea hollies (*Eryngium*), do not need heavy feeding. ▶

SIMPLE
SHAPES

In the context of this book, to describe flowers
as simple is an aesthetic judgment, not a
botanical comment. And yet in their clean lines
and unelaborated forms many flowers of
cultivated plants are close to plants that are
sometimes described as primitive because of
their open structure and straightforward method
of pollination. In some cases wild plants of
ancient ancestry have made the transition from
prairie, meadow or woodland to garden plot
with apparent ease. Many more garden plants
are the result of selection and breeding, often
with the essential qualities of the flower
retained, perhaps even enhanced. With their
lack of pretension, their fine proportions and
their elegance, all these flowers have the power
to please. Some are so exquisite or magnificent
that they rank among the supreme beauties of
nature and the garden.

Various Asiatic lily species have been used in the breeding of magnificent summer-
flowering hybrids with trumpet-shaped and usually scented flowers. The tall-
growing Pink Perfection Group is suitable for borders, for planting among shrubs
and for containers. The stout stems, each carrying several nodding flowers, are
superb for cutting.

SIMPLE SHAPES

Since the discovery in the eighteenth century that flowers are the sexual organs of plants, much scientific study has focused on their structures, which are key features in their classification. In their scale and outward form flowers are enormously varied and the mechanisms by which they ensure pollination (in most cases cross-pollination) run the gamut from the relatively straightforward to the preposterously ingenious. These are the result of evolutionary processes in the world's flora that have taken millions of years. By comparison, changes brought about by the cultivation, selection and breeding of plants have occurred in a relatively short period. In the case of many ornamentals the exploitation of a naturally occurring mutation has been very rapid. Some of the finest plants we grow for the ornamental value of their flowers are part of the world's wild flora. They provide points of reference against which we tend to measure flowers that are the result of cultivation: these are usually larger, more brightly coloured and more extravagantly shaped.

DECEPTIVELY SIMPLE

Flowers with relatively few petals generally convey an impression of simplicity, although this can be misleading. This is so with the crucifers (*Brassicaceae*, formerly *Cruciferae*), mainly annuals, biennials and perennials, which make up a large family that includes such important food plants as cabbages and some popular ornamentals. The most easily recognizable and constant feature of their flower structure is that there are eight segments arranged in two whorls, the inner whorl of four petals arranged in a cross constricted at the base by the four outer segments, the sepals. In fact, because the sepals are elongated and held tightly together, the flowers of many crucifers – wallflowers (*Erysimum*), for example – are tube-like and their plentiful supply of nectar accessible only to relatively long-tongued insects. Crucifers of ornamental value make an impact because, as with aubrietas, they produce flowers in great quantity and sometimes, as with wallflowers, are well scented.

At the least, many flowers with only three petals have a curiosity value. A few are of exceptional beauty, among them the wake robin (*Trillium grandiflorum*), a woodland perennial from eastern North America that excels as a garden plant in shade where the soil is moist and lime free. The flowers of the wake robin consist of six segments arranged in two whorls of three, the petals brilliant white, the three sepals small, green and leaf-like.

An arrangement of six segments divided into two distinct groups is the underlying structure of other flowers with three petals. All members of the iris family have six segments, and in the genus *Iris* they are arranged in two groups of markedly different appearance, the outer three each partially covered by a crest and horizontal or angled upwards, the inner segments upright. Iris relatives typifying the arrangement of floral segments in two sets of three, one set more conspicuous than the other, include the showy *Tigridia pavonia* and various species of *Libertia*.

RECEPTACLE SHAPES

Many flowers of great ornamental value are easily related to the textbook cross-section illustrating various floral parts: radially symmetrical flowers with well-defined segments surrounding the sexual parts of the flower, the overall shape suggesting a receptacle. The hardy geraniums, with saucer-shaped flowers in which the sepals and petals are arranged in fives, are good examples. Most have several qualities that make them good garden plants: tolerance of a range of growing conditions, excellent foliage, good ground-covering ability and nice balance between flowers and foliage. What clinches their popularity is the simple frankness, the direct appeal of the open saucers.

Other annuals and herbaceous plants with saucer-shaped to globular flowers include various poppies (among them species of *Meconopsis* and *Papaver*), many members of the buttercup family (*Ranunculaceae*), including moisture-loving globe flowers (*Trollius*), and peonies. A large number of the hybrid perennial peonies and also forms of the tree peonies (cultivars of *P. suffruticosa*) have double flowers and the proliferation of the petals obscures the simple form. These doubles have the advantage of being longer lasting than the singles but Mollie-the-witch (*P. mlokosewitschii*) and several other species are of a poignantly fleeting beauty that puts them in a class of their own.

The tulips are among the most valuable of all the spring-flowering bulbs and countless hybrids have been raised since the first bulbs were sent from Turkey to Europe in the sixteenth century. Some of the species have quite starry flowers but most of the hybrids are of bowl, cup or globular shape. The consistency and reliability of the hybrids and their generous forms, showing off well their extraordinary colour range, have made them the most popular of all spring bedding plants and also favourite cut flowers. More elegant in form than the majority are those belonging to the Lily-flowered Group. The goblet-shaped flowers have pointed segments that are slightly pinched near their mid-point and then curve out. They make an excellent contrast to tulips of more dumpy shape.

There are few flowering shrubs and trees that are more magnificent than the magnolias. They belong to a family that is regarded by many botanists as the most primitive of those living today but the species as well as the hybrids have large showy flowers. Some, including *Magnolia stellata*, have starry flowers but many other magnolias have flowers suggesting upright well-proportioned vessels.

NARROW AND TAPERED SHAPES

From the first daffodils of early spring, through the crescendo of lilies at the height of summer and until the last nerines of autumn, trumpet flowers play an important part in the ornamental garden. The trumpet shape is best not defined too closely, for it transmutes effortlessly into a funnel or even a tube. Because of their bold form, trumpet and funnel flowers – whether nodding, outward-facing or upturned – stand out well against foliage and the massed effect of small flowers in the garden or in a vase.

All the narcissi have a corona, an outgrowth from the petal-like segments, but this can vary from a small cup to a long trumpet and in some cultivars is split. The common name 'daffodil' is usually applied only to those narcissi with a trumpet that is as long or longer than the surrounding segments. In the course of the last 400 years or so vast numbers of hybrids have been produced, many breeders putting a premium on sheer size. A recent trend favours some of the species and the smaller hybrids, particularly the well-proportioned Cyclamineus daffodils (derived from the *Narcissus cyclamineus*) with trumpets thrusting forward from swept-back segments.

The lilies (and their close relatives such as *Cardiocrinum giganteum*) with trumpet- or funnel-shaped flowers are among the most splendid bulbs of the summer garden and make superb flowers for containers and for cutting. They go well with many perennials and shrubs, most doing best with the base of the plant in shade. They can be attacked by various pests and diseases. Viruses, for example, cause distortion and loss of vigour on affected plants. Control of aphids and other sucking pests reduces the risk of virus attack.

The luminously beautiful trumpet gentians are on a much smaller scale, although the flowers are large for the size of the plants. An intriguing feature of many, including *G. sino-ornata*, is that panels in the side of the trumpet serve as windows, providing light for pollinating bees extracting nectar from a deep-set ring of narrow tubes – like the chambers of a revolver – and picking up copious quantities of pollen in the process.

HANGING FLOWERS

A number of popular ornamentals have hanging flowers that are more or less bell-shaped, often with the segments joined. The campanulas, commonly known as bellflowers, provide many examples, some with the bells extended into rather narrow tubes, some rather broad and saucer-shaped. In the down-turned flower the sexual parts are to some extent protected and the inversion goes some way to concealing the nectar. In the case of bellflowers some pollinators may be discouraged but not various bees, which are especially attracted to blue, a predominate colour in the campanulas.

Among bulbous plants, the fritillaries are a particularly interesting group of plants (see also p.38) with bell-shaped flowers. The most impressive species, the crown imperial (*Fritillaria imperialis*), was introduced to European gardens from Turkey in the late sixteenth century and immediately recognized as a plant of distinction. The orange or yellow bells, clustered at the top of a stout stem beneath a curious tuft of leaves, are made up of six more-or-less equal segments, each having at its base a glistening nectary to attract insect pollinators. The herbalist John Gerard described these as 'resembling in shew faire orient pearles'. According to legend, of all the flowers lining the route to Calvary, only the crown imperial failed to bow to the cross-laden figure of Christ. Repenting of its arrogance, the plant has ever since remained bowed, its flowers heavy with unshed tears.

THREESOMES & FOURSOMES

The simple arrangement of flower parts in threes looks unusual and can be deceptive, for it is commonly two sets of three, one more conspicuous than the other. The cross arrangement of four petals is more straightforward and often pleases because the flowers are unpretentious and produced in great quantity.

Aubrieta 'Doctor Mules'

Evergreen perennial H 10cm/4in, S 60cm/2ft Z7

Full sun Well-drained, preferably alkaline, soil

Numerous forms and hybrids of *Aubrieta deltoidea* are popular and easy rock garden perennials. The small four-petalled flowers, borne in profusion over several weeks in spring, almost hide the mat of hairy wedge-shaped leaves. *A.* 'Doctor Mules' is an old favourite with violet-purple flowers. More recent hybrids include the richly coloured 'Greencourt Purple' and others in shades of blue, red and pink. In some, for example the blue-flowered 'Silberrand', variegation brightens the foliage in summer. The simple cross is obscured in floriferous doubles, such as the mauve 'Joy'.

All are seen to best advantage cascading from a ledge or spilling from a crevice. To keep compact, trim immediately after flowering.

Erysimum 'Bowles' Mauve'

Evergreen subshrubby perennial H 75cm/30in, S 60cm/2ft Z8

Full sun Well-drained, preferably alkaline, soil

This grey-green shrubby wallflower is usually short-lived and lacks the blissful scent of its relatives grown as biennial bedding plants, but over several months, from as early as late winter, it produces numerous short spikes packed with cross-shaped rich mauve flowers. It combines well with sun-loving Mediterranean plants. Take softwood cuttings in spring or summer to maintain stocks.

See also *Erysimum cheiri*, p.145, and *E.* 'John Codrington', p.116.

Tradescantia Andersoniana Group

Perennial H 50cm/20in, S 60cm/2ft Z7

Sun or partial shade Moist but well-drained soil

The clumps of curving lance-shaped leaves of this plant lack elegance but for weeks in summer and autumn three-petalled flowers, each forming a triangle around a tuft of fluffy stamens, open a few at a time from clusters formed at the junction of the leaves and stems. The colour range includes blue, such as the dark 'Isis', purple, pink, wine red and white. *Tradescantia* Andersoniana Group 'Osprey' has a blue tuft contrasting with the white petals.

▲ *Aubrieta* 'Doctor Mules'
◀ *Erysimum* 'Bowles' Mauve'

Trillium grandiflorum

Wake robin

Perennial H 40cm/16in, S 30cm/1ft Z4

Partial to deep shade Moist but well-drained soil, preferably neutral to acid

The trinity flowers are woodland plants with leaves, flowers and calyces all arranged in threes. This species is the unrivalled beauty of the genus. In late spring or early summer it bears clean white flowers, later sometimes tinted pink, of triangular shape blunted by the recurved tips of the petals. It is tempting to cut them because they last well but the loss of leaves as well as flowers weakens the plant. The arrangement in threes is less obvious in the flowers of the double 'Flore Pleno', but this is an exquisite plant.

More sombre species include birth root or stinking Benjamin (*Trillium erectum*), with nodding maroon flowers over large leaves, and toad-shade (*T. sessile*), with upright maroon flowers sitting at the centre of blotched leaves.

OTHER GOOD PLANTS

Aethionema 'Warley Rose'
Evergreen subshrub making a strong splash of rich pink in rock gardens during late spring and early summer when covered by numerous heads of four-petalled flowers.

Arabis alpina subsp. *caucasica* 'Schneehaube'
Low and vigorous evergreen perennial rock cress thriving on sunny banks or dry walls and covered with single four-petalled flowers of brilliant white from late winter to early summer.

Aurinia saxatilis 'Gold Dust'
Mound-forming evergreen perennial covered in late spring and early summer with dense heads of four-petalled flowers, commonly bright yellow but in 'Citrina' lemon yellow and in 'Dudley Neville' buff-orange.

Calochortus venustus
This medium-sized bulb, one of the largest of the mariposa lilies, bears in summer up to three flowers per branching stem, each cup formed from the three inner petals, usually white, with dark red blotches in the centre.

Iberis sempervirens 'Schneeflocke'
Mound-forming evergreen subshrub for sunny banks and rock gardens covered with heads of brilliant white four-petalled flowers in late spring and early summer.

Iberis umbellata
Common candytuft
Mound-forming annual, good even on poor soils, producing in summer flattened heads of white (in the Fairy Series also pink, red and purple) four-petalled scented flowers.

Libertia ixioides
Evergreen rhizomatous perennial making dense clumps of narrow sword-like leaves through which rise (to 90cm/3ft) in late spring or early summer dark stems carrying small flowers with three clean white inner petals and inconspicuous outer petals.

Tigridia pavonia: see p.128.

Trillium grandiflorum ▲
Tradescantia Andersoniana Group ▶

STARS

The many plants with starry flowers have in common the clarity of an outline defined by points. But the number of points varies considerably. There can be as few as five, as with the deutzias; there are commonly six, as in the case of alliums and scillas, but in the star magnolia there may be more than twice this.

Allium cristophii

Bulb H 45cm/18in, S 20cm/8in Z4

Full sun Well-drained soil

Many ornamental members of the onion family produce rounded heads of starry flowers, predominantly in shades of mauve and purple. In some cases the heads are suitable for drying. *Allium cristophii* is one of the best for this purpose, with a sphere as much as 20cm/8in in diameter composed of up to fifty metallic purplish blue stars.

Even more attention-seeking but also more tender is *A. schubertii*, with an enormous head (as much as 30cm/1ft across) of starry flowers on a stem 40–60cm/16–24in high. The stalks of the pale purple flowers are of very unequal length, creating an effect of an arrested explosion.

The strap-shaped leaves of these species wither before the flowers open, so it is best to plant the bulbs behind low-growing shrubs or perennials.

See also *A.* 'Globemaster', p.166.

Asphodeline lutea
King's spear, yellow asphodel

Perennial H 1.2m/4ft, S 25cm/10in Z6

Full sun Well-drained soil

At home in dry sunny borders or gravel gardens where conditions resemble those of stony Mediterranean landscapes, the yellow asphodel sends up tall stems surrounded by grassy blue-green basal and stem leaves. In late spring it has a flower spike of silky yellow fragrant stars. Later this becomes a rod topped with round green seed pods that dry crinkled and brown.

Camassia leichtlinii subsp. *suksdorfii*

Bulb H 1m/3ft, S 60cm/2ft Z4

Sun or partial shade Fertile, moist but well-drained soil

Most species of the North American genus *Camassia* are found in moist meadow-like habitats. The large bulbs produce linear or strap-shaped leaves and spikes of creamy white or blue starry flowers. Plants can be naturalized in grass or grown in borders, where they are best placed so that other plants hide their foliage. The late-spring flowers of *C. leichtlinii* are creamy white but those of this subspecies are blue or violet and most strongly coloured in the Caerulea Group.

C. cusickii 'Zwanenburg', also flowering in late spring, bears more cup-shaped deep blue flowers, with a star of light blue rays.

⬆ Asphodeline lutea
▲ Camassia leichtlinii subsp. suksdorfii

Allium cristophii ▶

▲ *Chionodoxa luciliae* Gigantea Group   ▲ *Deutzia* × *elegantissima*   ▲ *Pelargonium* 'Bird Dancer'   ▲ *Saxifraga fortunei*

Chionodoxa luciliae Gigantea Group

Bulb H 20cm/8in, S 8cm/3in Z4

Full sun Well-drained soil

The common name glory of the snow given generically to the handful of species in the genus *Chionodoxa* refers to their flowering in the mountain regions of Crete and western Turkey as the snows melt. Colonies are easily established in rock gardens or as a skirt to deciduous trees and shrubs and they also do well in containers. As cut flowers, all make lovely additions to miniature spring posies. *C. luciliae* Gigantea Group is the largest flowered of these bulbs, producing small sprays of pale blue white-centred stars in late winter or early spring as the blunt-tipped and strap-shaped leaves develop.

Slightly stronger in colour but with smaller stars in sprays of up to twelve, *C. forbesii* flowers at the same time. The more vivid blue nodding stars of *C. sardensis*, with tiny white eyes, are true spring flowers.

Deutzia × *elegantissima*

Deciduous shrub H 1.2m/4ft, S 1.5m/5ft Z6

Full sun Well-drained, reasonably moist soil

There are many deutzias of great garden value that produce masses of starry flowers in late spring and early summer to brighten mixed and shrub borders. The main colours are white, mauve and pale pink. This hybrid has lightly fragrant pale pink flowers. Those of its cultivar 'Rosealind' are a deeper shade of pink.

Other hybrids of similar size include *D.* × *hybrida* 'Mont Rose', with mauve-purple flowers, and *D.* × *rosea*, with flowers that are tinged pink, darker on the outside. *D. ningpoensis* makes a larger bush and bears its numerous white or pink-tinted nodding stars in mid-summer.

Prune these shrubs immediately after flowering, cutting back old flowered shoots.

Magnolia stellata
Star magnolia

Deciduous shrub H 3m/10ft, S 4m/13ft Z5

Sun or partial shade Humus-rich, moist but well-drained soil

This slow-growing shrub takes many years to reach its ultimate dimensions but starts flowering when young. In early to mid-spring grey-green buds, which have been sombrely attractive for many weeks in winter, open into somewhat limp and many-pointed fragrant stars composed of up to fifteen petals. Several forms of *Magnolia stellata* with even more petals include 'Royal Star', which is pink in bud, and 'Waterlily', with large flowers and numerous petals.

M. × *loebneri*, a deciduous hybrid of *M. stellata* and *M. kobus*, is a large shrub or small tree, which produces starry flowers in mid-spring. Those of 'Leonard Messel' (illustrated on p.1) are mauve-pink and somewhat goblet-shaped as the buds open.

The willow-leaved magnolia (*M. salicifolia*), a deciduous tree growing to 10m/30ft, has flowers of a crisper starry shape, which are fragrant. It does not tolerate alkaline soils.

Pelargonium 'Bird Dancer'

Evergreen perennial H 20cm/8in, S 15cm/6in Z9

Full sun Soil-less or soil-based compost (John Innes No. 2)

The Stellar pelargoniums are a group of hybrids with flowers of irregular star-like form. The three lower petals are strap-shaped, the two upper petals narrower and spindly. They are carried in rounded clusters above

▲ *Magnolia stellata*

usually dark-zoned leaves of jagged outline. They are ideally used as container plants, their minimalist effect in marked contrast to the clotted heads of many Zonals. 'Bird Dancer' is dwarf, with pale pink flowers, the upper petals shaded salmon.

A brick-red Stellar with broader petals is 'Vancouver Centennial', which has lime-green leaves heavily overlaid with bronze.

Saxifraga fortunei

Deciduous to semi-evergreen perennial H and S 30cm/1ft Z7

Full or partial shade Humus-rich, moist but well-drained soil

As well as numerous small species and hybrids that excite alpine gardeners, there are taller saxifrages, usually shade tolerant, suitable for growing in borders or among shrubs. One that does well even in poor conditions is London pride (*S. × urbium*), which has attractive evergreen foliage and sprays of tiny pink-tinted stars in summer. Give *S. fortunei* better treatment. The scalloped leaves, red-purple on the underside and taking on red tints as they age, make a pleasing clump through spring and summer. In autumn branched stems carry showers of starry white flowers, consisting of three short upper petals and two longer lower petals. *S.* 'Rubrifolia' is more compact, with glossy copper-red leaves.

OTHER GOOD PLANTS

Amelanchier × grandiflora 'Ballerina'

Deciduous shrubby tree with starry white flowers in spring, usually coinciding with the emergence of bronzed young leaves that colour brilliantly in autumn. The blue-black fruits are edible.

Gentiana verna: see p.97.

Isotoma axillaris

Compact perennial often grown as a container plant, bearing a profusion of blue flowers with five narrow petal lobes over a long season in summer.

Malus transitoria

A crab apple making a small deciduous tree, with pink buds opening to white stars in spring. The lobed leaves turn yellow in spring and it produces pea-sized yellow crabs.

Phlox adsurgens 'Wagon Wheel'

Creeping semi-evergreen perennial in late spring and early summer well covered with pink flowers with five narrow spoke-like lobes.

Tiarella wherryi 'Bronze Beauty'

A foam flower that makes a clump of handsomely bronzed hairy leaves and in late spring and early summer carries tiny blushing stars on dark brown stems.

Tulipa tarda

Short-growing bulb producing in early spring starry flowers that are yellow with white tips.

BOWLS, CUPS & SAUCERS

Many flowers have centrally positioned sexual organs surrounded by petals and sepals that curve upwards. In this formula doubling of the segments is common in plants of great ornamental value, notably roses. However, the open frank quality of single flowers is immediately appealing, particularly when they are borne profusely.

Chaenomeles speciosa
Flowering quince, Japanese quince, japonica

Deciduous shrub H 2.5m/8ft, S 4m/13ft Z5

Sun or partial shade Well-drained soil

The flowering quinces consist of a small group of species and their various hybrids, most of which make spiny spreading tangles. The numerous cup-shaped flowers, sometimes on bare wood but continuing when the leaves have opened, are often followed by more-or-less fragrant fruit, which can be used to make preserves. The cultivars of *Chaenomeles speciosa* cover a colour range from white to dark red. 'Moerloosei' has often been sold under the name 'Apple Blossom', which conveys the delicate mixture of pink and white of its densely clustered flowers. 'Nivalis' is pure white.

A number of the hybrids grouped under the name *C. × superba*, which are generally smaller, have vivid scarlet or red flowers. 'Knap Hill Scarlet' bears glowing orange-red flowers over a long season. Some are less fiery. 'Pink Lady' bears red-pink flowers early in the season.

When picked in bud, the flowers of all these will open in a warm room.

Cut back flowered shoots of these shrubs and remove old wood immediately after flowering. Spur-prune wall-trained specimens, cutting back flowered stems close to a framework of permanent branches.

Chaenomeles speciosa 'Moerloosei' ▲

▲ *Geranium* 'Johnson's Blue'   ▲ *Helleborus* × *hybridus*   ▲ *Kalmia latifolia*

Geranium 'Johnson's Blue'

Perennial H 40cm/16in, S 75cm/30in Z4

Sun or partial shade Well-drained soil

The rise in popularity of the cranesbills seems unstoppable. In general they are easy to grow; most have attractively lobed leaves, often highly effective as ground cover; and in a flowering season that in some cases lasts for several months they produce masses of saucer-shaped five-petalled blooms in a range of delicate and vivid colours. *Geranium* 'Johnson's Blue' is a rhizomatous hybrid that for weeks in mid-summer produces masses of light blue saucers, which float above a mat of elegant leaves.

The mourning widow (*G. phaeum*) is a useful shade-tolerant species with maroon-purple flowers. Even better for lighting a dark corner is its white form *G.p.* 'Album'. See also *G. pratense* 'Mrs Kendall Clark', p.126, and *G. psilostemon*, p.123.

Helleborus × *hybridus*

Lenten rose

Perennial H and S 45cm/18in Z4

Partial to full shade Well-drained neutral to alkaline soil

The various hybrids derived in part from the true Lenten rose (*Helleborus orientalis*) are key perennials for the second half of winter and early spring. The saucer-shaped flowers, borne several to a stem, are drooping or outward-facing, in a range of subdued but beautiful colours from green and yellow to pink and deep plum. Many are handsomely speckled maroon or crimson. Each flower is finished with a showy boss of pale yellow stamens. Named selections include Ashwood Garden hybrids and Ballard's Group. Excellent plants can be chosen from unnamed hybrids sold in flower, or you can build up interesting colonies by selecting from the numerous seedlings garden-grown plants produce.

The flowers do not last well indoors. The most attractive way of displaying them is to float the flowers in a shallow bowl of water.

The Christmas rose (*H. niger*), a smaller plant, bears saucer-shaped white flowers, usually green- or pink-tinted from early winter. A good specimen is handsome but plants often disappoint after their first season.

Remove the overwintering fingered leaves of these hellebores if their shabbiness detracts from the flowers.

See also *H. argutifolius*, p.109.

Kalmia latifolia

Calico bush, mountain laurel

Evergreen shrub H and S 3m/10ft Z4

Sun or dappled shade Humus-rich, moist but well-drained acid soil

Where the soil is lime free, this North American shrub makes a striking addition to woodland gardens and shrub borders, flowering best when it gets plenty of light. In early summer large clusters of pink buds, curiously crimped and pointed, are set among the glossy leaves. When open the flowers are saucer-shaped, paler than the buds and it can be seen that the very distinctive bud shape is defined by ten evenly spaced stamen pouches.

Kalmia latifolia 'Ostbo Red' is a selection with bright red buds. These open to pale pink flowers that fade to near white except for the stamens. The compact 'Minuet' has pale pink flowers with an inner maroon band.

▲ *Limnanthes douglasii*

▲ *Rubus 'Benenden'*

Limnanthes douglasii
Poached egg plant

Annual H 15cm/6in, S 20cm/8in

Full sun Moist but well-drained soil

This easy annual, which is a genial self-seeder, is best sown in autumn or spring where plants are to flower, for example as a filler at the edge of a path. In summer the fleshy deeply cut leaves are almost hidden by cup- to saucer-shaped flowers with bright yolk-yellow centres surrounded by a scalloped white margin, each of the five petals having a central notch. The flowers are lightly fragrant and are assiduously worked for their nectar by bees.

Magnolia grandiflora
Bull bay

Evergreen tree H 18m/60ft, S 12m/40ft Z7

Full sun Well-drained soil

The size of its glossy green leaves, often rusty and felted on the underside, makes *Magnifolia grandiflora* an impressive foliage plant although it is only in a favourable climate that the tree will reach its potential dimensions in an open position. Given the protection of a warm wall it makes a large and handsome shrub. It produces sensational cup-shaped flowers, creamy white, fragrant and up to 25cm/10in across, in late summer and autumn. They do not last well when cut but are splendid floated in a bowl to scent a room.

'Exmouth' is a fine clone that comes into flower when young and produces large blooms. 'Goliath', another clone that starts to flower when young, produces large somewhat globular blooms. The underside of the leaves has no rusty felt.

Prune, if necessary, in late winter or early spring.

Rosa 'Complicata'

Deciduous shrub H and S 2.5m/8ft Z6

Full sun Humus-rich, moist but well-drained soil

The direct appeal of the single roses is exemplified by this Gallica, which masquerades as a larger-than-life wild rose. A vigorous thorny shrub or climber with lustrous foliage, it makes a spectacular display in early to mid-summer, when cup- to saucer-shaped flowers are clustered along the length of its arching stems. The flowers are bright pink with a paler centre around the golden stamens.

Many other fine single roses bear flowers of similar shape. *R.* 'Ballerina', a Polyantha shrub rose that grows to about 1.5m /5ft, bears large heads of small white-centred light pink flowers through summer and early autumn. More wild rose in character, the shrub *R.* 'Frühlingsmorgen' makes a spiny bush up to 1.8m/6ft high, lit in early summer – and in a later though minor flush – with deliciously scented flowers that shade from soft pink to a pale yellow centre around crimson stamens.

Another handsome but spiny modern shrub rose is 'Golden Wings'. The shallow cup shape of its soft yellow flowers, which are borne throughout summer, is sometimes partly obscured by the wavy and irregular petals surrounding the amber stamens. The flowers are scented.

Among the Ramblers, the most vigorous of all the roses, there are many with single or semi-double cup-shaped small flowers borne in profusion. The white semi-double 'Bobbie James' has a scent that carries well.

Rubus 'Benenden'
Deciduous shrub H and S 3m/10ft Z5
Sun or partial shade Well-drained soil

Apart from the brambles grown for their edible fruits, there are a number of ornamental value, some, such as *Rubus biflorus* and *R. cockburnianus*, with 'white-washed' stems that stand out in the winter garden and a few with conspicuous saucer-shaped flowers in late spring and early summer.

R. 'Benenden' is the pick of those grown for their flowers. It makes a wide-spreading clump of thornless arching stems set along their length in late spring with pristine white flowers that are about 5cm/2in across and have a central boss of yellow stamens.

Cut back if necessary immediately after flowering.

▲ *Rosa* 'Complicata'

OTHER GOOD PLANTS

Abutilon vitifolium
Downy deciduous shrub for a warm sheltered position carrying saucer-shaped flowers about 5cm/2in across from late spring to mid-summer. 'Tennant's White' is a fine pure white, 'Veronica Tennant' an exquisite mauve.

Cistus x *cyprius*: see p.86.

Eucryphia x nymansensis 'Nymansay'
Fast-growing evergreen tree producing numerous cup-shaped cream flowers with a conspicuous boss of stamens among lustrous and serrated dark green leaves in late summer and early autumn.

Meconopsis betonicifolia: see p.83.

Paeonia lactiflora
'Bowl of Beauty': see p.70.

Papaver commutatum 'Ladybird': see p.128.

Papaver nudicaule: see p.86.

Potentilla fruticosa
The numerous cultivars are twiggy deciduous shrubs that produce masses of small saucer-shaped flowers in summer and early autumn, even on poor soils. 'Tilford Cream' has rich green foliage and relatively large creamy white flowers. 'Manchu' is dwarf and the flowers are white.

Saxifraga x irvingii 'Jenkinsiae'
This Kabschia saxifrage is an evergreen alpine that forms a miniature tight mound of silver-encrusted leaves. In early spring the foliage is almost hidden by cup-shaped flowers, pale pink with a darker centre, that are quaintly out of scale with their base.

Tulipa 'Prinses Irene': see p.133.

Waldsteinia ternata
Creeping semi-evergreen perennial with dark, lobed and toothed leaves making good ground cover. In summer there are small sprays of bright yellow saucer-shaped flowers.

▲ *Magnolia grandiflora*

GLOBES, GOBLETS & CHALICES

The balanced proportions of many elegant flowers such as the magnolias are defined by long tapering stems, outlines that are subtly waisted and incurved petals. They suggest vessels of quality and as flowers of quality deserve careful placing in the garden.

▲ *Crocus speciosus*

▲ *Colchicum speciosum* 'Album'

▲ *Rosa* Constance Spry

Colchicum speciosum
Corm H 15cm/6in, S 10cm/4in Z6

Sun or dappled shade Well-drained soil that is moist in the growing season

The best known of the colchicums are autumn-flowering perennials with large corms that produce their goblet-shaped flowers, which resemble large crocuses, before the leaves – hence the common names autumn crocus and naked ladies. Many have purplish pink flowers, some with chequered patterns. Each corm of *C. speciosum* produces several white-throated purple-pink flowers and large bright green leaves in spring. A more striking and elegant plant is the form 'Album', with well-shaped white goblets teetering on pale green slender tubes.

Other robust colchicums suitable for naturalizing in grass or growing among shrubs include *C.* 'Lilac Wonder', deep mauve-pink with narrow segments, and *C.* 'Rosy Dawn', white-throated, with lightly scented violet-pink flowers.

If growing colchicums in grass, do not cut down the leaves until they have withered.

See also *C. agrippinum*, p.127.

Crocus speciosus
Corm H 15cm/6in, S 5cm/2in

Full sun Well-drained, gritty soil Z4

This species is the best of the autumn-flowering crocuses for general garden use. It multiplies freely from seed and from offsets when naturalized in grass or in mixed borders. It is also suitable for broad planting in large rock gardens, but not among the choicest miniatures. The fine-stemmed goblets, produced in early to mid-autumn before the leaves, are mauve to violet-purple and heavily veined. The much-divided styles cradled in the flowers are bright orange. There are several named forms of *Crocus speciosus*, including the deep violet-mauve 'Oxonian', and 'Albus', which is elegant and white.

A counterpart to this species, flowering in late winter and early spring, is *C. tommasinianus*, which often naturalizes most freely in paths and among paving. The outer segments are usually silvery mauve, the inside deeper purplish mauve. 'Ruby Giant' has red-purple flowers.

See also *C. chrysanthus* 'Zwanenburg Bronze', p.132, and *Crocus sieberi* subsp. *sublimis* 'Tricolor', p.130.

Magnolia × *soulangeana*

Deciduous shrub or tree H and S 6m/20ft Z5

Sun or partial shade

Humus-rich and moist but well-drained soil that is neutral to acid

The magnolias include many flowering trees and shrubs of outstanding quality – of a very primitive family – but few outclass the clones of this magnificent hybrid. The wide-spreading branches of the typical form carry numerous upright goblet-shaped flowers in mid- to late spring before the leaves develop. The flowers are up to 15cm/6in across, white and flushed purple-pink at the base of the outer petals. M. × *soulangeana* 'Alba' is almost pure white and the widely planted 'Lennei' pink-purple outside with a creamy white inside lightly stained purple. It continues to produce occasional flowers throughout the summer.

An advantage of the late-flowering clones is that they stand a good chance of escaping frost damage. These include 'Brozzonii', with very large white flowers stained with purple at the base, and 'Rustica Rubra', with reddish pink flowers.

M. × *liliiflora* 'Nigra', which bears wine-red chalices, paler inside, in early summer, with occasional flowers to follow, stands a good chance of escaping frosts and has the added advantage for the smaller garden of rarely growing more than 2.5m/8ft high.

Paeonia mlokosewitschii

Perennial H 75cm/30in, S 90cm/3ft Z5

Sun or partial shade Humus-rich, moist but well-drained soil

Although they last only a few days in late spring or early summer, the trembling lemon-yellow globes, filled with yellow stamens, of Mollie-the-witch – as this peony is familiarly known – are of an ethereal, spellbinding beauty. The copper-pink young foliage is outstanding as it emerges, well above average in ornamental value when the divided leaves turn grey-green, and in autumn the gaping seed pods reveal a startling combination of glossy black and scarlet.

Other peony species with incurved petals that give the single flowers a globular form include P. *peregrina*, sheeny scarlet with golden stamens, and P. *wittmanniana*, pale yellow with richer yellow anthers and deep pink filaments.

Rosa Constance Spry ('Austance')

Deciduous (shrub rose) H 2m/6½ft, S 1.5m/5ft Z5

Full sun Humus-rich, moist but well-drained soil

Although their flowers are double, many of the hybrid roses are appealing on account of the simple shape of their globular blooms. One such is Constance Spry, a remarkable modern Shrub rose that can be trained as a climber up to about 3m/10ft. The lightly scented and refined flowers are clear pink and up to 15cm/6in across. It does not repeat but is worth a place in the garden for its magnificent display in mid-summer.

▲ *Magnolia* × *soulangeana*

The China roses are rather lightweight twiggy shrubs with flowers varying considerably in form but having the useful attribute of repeating in summer and autumn. 'Hermosa', an example dating from the first half of the nineteenth century, has scented globular pale pink flowers. It is an old rose that is suitable for a small garden, but to make an impact it is best planted in a group of two or three.

The Bourbons are also old roses that produce several flushes in summer and autumn. Two of great refinement with scented globular flowers are the mauve-pink 'Reine Victoria' and the silvery pink 'Madame Pierre Oger'. These grow to about 1.2m/4ft and need some support.

Prune Constance Spry after flowering and the other roses mentioned in late winter or early spring.

Trollius × cultorum

Perennial H 60–90cm/2–3ft, S 45cm/18in Z4

Sun or partial shade Moist soil

Globe flowers are buttercup relatives that make clumps of divided or lobed leaves and bear flowers in late spring or early summer in shades of lemon, yellow and orange, most of globular shape defined by incurved petals. The strongest and palest shades are found among the hybrids listed under *Trollius × cultorum*. Among those of strong colour is 'Feuertroll', with warm orange flowers. A less vigorous plant with ivory globes is 'Alabaster'. One of the first to flower is the bright yellow 'Earliest of All'.

The common European globe flower (*T. europaeus*), itself a good garden plant with lemon-yellow flowers, and other parents of these hybrids are found wild in moist meadows and marshy ground. All these plants look well when established near water but will thrive in borders where the soil does not dry out and are excellent on heavy ground.

Globe flowers will usually last for a few days when cut.

Tulipa 'West Point'

Bulb H 50cm/20in, S 8cm/3in Z4

Full sun Well-drained soil

The distinctive Lily-flowered Group tulips produce elegantly waisted flowers with turned-back tips in late spring. 'West Point' is an almost uniform light yellow and it has finely tapered tips that are strongly recurved. Another single-colour favourite that is slightly taller is the pure 'White Triumphator'. Several of these tulips have contrasting edges that show up the refined shape. The scarlet flowers of 'Aladdin' have yellow margins while those of 'Ballade' are red-magenta outlined in white. The stems of 'Marilyn' are less sturdy than those of many in the group but the cream flowers are prettily flamed soft red.

All these are excellent flowers for cutting. Lift the bulbs when foliage has died down and store in a dry warm place before replanting in the autumn.

◀ CLOCKWISE FROM LEFT
Paeonia mlokosewitschii
Tulipa 'West Point'
Trollius × cultorum 'Earliest of All'

OTHER GOOD PLANTS

Camellia × williamsii
'E.G. Waterhouse'
The Williamsii hybrid camellias are medium-sized evergreen shrubs, some of which, like this example, have formal double flowers that are globular when they first open. All the hybrids require lime-free soil.

Escallonia 'Apple Blossom'
The genus contains several evergreen hybrid shrubs often grown as informal hedges and valued for their generous display of small chalice-shaped flowers in summer and autumn. This hybrid grows to about 1.8m/6ft high and its flowers are delicate pink.

Tulipa 'Madame Lefeber':
see p.84.

Meconopsis integrifolia
Tall poppy that takes several years to reach flowering maturity but dies after flowering. It is covered with reddish hairs and bears globular upward- or outward-facing yellow flowers in late spring to mid-summer. Grow in moist and humus-rich soil.

Papaver orientale 'Watermelon'
The Oriental poppies are long-lived perennials flowering in early summer. This single cultivar has flowers that are an unusual shade of pink and globular when they first open but some become more bowl-shaped.

Sternbergia lutea
Autumn-flowering bulb with deep green leaves and satiny golden flowers that are goblet-shaped and grow to about 15cm/6in. Needs sun and good drainage.

TRUMPETS & FUNNELS

The first clarions of spring in the garden are the spring daffodils, probably the most loved and commonly grown of all the trumpet flowers. Large or small, the trumpet shape in flowers is bold, and so, too, are evenly tapered and open funnel shapes.

◂ *Cardiocrinum giganteum*

Agapanthus hybrids
Perennial H 45cm/18in, S 30cm/1ft Z7–Z8
Full sun Moist but well-drained soil

The African lilies are perennials from southern Africa, most of which flower in the second half of summer, when they make a strong impact in borders or in containers. The base of strap-shaped leaves is topped by rounded heads, sometimes with rather drooping flowers, which can be tubular, bell- or trumpet-shaped. Many hybrids have been raised and a fine range of selected seedlings was distributed in the 1950s and 1960s as Headbourne Hybrids. The name has since been misapplied to lower mixed seedlings that vary greatly in quality. Among the hybrids, most of which are deciduous, there is considerable variation in scale but in all sizes the flower colour is white or more commonly a shade of blue. *Agapanthus* 'Midnight Blue' is a hybrid with heads of trumpet flowers that are deep indigo blue in the second half of summer. The more compact 'Lilliput' is another hybrid with deep blue trumpets in late summer.

'Loch Hope' is an example of the larger clump-forming African lilies. It grows to about 1.5m/5ft and its trumpets are deep blue. A good choice among the non-blues is 'Bressingham White', which grows to about 90cm/3ft.

The flower stems of all African lilies are good for picking and the seedheads, whether green or dried, are highly ornamental.

Cardiocrinum giganteum
Giant Himalayan lily
Bulb H 3m/10ft, S 50cm/20in Z8
Dappled shade Fertile, humus-rich, moist but well-drained soil

From seed it takes about eight years before this lily relative is ready to send up a stout flowering stem from a base of large heart-shaped leaves. But then in a colony it makes a stupendous effect, especially in a glade among rhododendrons, as it might grow in its native Himalayan woodland. The richly scented trumpets, up to twenty per stem and hanging stiffly at an angle, are 15cm/6in long, greenish white and stained red-purple at the base inside. The upright seed pods that follow are also highly decorative.

Although the main bulb dies after flowering, the plant produces offsets. Replant these with the tops just below the surface. Pander to their greed and bring them into flower in about four years by feeding generously with well-rotted manure. Plants raised from seed may take seven or more years to reach flowering maturity. The ideal is to establish a colony with plants of different ages raised from seed and offsets so that you have flowers annually in mid- to late summer.

Gentiana × macaulayi 'Kingfisher'

Semi-evergreen perennial H 5cm/2in, S 30cm/1ft Z4

Sun or dappled shade Lime-free, humus-rich, moist but well-drained soil

The low-growing and autumn-flowering gentians, including hybrids of Asiatic species, are elite plants of the rock garden and well suited to growing in troughs. Their brilliant blue trumpet- to funnel-shaped flowers, large in relation to the scale of the plants, are often beautifully marked.

This Asiatic hybrid makes a mat of narrow leaves and produces vivid blue trumpets that are purplish in the throat, with pale panels outlined and divided by dark lines on the outside. The season of this and similar hybrids requiring the same conditions, such as *Gentiana* 'Inverleith' and *G.* 'Strathmore', often extends into late autumn.

A parent of many of the autumn-flowering hybrids is *G. sino-ornata*, which is a superb plant in its own right. The trumpets are bright blue with purplish stripes and pale green panels on the outside. It is lime-hating.

By contrast, the spring-flowering trumpet gentian (*G. acaulis*) is lime tolerant. This European species is whimsical in its flowering but when produced the deep blue trumpets, green-spotted inside, are sumptuous.

Hemerocallis hybrids

Semi-evergreen perennial H and S 1m/40in Z3–Z4

Full sun Fertile, moist but well-drained soil

The day lilies in cultivation are mainly tough clump-forming perennials with strap-shaped leaves through which rise erect stems carrying several upward-facing flowers. Although individual flowers are short-lived, they follow one another in rapid succession over a long season in summer. There are thousands of hybrids, with flowers in a wide range of colours and shapes. Singles are described as spider-shaped, star-shaped, triangular or circular. Some of the modern hybrids have coarsely gross flowers but the most refined of the singles have flowers of clean trumpet outlines. A good example is the rich scarlet and yellow-centred *Hemerocallis* 'Stafford'. Others are 'Red Rum', which has brick-red flowers, and 'Corky', yellow with exterior red-brown stains.

Most of the species have flowers of trumpet shape, though the segments tend to spread wide at the mouth to form a star. A plant of exceptional refinement is *H. lilioasphodelus*, which produces sweetly scented yellow trumpets in early summer.

FROM TOP ▶
Agapanthus hybrid
Gentiana × *macaulayi* 'Kingfisher'
Hemerocallis hybrid

▲ *Lilium* Golden Splendor Group

▲ *Narcissus* 'February Gold'

Lavatera × clementii 'Barnsley'

Semi-evergreen subshrub H and S 1.8m/6ft Z8

Full sun Well-drained soil

The shrubby mallows tend to be short-lived but their value is as fast-growing and free-flowering fillers that thrive even on relatively poor soils and in coastal conditions. *Lavatera × clementii* 'Barnsley' has grey-green leaves and produces funnel-shaped flowers with notched petals non-stop through summer and into autumn. The flowers open pink with a red eye and age to white, the variation in white and pink giving a blooming bush a lively appearance.

Similar cultivars include 'Burgundy Wine', with rich pink flowers darkened by heavy veining, and 'Rosea', with pink flowers.

Buy young plants, for older specimens of all these mallows tend to root poorly when planted out. Prune out growths that spoil the plant's balance. Plants can be cut back annually to near ground level.

See also *L. trimestris*, p.83.

Lilium Golden Splendor Group

Bulb H 1.2–1.8m/4–6ft, S 20cm/8in Z4

Sun with base in shade Humus-rich, moist but well-drained and preferably lime-free soil

Many hybrids of Asiatic and East Asian lilies have trumpet flowers. The Golden Splendor Group provides a magnificent example with fragrant flowers. Strong erect stems carry pyramids of nodding or outward-facing large trumpets that are yellow with dark red markings on the outside.

Trumpet hybrid lilies of comparable quality include *L.* 'Black Dragon' and Pink Perfection Group (illustrated on pp.14–15).

All these hybrids are suitable for the garden or for containers, planted where they get good light but with the base in shade. They are stem-rooting – that is to say they produce roots above the bulb as well as from it – and should be planted at least 10cm/4in deep.

See also *L. regale*, p.143.

Narcissus 'February Gold'

Bulb H 30cm/1ft, S 8cm/3in Z5

Sun or partial shade

Well-drained soil with plentiful moisture in the growing season

A valuable group of neat trumpet-flowered hybrid daffodils 20–40cm/8–16in high derived from *Narcissus cyclamineus* are characterized by the way the trumpet thrusts forward from swept-back segments. *N.* 'February Gold' is one of the most reliable of these and excellent for naturalizing. In the northern hemisphere it does not often flower as early as its name might suggest but its rich yellow trumpets are long-lasting.

Two tall Cyclamineus daffodils with exceptionally long and slender yellow trumpets are 'Bartley' and 'Peeping Tom'. The jaunty 'Jack Snipe' has a shorter lemon-yellow trumpet and the swept-back segments are white.

Good trumpet species flowering in early spring that are suitable for naturalizing include the graceful Tenby daffodil (*N. obvallaris*). This is a robust, upstanding plant with flowers of a uniform rich yellow that are horizontal or slightly upward-tilting when they open from their papery sheaths. The trumpet, flaring but lobed rather than frilled at the mouth, can be more than 5cm/2in long. Another is the variable *N. pseudonarcissus*. The twisted segments of the nodding flowers are creamy yellow and the trumpet a richer colour.

Flowering earlier than any of these is *N.* 'Cedric Morris', a small yellow daffodil, usually under 25cm/10in high, that often heralds the arrival of spring as early as mid-winter.

Where daffodils are naturalized, leave the grass unmown until the foliage of the bulbs dies down.

Petunia Surfinia Purple ('Shihi Brilliant')

Annual H 15cm/6in, S 90cm/3ft

Full sun Well-drained soil; in containers either soil-less

or soil-based compost (John Innes No. 2)

Petunias are annuals that produce prodigious quantities of trumpet-shaped flowers over a long season in summer and early autumn. Most can be raised from seed but not the trailing Surfinia Series, which are raised annually from softwood cuttings. They are excellent for container gardening, bearing single weather-resistant flowers for months in a colour range that includes white and shades of pink, red and blue.

The relatively small-flowered Multiflora petunias produce masses of trumpet-shaped blooms over a long summer and autumn season and are generally less prone to rain damage than the large and rather floppy Grandifloras. The Wave Series is a popular seed strain of single-flowered Multifloras in a good colour range that includes the pale mauve-pink of 'Pearly Wave' and the intense violet-purple of 'Purple Wave'.

A Grandiflora seed strain bred for weather resistance is the Storm Series, available in a mixture of soft colours.

OTHER GOOD PLANTS

Alcea rosea 'Nigra': see p.16.

Amaryllis belladonna
Autumn-flowering bulb with six or more pink, scented and funnel-shaped flowers bunched at the tip of a bare stem.

Campsis × tagliabuanum 'Madame Galen'
Vigorous and partially self-clinging deciduous woody climber for warm gardens bearing clusters of salmon-pink trumpets on new growth in late summer and early autumn.

Convolvulus cneorum: see p.74.

Crinum × powellii
Summer- and autumn-flowering bulb with up to ten funnel-shaped and scented pink or white ('Album') flowers arching from the top of stout stems.

Crocosmia 'Lucifer': see p.152.

Gladiolus communis subsp. *byzantinus*
Summer-flowering corm with spikes of up to twenty vivid magenta funnel-shaped flowers.

Hibiscus syriacus 'Woodbridge'
Deciduous shrub growing to 3m/10ft and producing in late summer and early autumn trumpet- to funnel-shaped flowers that are rich pink with a darker centre and maroon veining.

Ipomoea purpurea 'Star of Yalta'
Annual twining climber growing to about 3m/10ft and producing throughout summer funnel- to trumpet-shaped flowers that are intense blue rayed red-purple.

Zantedeschia aethiopica Arum lily
Rhizomatous perennial making an evergreen clump of arrow-shaped leaves with stems bearing white funnel-shaped flower-like spathes.

▲ *Lavatera × clementii* 'Barnsley'

▲ *Petunia* Surfinia Purple

BELLS, THIMBLES & URNS

The common and attractive bell shape is found in flowers from different families in many parts of the world. By definition, the bell or thimble is open-mouthed but in the heaths (*Erica*) and in several other genera there is a gradation from fully open bells to urn shapes that are constricted at the mouth.

Bergenia 'Silberlicht'

Evergreen perennial H 40cm/16in, S 50cm/20in Z3

Sun or partial shade Moist but well-drained soil

Elephant's ears, the common name applied loosely to bergenias, refers to the large leathery leaves that are often thought of as the principal feature of these tough perennials. At its best the foliage of many is ground-covering and handsome, the burnished bronze and purple tints that develop in winter adding a rich patina to the garden floor. The sprays of bell-shaped flowers held well above the leaves are, however, far from inconsequential and welcome in early spring. Most are in shades of pink or purplish red; the less strident whites and pale pinks are easier to place with other spring flowers. The hybrid 'Silberlicht' bears large sprays of white flowers that develop delicate pink tints as they age. Another hybrid, 'Beethoven', which flowers freely in late spring and into summer, has white bells held in greenish red or pink calyces.

Among bergenias with strongly coloured flowers is the large hybrid 'Ballawley'. Its leaves are richly tinted in winter and its tall red stems carry rich pink bells in early spring.

The winter leaves of bergenia are beautiful in arrangements and the flowers are suitable for cutting.

Campanula 'Burghaltii'

Perennial H 60cm/2ft, S 30cm/1ft Z4

Sun or partial shade Moist but well-drained soil,

preferably neutral to alkaline

Despite their generic common name of bellflowers, the flower shape of the numerous campanulas varies. Several species and hybrids that are good summer-flowering perennials have somewhat tubular bells. Those of *C.* 'Burghaltii' are elegantly shaped and pale grey-blue hanging from erect stems. *C. takesimana* 'Elizabeth' is a shorter-growing rhizomatous perennial that may need to have its spread checked. The long pendent bells are cream, flushed red outside and speckled red within.

Of the tall-growing perennial bellflowers *C. lactiflora* is the most versatile. Its stout and leafy stems carry great heads of small pale blue bells for several weeks from mid-summer on plants that can grow to a height of 1.5m/5ft or more. It needs staking in exposed gardens. Several somewhat shorter-growing forms extend the colour choice: 'Alba' is laundry white, 'Loddon Anna' mauve-pink and 'Prichard's Variety' rich violet-blue.

Enkianthus campanulatus

Deciduous shrub H and S 3m/10ft Z5

Sun or partial shade Humus-rich, moist but well-drained neutral to acid soil

In late spring, when this shrub is already in leaf, it bears numerous drooping clusters of bell-shaped flowers, which are pale yellow warmed by red veins. Their subtle beauty shows well when they are cut. The shrub, a native of Japan, gives an eye-catching turn in autumn, when the foliage turns brilliant shades of yellow and red, rivalling in brilliance the colours of Japanese maples such as *Acer japonicum* and *A. palmatum*.

The more compact *Enkianthus perulatus*, with red-brown shoots, has smaller flowers that are urn-shaped and white. Its autumn reds outclass even the intense colours of *E. campanulatus*.

Erica carnea
Winter heath

Evergreen shrub H 20–30cm/8–12in, S 35–60cm/14–24in Z6

Full sun Well-drained soil

The numerous cultivars of this dwarf shrub have short linear leaves, far from always a standard dark green, and in late winter to early spring one-sided spikes of urn-shaped flowers, generally rather elongated, from which the anthers protrude. As well as the dominant purplish-pink, the range includes white, pale pink and shades of crimson and red. Even when the flowers are dead they warm the garden with a rich brown. Two outstanding mid-season cultivars of *Erica carnea* are the clean 'Springwood White' and the pink to carmine 'Vivellii', which has dark foliage that turns bronze in winter. 'Praecox Rubra' is early and deep reddish pink. 'Rosalie' is bright pink and late-flowering. Unlike many heaths, these will tolerate lime in the soil.

The bell heather (*E. cinerea*), a species for lime-free soils, is another low evergreen shrub, generally with foliage that is a rich deep green. The neat urn-shaped flowers, borne profusely throughout summer and into autumn, are white or shades of pink and red. The flowers of 'C.D. Eason' are vivid magenta pink, those of 'Eden Valley' pink and white. One of the most richly coloured, 'Pentreath', has beetroot-red flowers.

Trim these heaths after flowering or in spring.

CLOCKWISE FROM LEFT ▶
Campanula 'Burghaltii'
Bergenia 'Silberlicht'
Erica carnea 'Springwood White'
Enkianthus campanulatus

▲ *Fritillaria imperialis*

Fritillaria imperialis
Crown imperial
Bulb H 1.2m/4ft, S 25cm/10in Z5

Full sun Well-drained soil

The crown imperial is a spectacular mid-season spring bulb, with a stout dark stem surrounded by whorls of glossy leaves for half its height then rising bare to a ring of up to eight pendulous bells, commonly brick-red but in *Fritillaria imperialis* 'Maxima Lutea' yellow and in 'Rubra Maxima' orange-red with dark veining. The bells are 5cm/2in or more long and inside, at the base of each segment, is a glistening nectary. Above the carillon is a curious topknot of leaves. The plants have a somewhat rank scent.

The fritillaries, many of which have bell-shaped flowers of subtle colouring, have an enthusiastic following among specialists. Some are demanding but good garden plants include *F. michailovskyi*, usually under 20cm/8in in height, with dark purple-brown bells tipped yellow, and *F. pallidiflora*, 40cm/16in high, with green-tinted pale yellow nodding bells. These species flower in late spring or early summer.

See also *F. acmopetala*, p.108, *F. meleagris*, p.126 and *F. persica* 'Adiyaman', p.111.

Galtonia candicans
Bulb H 1.2m/4ft, S 20cm/8in Z7

Full sun Well-drained soil that is moist in the growing season

The galtonias are South African bulbs that in mild areas can be planted in autumn to flower in late summer to autumn the following year. In colder regions it is best to plant in spring and lift in autumn after flowering. From a base of strap-shaped leaves, *G. candicans* sends up an erect stem, from which dangle numerous well-spaced, lightly scented white bells.

The shorter-growing *G. viridiflora*, with light green bells, is a favourite of flower-arrangers.

Leucojum aestivum
Summer snowflake
Bulb H 50cm/20in, S 15cm/6in Z4

Sun or partial shade Reliably moist soil

In spite of its common name, this bulb flowers in the second half of spring. A sturdy leafless stem rises from a clump of strap-shaped leaves carrying several drooping white bells. The six petals, unlike those of the

▲ *Leucojum aestivum* 'Gravetye Giant'

▲ *Galtonia candicans*

▲ *Muscari botryoides* 'Album'

snowdrops (*Galanthus*), are of equal length and all have green marks just above the tips. The form of *Leucojum aestivum* generally grown is 'Gravetye Giant', which in good moist soil can reach a height of 90cm/3ft.

The shorter-growing spring snowflake (*L. vernum*) flowers several weeks earlier, even in late winter, the robust form var. *wagneri* usually with two large flowers per stem. Much more slender than either of these is the autumn-flowering *L. autumnale*. It produces pink-tinged white bells before the grass-like leaves. It thrives in drier conditions than the other species and needs sun.

Muscari botryoides 'Album'

Bulb H 15cm/6in, S 8cm/3in Z3

Full sun Moist but well-drained soil

The grape hyacinths in cultivation are dwarf bulbs showing a strong family resemblance. In spring they produce short spikes packed with small bells, in most species blue, that are constricted at the mouth. The leaves are present at flowering, usually starting into growth in autumn. Some grape hyacinths spread by offsets rather too freely; this is particularly the case with the dark-flowered and very leafy *Muscari neglectum*. The bright blue *M. armeniacum* can also be invasive but is a useful bulb for planting as a skirt to deciduous trees and shrubs and is a particularly beautiful companion for spring-flowering magnolias.

One of the most suitable grape hyacinths for rock gardens is *M. botryoides* 'Album'. It is a refined plant that does not spread aggressively. In mid- to late spring it produces slender spikes of fragrant white bells, which are rather globular in shape.

M. aucheri 'Tubergenianum' is another grape hyacinth suitable for rock gardens. The lower, somewhat tubular bells, with a white rim at the mouth, are bright blue and above them is a crown of pale blue sterile flowers. On the basis of this contrast it is sometimes known as the Oxford and Cambridge grape hyacinth, an allusion to the colours of the two universities.

OTHER GOOD PLANTS

Calluna vulgaris **Heather, ling**
Low evergreen shrub with scale-like leaves and spikes of small bell-shaped flowers in white or shades of pink and purple in late summer or autumn. The many named cultivars, long-lasting in flower and some with ornamental orange or red foliage, all need lime-free soil.

Clematis rehderiana
Vigorous deciduous woody climber producing in late summer and autumn sprays of pendent yellow thimble-shaped flowers that are lightly scented.

Cobaea scandens: see p.116.

Convallaria majalis: see p.138.

Dierama pulcherrimum: see p.152.

Digitalis x *mertonensis*: see p.155.

Halesia carolina **Snowdrop tree**
Large evergreen shrub for lime-free soils bearing in late spring clusters of pendulous white bells just as the leaves begin to unfurl.

Hosta 'Honeybells'
Like most hostas, this perennial has handsome leaves, which are strongly veined and pale green. In late summer it bears a tall spike of fragrant white or mauve-tinted bells.

Hyacinthus orientalis: see p.142.

Nectaroscordum siculum **subsp.** *bulgaricum*: see p.105.

Pieris japonica: see p.88.

Pulsatilla vulgaris: see p.71.

Rhododendron 'Bow Bells'
Compact evergreen shrub for lime-free soils with rounded leaves bearing in late spring trusses of pale pink bell-shaped flowers.

Yucca gloriosa
Evergreen shrub with rosettes of stiff blue-green or dark green sword-like leaves. In late summer or autumn spikes of pendent bell-shaped ivory flowers, usually tinged purple, stand well above the foliage.

ELABORATED SHAPES

Flowers of complex structure formed in nature have long fascinated gardeners. Elongated tubes, extended spurs and other beautiful and curious shapes are typically an indication of specialized relationships between flowers and pollinators. Some floral structures give a misleading appearance of being simple: the daisy flowerhead, for instance, looks and functions like a single flower but is in reality composite, consisting of a head packed with many small flowers. Some elaborations are the result of mutation and for early gardeners among the choicest flowers were sports of familiar plants in which the floral parts were multiplied. Many commonly grown ornamentals, including roses, are best loved in forms with double flowers.

The flowers of *Dicentra spectabilis* are of complex structure, inspiring various common names – including bleeding heart and lyre flower – that convey the direct charm of this perennial. The lockets, dangling elegantly from slender stems, appear just as the bulbs are finishing and before the great rush of summer perennials.

ELABORATED SHAPES

A marked feature of the evolution of flowering plants is the development of floral parts so that nectar, instead of being available to all comers, is to a lesser or greater extent concealed. This process has gone hand in hand with the evolution of pollinators. In highly developed flowers the size and shape of floral parts are standardized so that they match the standardized shape and dimensions of the body and, in the case of insects, the proboscis of a specific pollinator. Although in theory these refinements exclude all but a designated pollinator from getting at the nectar payload, they do not necessarily ensure pollination; and some insects, and also birds, are adept nectar thieves, getting at the supply by boring through the wall of the flower or by other devious means without making any contact with the sexual parts. Nonetheless, these evolutionary developments, reinforced by the behaviour of pollinators, which tend to return repeatedly to flowers of the same species as a source of nectar and pollen (a pattern that has helped to isolate populations of distinctive character), are evident in the astonishing range of flower structures that occur naturally. Many such plants owe their place in the garden to the fact that their intriguing flowers have fascinated one or other of the many plant hunters who have collected in the wild. But in addition other elaborately shaped flowers are the result of mutations that have been spotted and perpetuated or in other cases developed intentionally.

The happy consequence of evolutionary developments in the plant world and to a lesser extent the results of plant breeding is that our gardens can be full of very varied flowers. The irony is that variety is not what we always want. But though there is a place in gardening for the simplification that can be achieved with block or patterned plantings for bedding schemes, in which the character of particular flowers is subordinated to a general effect, I side with those who feel that making a coherent whole out of assembling plants of very varied character is gardening of a superior order.

THE ORCHID FAMILY

The fact that no members of the orchid family (*Orchidaceae*) are included needs some explanation for of all flowers these are the most remarkable and varied in structure. Most are tropical or subtropical and on that account are beyond the scope of this book. The slipper orchids (*Cypripedium*) are, however, a particularly beautiful group of hardy terrestrial orchids. The generic name, combining an allusion to Cyprus, the island sacred to Venus, and a corrupted form of the Greek *pedilon* (slipper), can be translated as Venus's slipper. The slipper is a pouch-shaped adaptation of the lip. It has slippery sides and insects that enter it in search of nectar can only get out by brushing against the stigma and pollinia, and in this way effect cross-pollination. The difficulty of propagating these plants has led to collecting from the wild on a devastating scale. The lady's slipper orchid (*C. calceolus*) is one of the most endangered of British natives. There are a few exceptions but it is fair to say that most of the terrestrial orchids from temperate parts of the world are plants for specialist collections.

THE SUNFLOWER FAMILY

The sunflower family (*Compositae* or *Asteraceae*), which includes the common daisy (*Bellis perennis*), is so numerous that it deserves a note of its own. All species in the family, and this is as true of weedy thistles and dandelions as it is of the numerous ornamental daisies, bear 'flowers' that in reality are heads, each of which is made up of numerous small flowers surrounded by bracts. The central or disk florets are radially symmetrical, and the outer or ray florets are irregular, and commonly tongue- or strap-shaped.

The daisy-flowered members of the family are sometimes treated ungenerously by gardening writers who find fault with the repetition of the daisy formula and claim to find garden daisies in the yellow, red-brown and bronze range too dominant in late summer and autumn. I would not want a garden entirely of daisies, although it would be an interesting experiment to try to create one. But to my mind there is enough variation in their scale, size and arrangement of flowers and colour to make daisies of various kinds welcome at any season of the year. In a mild climate the rather tender argyranthemums will flower for almost the full twelve months and, even where they can only be put outdoors for summer, make ideal plants for containers. Avoid, if you must, the yellows and copper-to-mahogany tones of daisies such as the heleniums, but a better policy is to keep them apart from the clashing colours of the most vibrant asters – another important group of daisies that help prolong summer well into autumn.

The sunflower family also includes the knapweeds (*Centaurea*), several of which are excellent plants for sunny alkaline gardens that are on the dry side. Their typical flowerheads are thistly at the centre, surrounded by dissected florets, and the conspicuous base of the flowerhead is composed of overlapping bracts. The cardoon (*Cynara cardunculus*), which also belongs to this tribe, is a perennial outstanding for its silver-backed, much divided glaucous leaves but also impressive in flower.

Cephalaria, *Knautia* and *Scabiosa* are all members of the family *Dipsacaceae*, which bears a superficial resemblance to the sunflower family in that what looks like a single pincushion flower is in fact composed of numerous small flowers, from which the anthers protrude, gathered together in a head and surrounded by bracts.

DOUBLE FLOWERS

Double flowers must have delighted the first gardeners and were certainly highly esteemed for their curiosity and ornamental value by sixteenth- and seventeenth-century writers on gardening. In their various forms the early doubles added significantly to the range of interesting ornamentals at a time when the flood of introductions from every corner of the world was just beginning.

In the wild the flowers of most plant species have relatively few petals, although their great differences in shape, scale and arrangement are the basis of enormously varied floral structures. There are, of course, exceptions. Among them are various species of waterlily (*Nymphaea*), which, like many of the hybrids derived from them, often have numerous segments.

In general, the multiplication of petals beyond the normal complement is the result of mutations involving the transformation of male or female sexual organs into additional segments. Whatever the degree of doubling, and it can vary considerably, the sports of nature with double flowers have little chance of producing similar progeny without human interference. Gardeners and plant breeders have, however, stepped in. Double seed strains of many

annual and biennial flowers have been stabilized and many other plants with double flowers are propagated vegetatively, for example from cuttings or by division.

The preference for double forms of many flowers remains strong. They are generally larger, more conspicuous, longer-lasting and less likely to self-seed than the singles from which they are derived. The shape and density of the doubled flower can have an intrinsic charm, as in the forms whose neatness is conveyed by the words 'button' and 'pompon', the latter derived from the French for a knot of ribbons. There is, however, no unanimous verdict on the beauty of numerous very full and shaggy double flowers. There is a great divide between gardeners who dismiss out of hand the compact and larger-flowered cultivars of bedding plants that breeders have been at such pains to produce and other gardeners for whom they are an indispensable part of a colourful garden. It is easy to be snobbish about these plants and the styles of gardening with which they are associated. But it is better to judge the flowers on their own merits. Even the most monstrous – some of the African marigolds (*Tagetes*), for example – might be useful where the aim is to create bands of solid colour.

In some categories of flowers there are different kinds of doubling and a special language is needed to describe them. There are, for example, specific classification systems to cover the numerous forms of chrysanthemums and dahlias, two genera from the sunflower family that have been enormously popular as flowers for competitive showing. Other highly cultivated plants with flowers showing various degrees of doubling include camellias. Those that are 'formal double' have numerous petals radiating from the centre and overlapping like meticulously placed tiles. These sophisticated blooms can look out of place in a 'wild' woodland garden but in a more formal architectural setting their artificial perfection does not strike a discordant note.

Among roses the doubles have long been in the ascendant and some cultivars with full flowers that are grown today are of very ancient origin. The rosette shape, predating the high-centred conical form of the Hybrid Teas, is characterized by flowers filled with overlapping petals, usually slightly uneven in length, that open flat. Some of the doubles that open flat are described as quartered, the petals at the centre being tightly packed in four more-or-less distinct sections. The entry on *Rosa* 'Königin von Dänemark' covers a number of old roses with flowers of this distinctive form.

TUBES, LIPS & LOBES

Many radially symmetrical flowers are tubular, opening at the mouth to a ring of lobes that are often petal-like. Flowers that are symmetrical in only one plane, as is the case with the large number that are lipped, usually have intriguing shapes, the origin of which is a snug adaptation to a particular pollinator.

▲ *Lonicera* × *brownii*

▲ *Penstemon* 'Evelyn'

Anchusa azurea 'Loddon Royalist'

Perennial H 90cm/3ft, S 50cm/20in Z4

Full sun Moist but well-drained soil

This perennial is not long-lived and its roughly hairy foliage is somewhat coarse, but any criticism goes out of the window when it flowers in early summer. The small tubular flowers, opening at the mouth to five spreading lobes, are borne freely on branching spikes. Their radiant blue, becoming more purple with age, is lit by a tiny white eye.

This relatively compact cultivar usually needs no staking. Cut out stems that have finished flowering to extend the season.

The dwarf *Anchusa cespitosa* is suitable for an alpine house or a rock garden. It has linear leaves, among which nestle the bright blue white-eyed flowers in spring.

Fuchsia 'Thalia'

Deciduous shrub H 75cm/30in, S 50cm/20in Z10

Sun or partial shade Moist but well-drained soil; in containers soil-less or

soil-based compost (John Innes No. 3)

The Triphylla Group of fuchsias, derived fom *F. triphylla*, are among the most tender of the fuchsias but in warm sheltered gardens they can be used for summer bedding or as container plants outdoors as well as under glass. They are upright in growth, generally with attractive velvety leaves, often bronzed or purplish on the underside, and throughout summer bear numerous tubular flowers, which are pendulous, long and narrow, opening to short pointed sepals and a skirt of petals that just shows. The small flowers of *F*. 'Thalia' are rich orange-scarlet and borne prolifically.

Other fuchsias in the same group include the salmon-pink 'Coralle', and 'Gartenmeister Bonstedt', with bronzed foliage and brick-red flowers.

Jasminum nudiflorum
Winter jasmine

Deciduous shrub H and S 3m/10ft Z6

Sun or partial shade Well-drained soil

When the garden is at its most bare the winter jasmine astonishes with its profusion of bright yellow flowers, which are tubular and five-lobed and open from buds tinged rust red. Although the flowers are unscented, short sprays are always welcome indoors as a promise of spring. This shrub has many virtues, including its tolerance of sun or

shade, but a shortcoming is its awkward appearance when the lax stems are trained up a wall. It looks much more comfortable when it is placed so that these trail over a retaining wall or down a bank.

Less hardy yellow-flowered jasmines usually trained as wall shrubs in warm and sheltered positions include the primrose jasmine (*J. mesnyi*), with unscented and usually semi-double flowers in spring, and a form of the yellow jasmine (*J. humile* 'Revolutum'), with small scented flowers in summer.

See also *J. officinale*, p.141.

Trim all these after flowering.

Lonicera × brownii

Deciduous woody climber H 6m/20ft, S 2.5m/8ft Z4

Sun or partial shade Humus-rich, moist but well-drained soil

Even honeysuckles that lack scent can be impressive ornamentals. The flowers, usually borne freely in pairs or whorls, may be tubular or of more spreading shape and either two-lipped or with five equal lobes at the mouth. The two-lipped flowers of this hybrid climber are orange-red and freely produced throughout summer against a background of oval blue-green leaves. 'Dropmore Scarlet', the most commonly grown form of this hybrid, has flowers that are more red than orange.

One of the parents, the semi-evergreen coral or trumpet honeysuckle (*Lonicera sempervirens*), is less hardy but long-flowering. The flowers are tubular rather than trumpet-shaped, scarlet-orange outside, more yellow within. The trumpet honeysuckle is also a parent of *L. × tellmanniana*, a vigorous deciduous hybrid, good in shade, which in late spring and early summer bears glowing amber flowers that have scarlet streaks and tips. The other parent of this hybrid, the deciduous *L. tragophylla*, is a showy climber with large bright yellow two-lipped flowers in early summer.

All these honeysuckles are less prone to aphid attack if grown in partial shade. Prune after flowering.

For scented honeysuckles, see *L. periclymenum*, p.143.

Penstemon 'Evelyn'

Perennial H 45cm/18in, S 30cm/1ft Z7

Full sun Moist but well-drained soil

In addition to the many penstemon hybrids that are overwintered as rooted cuttings and planted out as half-hardy annuals to flower in summer and early autumn, there are some that are reasonably perennial in suitable conditions, especially if protected by a mulch in winter. *P.* 'Evelyn', one of the most reliably hardy, is a narrow-leaved bushy plant with pastel pink tubular flowers.

Other hybrids of similar size that have proved hardy in many gardens include the blue-purple 'Margery Fish' and the purple-pink 'Lynette'. 'Hidcote Pink', pale pink with dark markings in the throat, and the bright scarlet 'Schoenholzeri' are of similar hardiness but often grow to 90cm/3ft. See also *P.* 'Stapleford Gem', p.106.

Cut back to new basal growth in mid-spring and replace plants every three or four years.

OTHER GOOD PLANTS

Antirrhinum majus Snapdragon
Short-lived perennial, usually grown as an annual, with spikes of dragon-head flowers consisting of a broad tube with two closed lips. There are dwarf (e.g. Royal Carpet Series), intermediate (e.g. Monarch Series) and tall (e.g. Coronette Series) seed strains in a wide colour range, the flowers often bicoloured.

Nemesia caerulea
Long-flowering perennial for containers or borders with spires of tubular two-lipped flowers that taper to a spur. Flowers are usually in shades of blue or mauve and yellow-throated.

Nicotiana sylvestris: see p.139.

Osmanthus delavayi: see p.140.

Phygelius × rectus 'African Queen'
Medium-sized evergreen shrub, often treated as an herbaceous perennial, sending up long stems from which in late summer dangle numerous tubular five-lobed red to orange-red flowers.

Primula Gold-laced Group: see p.133.

Primula japonica: see p.158.

Primula vulgaris: see p.72.

Salvia guaranitica
Tall subshrubby perennial bearing spikes of deep blue two-lipped flowers in late summer and autumn.

Vinca minor
Lesser periwinkle
Trailing evergreen shrub, useful as ground cover, bearing five-lobed flowers, usually a shade of blue (e.g. 'La Grave') but sometimes white, over a long season from mid-spring.

RIGHT, FROM TOP ▶
Anchusa azurea
Jasminum nudiflorum
Fuchsia 'Thalia'

SLIPPERS, SPURS & LOCKETS

Flowers conventionally described as slipper-shaped are pouched and somewhat inflated traps for pollinators. There is a devious beauty in the daintiness of spurred flowers, which set tough goals for pollinators, enticing them into their depths. The elaborate shape of dicentra flowers is conveyed by various fanciful common names, with references to hearts and lockets, and even Dutchmen's breeches.

▲ *Calceolaria* 'Kentish Hero'

▲ *Corydalis flexuosa*

▲ *Dicentra spectabilis* 'Alba'

Aquilegia McKana Group
Perennial H 75cm/30in, S 60cm/2ft Z5
Sun or partial shade Moist but well-drained soil

Most of the columbines show a strong family resemblance, the flowers, often nodding and with petals extending behind to form spurs, borne profusely above rosettes of prettily divided and lobed leaves. The generic name may be derived from the Latin *aquila*, meaning an eagle, a reference to the claw-like appearance of the spurs. The name columbine alludes to the shape of the flower, which suggests a group of doves. Aquilegias are short-lived, intermarry indiscriminately and self-seed freely but remain valuable plants for filling the gap between spring bulbs and summer perennials. Various long-spurred hybrids have been raised from species such as the yellow-flowered *Aquilegia chrysantha* and the similar but paler *A. longissima*, with spurs up to 15cm/6in long. The McKana Group have flowers in white or shades of blue, yellow and red, often bicoloured.

Shorter, tightly clustered hooked spurs are an attractive feature of the bell-like nodding flowers of granny's bonnet (*A. vulgaris*), usually blue-flowered but with a magnificent white, 'Nivea'. See also *A. viridiflora*, p.138.

Calceolaria 'Kentish Hero'
Perennial H 45cm/18in, S 25cm/10in Z10
Sun or partial shade Moist but well-drained, preferably acid soil; in containers soil-based compost (John Innes No. 2)

The calceolarias are a South American genus that gained enormous popularity in the nineteenth century. Vast numbers of plants were raised for elaborate bedding schemes or used as fascinating and colourful conservatory plants. Although the hybrid calceolarias have lost ground since their nineteenth-century heyday, their curiously pouched flowers still excite interest. The perennial and evergreen subshrubby *C. integrifolia*, with clusters of yellow flowers for several months in summer, is usually grown as an annual bedding or container plant, as are most of the hybrids related to it. *C.* 'Kentish Hero' is a richly coloured example of these, its orange-yellow flowers being darkened by rust-red veining. To maintain stocks, take semi-ripe cuttings in late summer.

The Multiflora calceolarias in the Herbohybrida Group produce dense domed heads of flowers in vibrant colours. Anytime Series, with plants 20cm/8in high suitable for bedding and for containers outdoors and under glass, can be sown at any time of the year to come into flower within sixteen weeks.

Corydalis flexuosa

Perennial H and S 25cm/10in Z5

Partial shade Humus-rich, moist but well-drained soil

Since its recent introduction this species from western China has had enormous success as a remarkably trouble-free and beautiful plant. The soft foliage is ferny and blue-green, sometimes tinged purple or with reddish marks. The clusters of spurred and tilted tubular flowers, freely produced in spring and early summer, look for all the world like little shoals of blue fish. There are variations in the intensity of the flower colour and the tint of the foliage. Flowers and leaves of 'Purple Leaf' have a purplish tint. 'China Blue' has pale flowers and the short-growing 'Père David' is a strong mid-blue with grey-green leaves. All flower in spring, sometimes into summer. These forms are generally planted out in the open garden, at their best forming large clumps in dappled shade, of deciduous shrubs that thrive in moist, well-drained soil. They are also excellent container plants, making a good contrast to spring-flowering bulbs.

The genus includes many other appealing plants, such as the beguiling yellow-flowered self-seeder *Corydalis lutea*. The unkind gardener may view this as a weed but when it lodges where it chooses in old walls it has the happy knack of looking perfectly placed. One of the great beauties of the genus is the temperamental blue-flowered *C. cashmeriana*. This species, cherished by alpine gardeners, is tuberous - rooted, makes a tuft 20cm/8in high and flowers in summer.

A much easier tuberous species is *C. solida*. A choice form of this is subsp. *solida* 'George Baker', which has vivid brick-red flowers in spring.

▲ *Aquilegia* McKana Group

Dicentra spectabilis
Bleeding heart, Dutchman's breeches,
lady's locket, lyre flower

Perennial H 1m/40in, S 50cm/20in Z3

Partial shade Moist but well-drained soil

The well-timed appearance of this perennial (see illustration on pp.40–41) – after most of the spring bulbs but before the main summer season – ensures that its full elegance is appreciated. It is a brittle plant, so give it a sheltered position where its divided grey-green leaves and sinuous stems will not be damaged by late squalls. From the arching growths dangle deep pink heart-shaped lockets, from which protrude the tips of white petals. Equally beautiful, and with a reputation for being more vigorous, is *Dicentra spectabilis* 'Alba', which has pure white lockets. Cut stems of these plants are beautiful in arrangements.

There are numerous smaller dicentras, usually less than 40cm/16in high, with pretty locket-like flowers and pleasing ferny foliage. All do best in moist, humus-rich soil. The wild bleeding heart (*D. formosa*) is a vigorous plant, making broad hummocks of divided leaves topped by clusters of mauve-pink lockets. The foliage of var. *alba* is paler and the lockets white. Two hybrids with blue-grey foliage are *D.* 'Langtrees', which has pinkish-white flowers, and 'Stuart Boothman', with deep pink lockets.

OTHER GOOD PLANTS

Diascia barberae
'Blackthorn Apricot'
Low sun-loving perennial producing loose spikes of twin-spurred salmon-pink flowers over many weeks in summer. The flowers of 'Ruby Field' are more purplish pink.

Epimedium grandiflorum
'Rose Queen'
Elegant ground-covering perennial about 25cm/10in high with beautifully tinted leaves in spring and also sprays of small pink flowers with white-tipped spurs.

Impatiens **New Guinea hybrids**: see p.100.

Linaria triornithophora
Short-lived perennial grown as an annual with branching stems up to 90cm/3ft high ending in tapered flights of bird-like purplish blue flowers, the spur forming a brown tail.

Linaria maroccana **'Northern Lights'**
Annual with foliage that is sticky to touch. This compact mixture produces a bright range of small and spurred colourful flowers, many of them bicoloured.

Nemesia **'Twilight'**: see p.114.

Viola cornuta **Horned violet, viola**
Low evergreen perennial thriving in sun or partial shade and in summer bearing masses of blue or white (Alba Group) spurred flowers with neatly separated petals.

Viola sororia **'Freckles'**: see p.129.

HATS, HOODS & HELMETS

A miscellany of attractive plants have flowers shaped in a way that suggests a head covering. Those with hanging flowers and petals curving back tightly have long been fancifully likened to turbans. In many cases the hood or helmet is a showy protective covering for the sexual parts of the flower.

▲ *Aconitum × cammarum* 'Bicolor'

Aconitum carmichaelii 'Arendsii'

Perennial H 1.2m/4ft, S 30cm/1ft Z3

Partial shade and sun Moist but well-drained soil

Despite the sinister aura that clings to them on account of the toxicity of all their parts, the monkshoods include border plants of great distinction, with handsome lobed leaves and erect stems of intriguing helmet-like flowers, which are excellent for cutting. *Aconitum × cammarum* 'Bicolor' flowers in the first half of summer, the helmets, clustered in dense sprays, shading from white to violet-blue.

For the end of the monkshood season there is *A. carmichaelii* 'Arendsii'. The dark foliage is good for many weeks before the sturdy branching stems carry spires of rich blue, hooded flowers in late summer and autumn.

Flowering midway between these in mid- to late summer is *A.* 'Spark's Variety', a slightly taller hybrid with deep violet flowers. It may need staking.

For late spring and early summer there is *A.* 'Ivorine', an appealing monkshood that is rarely more than 75cm/30in high and in a quite different colour range, for its slender flowers are creamy-white.

Lilium martagon
Common turk's cap lily

Bulb H 1.5m/5ft, S 20cm/8in Z4

Partial shade Well-drained soil

This species is the most widely distributed of all the lilies with turk's-cap flowers – that is with the segments rolled back – and is an adaptable garden plant, doing well in many positions and even naturalizing in grass. In early summer the stiff stems, set with whorls of lance-shaped leaves, carry up to fifty hanging flowers, usually a shade of pink-purple with darker spotting. The white var. *album*, waxy clean and with yellow anthers, shows well against dark foliage. If you use stems as cutting material, you will need to mask the somewhat rank smell of the flowers with the strong sweet scent of other blooms.

Another good turk's cap lily for naturalizing is *L. pyrenaicum*, with black-spotted green-yellow flowers that are also strong smelling. It likes neutral to alkaline soil, as does the taller *L. henryi*, which has stems, often more than 1.5m/5ft tall, in late summer carrying ten or more deep orange turkscap flowers that are spotted black.

Plant all these lilies deep, as they are stem-rooting.

More problematic in gardens because of their susceptibility to virus are the scarlet turk's cap lily (*L. chalcedonicum*) and the tiger lily (*L. lancifolium*). The former has bright scarlet flowers, the latter, best on acid soil, orange turk's caps spotted deep purple.

Lysichiton americanus
Yellow skunk cabbage

Perennial H 1m/40in, S 1.2m/4ft Z6

Sun or partial shade Humus-rich, reliably moist soil

The huge oar-shaped leaves of this plant, a native of western North America, make impressive clumps at the water's edge or in boggy ground throughout the summer but in early spring it is the flowers that are arresting, for they develop before the leaves. The 'flower' is in fact a protective greenish yellow bract, the spathe, up to 40cm/16in high, which hoods the spadix, the sturdy stem on which the minute true flowers are clustered tightly. Flowering plants give off an unpleasantly heavy smell.

The sweetly scented white skunk cabbage (*L. camtschatcensis*) is a slightly smaller plant with less hooded spathes that are white and surround pale green spadices.

Both species require permanently moist deep soil.

Roscoea cautleyoides

Tuber H 50cm/20in, S 15cm/6in Z7

Partial shade Humus-rich, moist but well-drained soil

Of the few woodland species of the genus *Roscoea* in general cultivation, this is generally the most adaptable, doing well in dappled shade under trees, in peat beds or in borders. It has narrow upright leaves topped in early to mid-summer by several pale yellow or purple hooded and lipped flowers of rather limp appearance.

The later-flowering *R. purpurea* is a smaller plant with flowers in shades of purple or bicoloured in purple and white and a large two-lobed lower lip.

The most compact of the commonly grown species is *R. humeana*, with orchid-like red-purple flowers in late spring and early summer.

Apply a generous mulch to protect the fleshy roots in winter.

OTHER GOOD PLANTS

Acanthus spinosus
Large perennial with rich green, deeply cut and spiny leaves forming an arching base for stiff stems that in late spring and early summer carry tiers of tubular white flowers hooded by purple bracts.

Delphinium grandiflorum 'Blue Butterfly'
Summer-flowering seed strain grown as border annual about 60cm/2ft high with airy sprays of bright blue elfin caps narrowing to upward-tilting spurs.

Gladiolus murielae
Tall perennial grown from corms with stiff linear leaves topped in late summer and early autumn by spikes of six to ten deliciously scented hooded flowers arching out on long tubes. They are white with deep purple throats.

Nicotiana langsdorffii: see p.109.

Phlomis russeliana
Hairy perennial with large basal leaves producing, mainly in early summer, tall erect stems set with whorls of hooded yellow flowers.

Salvia discolor
Medium-sized perennial, often grown as a container plant, with woolly foliage and branching stems carrying, in autumn, black flowers, each hooded by a woolly greenish white calyx.

▲ *Lilium martagon var. album*   ▲ *Lysichiton americanus*

▲ *Roscoea cautleyoides*

STANDARDS, WINGS & KEELS

The pea family is very large and contains many plants of great economic importance to man. Many members of this family are also highly ornamental, having five-petalled flowers of butterfly shape, with an upright standard, two lateral wings and two petals, more or less fused, that form a keel.

▲ *Cytisus* 'Lena'

▲ *Coronilla valentina* subsp. *glauca*

▲ *Baptisia australis*

Baptisia australis

Perennial H 1.2m/4ft, S 50cm/20in Z3

Full sun Well-drained, preferably acid soil

At a quick glance this looks like an etherealized version of a lupin, with a base of fresh green three-lobed leaves. In summer the uncluttered wavering spires are set with indigo-blue pea flowers. Clusters of swollen dark seed pods are left when frosts cut the foliage. This deep-rooted perennial may be slow to start but once established it is long-lived in a border.

Cercis siliquastrum
Judas tree

Deciduous tree H and S 10m/30ft Z6

Full sun Moist but well-drained soil

Its heart-shaped blue-green leaves, notched at the tip, are attractive in summer but it is in spring that this spreading and often multistemmed tree catches the eye. It is then the branches are covered with clusters of pink or magenta pea flowers, sometimes bursting directly out of old wood.

Another species of similar dimensions is the eastern redbud (*Cercis canadensis*). It has heart-shaped leaves and pink to crimson flowers, produced most freely in a Continental climate. It is often represented in gardens by 'Forest Pansy', which is grown for its red-purple leaves rather than its flowers.

Coronilla valentina subsp. *glauca*

Evergreen shrub H 90cm/3ft, 75cm/30in Z7

Full sun Well-drained soil

This rather lightweight shrub (formerly known as *Coronilla glauca*), is worth a sunny corner in a sheltered garden, preferably at the base of a warm wall. Its divided glaucous leaves show off the clusters of scented yellow pea flowers. The main flush is in spring with occasional clusters throughout summer but more valuable are the flowers that usually begin its prolonged season in winter. A more subtle plant is the pale yellow 'Citrina'. The leaves of 'Variegata' are cream-edged.

None of these is long-lived. Guard against losses in cold winters by taking cuttings.

Cytisus 'Lena'

Deciduous shrub H 1.2m/4ft, S 1.5m/5ft Z6

Full sun Well-drained soil

There is a group of hybrid brooms derived from *Cytisus scoparius* which are colourful shrubs in late spring and early summer, when their slender stems are densely set with pea flowers, which in many cases are bicoloured. These brooms are generally not long-lived but are fast-growing if planted out when small. *C.* 'Lena' is a compact example with dark yellow flowers with wings and standards shading into rusty red.

Cercis siliquastrum ▶

More upright hybrids include 'Hollandia', which has cream and deep pink flowers, and 'Zielandia', which has flowers in a combination of mauve, pink and cream. The bushy and slightly later flowering 'Windlesham Ruby' is deep red.

Several low-growing deciduous brooms are useful for frontal positions and for planting where they can spill from the shelf of a rock garden or the top of a retaining wall. They make an impact out of all proportion to their size with the profusion of their flowers in late spring or early summer. The downy stems of *C. × kewensis* are thickly set with creamy yellow flowers in late spring or early summer.

In the same season the slightly more upright and less spreading *C. × beanii* bears rich yellow flowers.

Prune these shrubs lightly immediately after flowering.

▲ *Galega × hartlandii* 'Lady Wilson'

Galega × hartlandii 'Lady Wilson'
Perennial H 1.5m/5ft, S 90cm/3ft Z4
Sun or partial shade Well-drained soil, preferably moist

Goat's rue (*Galega officinalis*) is a parent of several hybrid galegas that were once border plants popular for their long summer display of small pea flowers carried profusely in branching spikes above ferny blue-green leaves. They are less popular than they were, partly because they generally need staking and partly because they tend to spread freely in good soil. However, they remain graceful understated perennials for modern borders. The attractively bicoloured flowers of *G. × hartlandii* 'Lady Wilson' combine deep mauve-blue and white; 'Alba' is a good clean white.

Similar to these is *G.* 'His Majesty', a bicolour with white and pinkish mauve flowers.

Lathyrus latifolius
Everlasting pea
Perennial climber H 2.5m/8ft, S 90cm/3ft Z5
Sun or partial shade Well-drained soil

This tendril climber, with strongly winged stems, can be trained on supports such as trellis or a wigwam of canes but displays a nonchalant confidence when allowed to scramble over shrubs or tumble down a bank. It is widely naturalized on waste ground. The unscented flowers, sometimes more than ten to a spray, are usually bright purple-pink. Of a quite different order are the pure and glistening 'White Pearl' and the pale pink 'Rosa Perle'. The long summer season makes all forms of the everlasting pea useful for masking gaps left by plants that flower in spring and early summer.

The suckering *Lathyrus grandiflorus* can easily be distinguished by its wingless stems. The unscented flowers, one to four per spray and magenta pink with a red keel, are short-lived but are freely produced for many weeks in summer.

For sweet peas see *L. odoratus* 'Angela Ann', p.75, and *L.o.* 'Matucana', p.139.

Lathyrus vernus
Spring vetchling
Perennial H 40cm/16in, S 45cm/18in Z8
Full sun Well-drained soil

Among the relatively small number of spring-flowering perennials this non-climbing sweet pea relative is one of the most resilient. It has a tough rootstock and even on dry stony soils makes a ferny clump of divided leaves, flowers with the mid-season bulbs and, before it becomes a nuisance, dies down to make way for the main perennial season. In the usual form the flowers are in a mixture of crimson, magenta and purple shades. The bicoloured flowers of 'Alboroseus' are pink and white.

Lotus berthelotii
Coral gem, parrot's beak, pelican's beak

Evergreen subshrub H 30cm/1ft, S indefinite Z9

Full sun Well-drained soil; in containers soil-based compost (John Innes No. 2)

Trailing stems, finely divided silvery leaves and scarlet beaked flowers in summer have made this a popular container plant but it probably no longer survives in the wild on its native Tenerife. It is easy to propagate from cuttings taken in late summer and, if overwintered under glass, these will provide plants that are freer flowering than the parent for the following summer. A similar plant, *Lotus maculatus*, has yellow flowers with orange tips. The cross *L. berthelotii × maculatus* shares characteristics of the two species.

More erect and hardier than either of these is the hairy canary clover (*L. hirsutus*), a lightweight but appealing subshrub. It has grey-green softly hairy foliage and carries clusters of pink-tinged creamy white flowers over a long season. The flowers are followed by red-brown seed pods and in favourable conditions the plant may produce numerous self-sown seedlings.

OTHER GOOD PLANTS

Clianthus puniceus Lobster claw, parrot's bill
Lax evergreen shrub, which can be trained as a climber, with leaves composed of numerous leaflets and beaked brilliant red flowers in spring and early summer.

Genista aetnensis
Mount Etna broom
Almost leafless small tree bearing a profusion of fragrant yellow flowers on slender drooping stems in mid- to late summer.

Laburnum × watereri 'Vossii': see p.163.

Lupinus Band of Nobles Series: see p.114.

Polygola chamaebuxus var. *grandiflora*
Small evergreen shrub in late spring and early summer producing eye-catching flowers combining pink wings and yellow lips.

Spartium junceum Spanish broom
Almost leafless shrub growing to 3m/10ft bearing rich yellow and fragrant pea flowers over many weeks in summer and even into autumn. Does well in sunny dry gardens.

Thermopsis lupinoides
Lupin-like perennial that in summer holds spikes of yellow pea flowers over leaves divided into three.

Wisteria sinensis: see p.163.

▲ *Lathyrus latifolius* 'White Pearl'   ▲ *Lathyrus vernus*   ▲ *Lotus berthelotii × maculatus*

DISCS & FLORETS

Sunny gardens would be much less interesting without the contribution made by numerous daisies of ornamental value. Many are easy to grow and very free-flowering. The typical colour contrast between the disc and the surrounding rays creates a lively effect. And many daisies are excellent cut flowers.

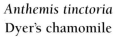
▲ *Anthemis tinctoria* 'Sauce Hollandaise'

▲ *Echinacea purpurea* 'White Lustre'

Anthemis tinctoria
Dyer's chamomile
Perennial H and S 75cm/30in Z4

Full sun Well-drained soil

The various cultivars of the golden marguerite have filigree leaves topped in summer by countless stiff-stemmed daisies in various shades of yellow. The easiest to mix with a wide range of other plants are those on the pale side. *Anthemis tinctoria* 'E.C. Buxton' is a cool lemon yellow with a deeper yellow disc. Those in creamy yellow include 'Sauce Hollandaise' and 'Wargrave Variety'.

Some plants previously listed under the species are probably hybrids between it and *A. sancti-johannis*, a similar but slightly taller plant bearing orange-yellow daisies with stubby ray florets. The daisies of *A.* 'Grallach Gold' are exceptionally bright.

For a frontal position, raised bed or rock garden a better choice than any of these is *A. punctata* subsp. *cupaniana*. In early summer its white daisies spangle a low mound of finely cut silvery leaves.

These marguerites flower so exuberantly that they tend to be short-lived. To encourage basal growth cut back after flowering and as a precaution against loss maintain stocks from basal cuttings taken in autumn or early spring.

All these plants, particularly the cultivars of *A. tinctoria*, provide excellent material for cutting.

Aster × *frikartii* 'Mönch'
Perennial H 75cm/30in, S 40cm/16in Z5

Full sun Moist but well-drained soil

The taller asters, loosely referred to as Michaelmas daisies (although this name strictly applies only to *A. novi-belgii*), help to revive borders in late summer and autumn and provide copious flowers for cutting. This refined and reliable hybrid is disease resistant, needs no support and for many weeks carries loose sprays of yellow-centred daisies with narrow purplish blue rays.

One parent is *A. amellus*, with a shorter flowering season; its numerous cultivars come in shades of pink, blue and purple. An old cultivar of proven quality is 'Veilchenkönigin', about 40cm/16in high and with large yellow-centred flowerheads of intense violet. 'Sonia' is mauve-pink with green-yellow centres.

Flowering of the true Michaelmas daisies suffers unless tarsonemid mite is controlled by spraying with a suitable pesticide. Some of the most attractive cultivars are of compact growth. *A.* 'Kristina' makes a low dome covered with double white flowerheads, those of the slightly taller 'Purple Dome' are rich purple.

The New England asters (*A. novae-angliae*) may also be attacked by tarsonemid mite and all need frequent division to remain free-flowering. If you find the red-pink of 'Andenkenan Alma Pötschke' too strident, you might prefer the clear and lighter 'Harrington's Pink', as well as the blues and whites among other cultivars, growing 1.2–1.8m/4–6ft high.

▲ *Aster × frikartii* 'Mönch'

Echinacea purpurea

Perennial H 1.2m/4ft, S 75cm/30in Z4

Full sun Humus-rich, well-drained soil

This, the best known of the coneflowers, is a sturdy daisy that flowers in late summer and autumn. It is a prairie plant in its native North America. The flowerheads, carried on stiff stems above rough-textured leaves, are remarkable for the central cone, typically greenish copper in tone. The surrounding petal-like ray florets, usually reflexed, are purple-pink. 'Magnus' is a richly coloured cultivar with ray florets held almost horizontal. The somewhat shorter 'White Lustre' holds up brassy cones surrounded by drooping creamy white ray florets.

The flowerheads of all cultivars are long-lasting when cut.

Helenium 'Coppelia'

Perennial H 90cm/3ft, S 60cm/2ft Z4

Full sun Well-drained soil

The hybrid heleniums provide copious daisies through summer and into autumn, and are good for cutting as well as adding warming tones to borders. The prominent disc florets are usually yellow or brown while the ray florets are in shades of yellow, rusty red and mahogany. Many heleniums need staking, it is true, and their strong colours require careful placing but their sustained vibrancy is an enormous asset in the garden. 'Coppelia', which starts flowering in mid-summer, has copper-red ray florets and brown disc florets. The earlier flowering 'Moerheim Beauty' has similar colouring but the ray florets reflex as the flowerheads age.

▲ *Helenium* 'Coppelia'

Others of similar height include the rich yellow 'Waldtraut' and the rust-red 'Dunkelpracht'. 'Rubinzwerg', long-flowering and with deep mahogany-red flowerheads, grows to about 75cm/30in.

Taller hybrids growing to about 1.5m/5ft include 'Septemberfuchs', in a similar colour range to 'Moerheim Beauty', with red-brown flowers streaked yellow. It needs support but 'Sonnenwunder', which carries open bunches of clear yellow flowerheads with notched ray florets and green to pale brown bosses, is reasonably self-reliant.

All these are best divided every two or three years.

Helianthus annuus
Sunflower
Annual H 45cm–4m/18in–12ft
Full sun Moist but well-drained soil

Many gardeners retain their childhood attachment to a plant that provided the first demonstration of meteoric growth. But height is not everything. Many new cultivars of the plant are 1.5m/5ft or less and a few are dwarf, and an attractive feature is the large beautifully patterned central disc, surrounded by the petal-like ray florets, usually a shade of yellow. Most are excellent for cutting and the dried seedheads are attractive.

Grow 'Russian Giant' for its large flowerheads and to show how sunflowers can streak to 3m/10ft or more. For a group planting in a border select those growing to about 1.5m/5ft. A hybrid of similar size, *H.* 'Valentine' has creamy yellow flowerheads with brown centres, the very dark-centred 'Velvet Queen', flowerheads in shades of red-brown and copper. The dwarf 'Teddy Bear', only 45cm/18in, is a curiosity with very double orange-yellow flowerheads.

All the taller sunflowers need staking.

Leucanthemum x *superbum*
Shasta daisy
Perennial H 45–90cm/18–36in, S 45–60cm/18–24in Z4
Sun or partial shade Moist but well-drained soil

The colour range of the Shasta daisies is limited to white and off-white except for their yellow centres but despite this limitation these retain their popularity as dependable and easily pleased perennials. They provide flowers for the garden and for cutting over a long season in summer, and the range of singles and doubles come in a useful range of sizes.

Many need support but the large single 'Beauté Nivelloise' carries its flowers high on strong stems. The fully double 'Wirrall Supreme' is a daisy of comparable height, needing staking. Even shorter plants need some help, among them the single 'Phyllis Smith', which has narrow twisted ray florets, and the semi-double 'Aglaia'. One of the best for the front of a border is the single 'Snowcap', about 45cm/18in high and capable of looking after itself.

For good results plants need to be divided every few years.

Rudbeckia laciniata 'Herbstsonne'
Perennial H 1.8m/6ft, S 90cm/3ft Z3
Full sun Moist but well-drained soil

Provided it gets plenty of moisture, from mid-summer to early autumn this giant among the coneflowers produces masses of flowerheads more than 10cm/4in across, with broad yellow ray florets reflexed from the conical yellow-green centres.

The black-eyed Susans or rudbeckias are more compact perennials that also have a long late season. The pick of these is *Rudbeckia fulgida* var. *sullivantii* 'Goldsturm', which makes a mound 60cm/2ft high topped by rich yellow flowerheads with black studs. The slightly taller *R.* 'Goldquelle' has fully double lemon-yellow flowerheads but as they open from green buds they show a green-tinted centre.

Tithonia rotundifolia
Mexican sunflower
Annual H 1.8m/6ft, S 30cm/1ft
Full sun Moist but well-drained soil

Its height and vivid orange-red ray discs circling a yellow centre are attributes to be seized on in this gangling and handsome annual. A stand of the Mexican sunflower makes an impressive addition to a hot-coloured border in late summer or early autumn, when many annuals are past their best. It is not a plant for an exposed position; even in a sheltered border it needs the support of other plants or, more commonly, the main stems require staking.

Several shorter growing cultivars are available. The shortest are hardly worth considering. If you are not up to plants of full height, consider the slightly bushier 'Torch', which grows to about 1.2m/4ft, and 'Goldfinger', which is about 90cm/3ft high. The taller cultivars especially are good for cutting.

OTHER GOOD PLANTS

Argyranthemum 'Vancouver': see p.60.

Bellis perennis Pomponette Series: see p.60.

Brachyglottis (Dunedin Group) 'Sunshine'
Grey-leaved evergreen shrub, growing to about 1.5m/5ft, spangled with yellow daisies in summer.

Calendula officinalis Marigold, pot marigold
Easily raised summer annual, growing to about 75cm/30in, with bright orange single flowerheads. Usually represented by more subtle cultivars, often double, such as the richly shaded 'Touch of Red'.

Coreopsis verticillata 'Moonbeam'
Bushy perennial growing to about 50cm/20in and producing numerous lemon-yellow flowerheads over finely cut leaves for many weeks in late summer and autumn.

Cosmos atrosanguineus: see p.111.

Erigeron 'Foersters Liebling'
One of several closely related sun-loving hybrid perennial daisies of medium height flowering profusely in summer. The semi-double flowerheads are reddish pink with yellow centres.

Ligularia 'The Rocket': see p.155.

Olearia macrodonta
Evergreen holly-like shrub or small tree covered in early summer with heads of fragrant white daisies. Good for seaside gardens.

Osteospermum 'White Pim': see p.123.

Tagetes Gem Series
The Signet marigolds are annuals making low mounds radiant with small flowerheads (light yellow in 'Lemon Gem') over many weeks in summer and autumn. Good for frontal positions and containers.

▲ *Helianthus annuus* 'Velvet Queen'

Rudbeckia laciniata 'Herbstonne' ▼

▲ *Leucanthemum* × *superbum* 'Phyllis Smith'

Tithonia rotundifolia ▲

PINCUSHIONS & TUFTS

The pincushions of plants such as scabious are in reality compound flowerheads, with a dome of central florets surrounded by larger florets. The flowerheads of many knapweeds and thistles consist of tufty florets but the small fluffy tufts of the meadow rues are petal-less clusters of stamens.

▲ *Cynara cardunculus*

▲ *Knautia macedonica*

Cynara cardunculus
Cardoon
Perennial H 2m/6½ft, S 1.5m/5ft Z7
Full sun Well-drained soil

As well as being a connoisseur's vegetable (the young leaf stems can be blanched), the cardoon is an ornamental perennial of impressive size, with large and arching jagged leaves of silvery grey. By all means grow it for its magnificent foliage or even as a choice and unusual vegetable but do not ignore the thistle-like flowerheads carried high on branching stems. The tuft is an intense violet- or purple-blue and the spiny bracts below it are green with purple tints. The heavy flowerheads can be dried.

Knautia macedonica
Perennial H 75cm/30in, S 40cm/16in Z5
Full sun Well-drained, preferably alkaline soil

It comes as no surprise that this good-natured and long-flowering perennial was previously classified as a scabious (*Scabiosa rumelica*). The branching stems that rise from the basal leaves terminate in domed buds surrounded by green bracts. The open pincushion flowerheads, which are very attractive to bees, are a deep and unusual shade of red-purple.

To maintain vigorous free-flowering young stock, propagate every few years from seed or take basal cuttings in spring.

Scabiosa caucasica

Perennial H 60cm/2ft, S 45cm/18in Z4

Full sun Well-drained neutral to alkaline soil

Commercial interest in this scabious as a cut flower has waned but gardeners still rate it for cutting and for the long season it gives in the garden. Rigorous cutting to the base of spent flowers keeps plants blooming from mid-summer to autumn. The long-stalked flowers, one per stem, have large slighty waved outer florets, surrounding a paler pincushion dome of central florets. 'Clive Greaves' is soft mauve-blue, 'Moerheim Blue' several shades darker and 'Miss Willmott' white.

Shorter-growing than these is *Scabiosa* 'Butterfly Blue', a plant with mauve-blue flowers that is said to be a hybrid of the small scabious (*S. columbaria*). It makes an attractive addition to a rock garden.

For vigorous free-flowering plants, divide these perennials every three years.

Thalictrum aquilegiifolium

Perennial H 1.2m/4ft, S 45cm/18in Z5

Partial shade Humus-rich, moist but well-drained soil

The meadow rues are graceful plants with divided leaves that are well above the ordinary in beauty, as are their branching sprays of fluffy petal-less flowers in early to mid-summer. The specific name of *Thalictrum aquilegiifolium* indicates how strongly its leaves resemble those of columbines such as *Aquilegia vulgaris*. They are light green and from their elegant clump ascend branching stems terminating in heads of purplish pink fluffy flowers. There is a good white, var. *album*, and 'Thundercloud' is a splendidly rich purple.

The taller *T. flavum* subsp. *glaucum* combines glaucous sea-green foliage and pale yellow fluffy flowers to perfection.

These plants look awkward when staked and are at their best supported by companionable shrubs.

OTHER GOOD PLANTS

Astrantia major subsp. *involucrata* 'Shaggy': see p.68.

Centaurea hypoleuca 'John Coutts' Sturdy perennial knapweed growing to 60cm/2ft and bearing warm-pink flowerheads, with paler centres and prettily tufted florets in late summer and early autumn.

Centaurea macrocephala Coarse-leaved perennial carrying impressive glossy brown buds on thick stiff stems 1.2m/4ft high in the second half of summer. The base of overlapping papery bracts retains its shape when the yellow tufts burst from the top. The heads dry well when the tufts have faded.

Cephalaria gigantea Back-of-the-border perennial growing to 2.5m/8ft with tall branching stems carrying pale yellow pincushion flowerheads in summer.

Pterocephalus perennis Sun-loving evergreen mat-forming perennial for a rock garden or frontal position. The purple-pink flowerheads of summer are followed by papery seedheads.

Scabiosa atropurpurea Pincushion flower, sweet scabious Biennial producing a compact rosette of leaves from which rise slender stems bearing fragant pincushion dark crimson flowers.

▲ *Scabiosa caucasica*

▲ *Thalictrum aquilegiifolium*

ROSETTES, BUTTONS & POMPONS

Double flowers are no longer just choice rareties, as once they may have been, but play a dominant role in the modern garden. Whether neatly layered, fancifully flamboyant or simply quaint, double flowers create opulent effects in gardens and also in arrangements of cut flowers.

Achillea ptarmica 'The Pearl'
Perennial H 75cm/30in, S 60cm/2ft Z6
Full sun Moist but well-drained soil

Sneezewort is a weedy plant, too quick to take over ground, and its heads of loose flowers are an unlaundered white. Although some still need to be watched because they spread at the roots, the double forms are in a different class, the sprays thick with white buttons livening borders in summer and providing good material for cutting. *Achillea ptarmica* 'The Pearl', a non-spreading clone that needs to be propagated vegetatively, is strong-stemmed with tight buttons. The buttons of the shorter-growing 'Perry's White' are slightly larger. The seed-raised The Pearl Group is similar to 'The Pearl' but is invasive and shows some variation.

Argyranthemum 'Vancouver'
Evergreen subshrub H 90cm/3ft, S 75cm/30in Z9
Full sun Well-drained soil; in containers soil-based compost (John Innes No. 3)

Several of the argyranthemum hybrids have flowerheads described as anemone-centred, because the multiplication of the ray florets creates a dense centre, which is surrounded by a sparse ring of ray florets. These flowerheads are long-lasting on the plant and also when picked. Like all the argyranthemums, these hybrids have a very long season provided the conditions are frost free.

'Vancouver' has grey-green foliage and rich pink flowerheads surrounded by paler ray florets. 'Mary Wootton' is slightly taller with similar flowerheads but a paler shade of pink, fading with age to near white.

Both of these hybrids make excellent container plants and they are suitable for training as standards.

Bellis perennis Pomponette Series
Perennial/biennial H 10cm/4in, S 15cm/6in Z4
Sun or partial shade Well-drained soil; in containers soil-based compost (John Innes No. 1)

To the lawn perfectionist the common daisy is a curse but the double forms have delighted gardeners since the sixteenth century. The pink

Bellis perennis 'Dresden China', possibly of eighteenth-century origin, and *B.p.* 'Rob Roy', red and probably later, are some of those with the neatest button flowerheads. These plants, which have a period charm, need to be propagated by division.

Many daisies are raised from seed and treated as biennials. The heavier buttons of seed-raised plants provide quantity for bedding, edging and containers in late winter and spring. The white, pink and red flowerheads of the *B.p.* Pomponette Series, packed with narrow quilled 'petals', are about 4cm/1½in across. The Tasso Series comes in the same range of colours but the flowerheads are almost twice as large.

Camellia japonica formal double cultivars
Evergreen shrub H 2.5–6m/8–20ft, 2–4m/6½–13ft Z8
Partial shade Humus-rich, moist but well-drained acid soil; in containers, an ericaceous compost

Among the innumerable cultivars of *Camellia japonica* are formal doubles of a scrupulously crafted refinement that hold an appeal despite their air of artificiality. A number of elegant cultivars, most small-flowered by today's standards, were raised in Italy in the mid-nineteenth century. The unnamed cultivar illustrated is almost certainly one of these. As in other blotched and streaked formal doubles there is a curious tension between the rigorous symmetry of the rosetted flower and random markings in pink and red. 'Lavinia Maggi', another cultivar from the same period and one of the old formal doubles that has remained popular, has red and pink splashes and streaks on a pure white ground.

Other formal doubles cover the broad range of camellia colours. A particularly elegant example is the pure white 'Alba Plena'. The flowers of 'Desire' combine an intricate layering of petals with very subtle shading from an almost white centre through blush white to a stronger pink edging. 'Mathotiana Rosea' is a clear pink. 'Coquettii' is a slow-growing clone with bright red flowers of regular rosette form although not always of fully formal double shape.

Most of the Williamsii hybrids have single or relatively loose semi-double flowers. The formal double slightly cupped flowers of *C. × williamsii* 'E.G. Waterhouse' are composed of rounded and incurved light pink petals.

▲ CLOCKWISE FROM TOP LEFT *Achillea ptarmica* 'The Pearl', *Argyranthemum* 'Vancouver', *Bellis perennis* Pomponette Series, *Camellia japonica* cultivar

Dahlia 'Moor Place'
Tuber H 90cm/3ft, S 60cm/2ft Z9
Full sun Humus-rich, moist but well-drained soil

Most of the dahlias in cultivation are complex hybrids that are generally classified by the form of their flowerheads. The Pompon dahlias are an intriguing group with small symmetrically spherical flowerheads that are up to 5cm/2in across and composed of incurved florets. 'Moor Place' is one of these, a cultivar that is usually under 1.2m/4ft high, with deep wine-red flowerheads.

Another group, the Waterlily dahlias, have rosette-shaped flowerheads with broader and fewer ray florets than the large shaggy cultivars. 'Glorie van Heemstede' is a popular cultivar, usually just under 1.5m/5ft high. Its small bright yellow double flowerheads are about 10cm/4in across.

Dahlia cultivars in a wide range of sizes and colours come and go and it is as well to select from plants when they are in flower. All provide good material for cutting.

In frost-prone areas lift tubers when the foliage has been blackened by frost.

Geranium pratense 'Plenum Violaceum'
Perennial H 75cm/30in, S 60cm/2ft Z4
Sun or partial shade Well-drained soil

The double-flowered cranesbills have a distinctive, rather quaint charm. The ordinary meadow cranesbill (*Geranium pratense*) is beautiful, although a prodigious self-seeder, and 'Plenum Violaceum' is a really fine double that has much to offer. Cupped rosettes of intense violet-blue flowers, more purple at the centre, top clumps of fingered leaves. 'Plenum Caeruleum' is a pale mauve-blue double, and var. *pratense* f. *albiflorum* 'Plenum Album' is a double white.

Another fine double cranesbill, only 25cm/10in high but with spreading roots, is *G. himalayense* 'Plenum'. The blue flowers are tinted purple and pink.

Nymphaea 'Gonnère'
Perennial S 1.2m/4ft Z5
Full sun Aquatic compost

Waterlilies suitable for bodies of still water in temperate regions present their rosette flowers among the floating pads from early summer until the first autumn frosts. The vigour of waterlilies varies considerably and it is important to make your selection to suit the depth of water where the plants are to be grown. The surface spread is usually between one and two times the planting depth.

A suitable choice for a medium-sized pool with water 45–90cm/18–36in deep, is 'Gonnère', with fragrant flowers that have numerous overlapping white petals and yellow stamens. The pads are bronze when they first unfurl, then bright green. The vivid red-pink flowers of *N.* 'James Brydon'

◄ LEFT, FROM TOP
Dahlia 'Moor Place'
Geranium pratense 'Plenum Violaceum'
Rosa 'Königin von Dänemark'

▲ *Nymphaea 'Gonnère'*

are more cup-shaped, as are those of the yellow 'Marliacea Chromatella'. Both these have pads with purple to bronze markings.

There is a surprisingly wide choice of waterlilies for small pools and containers with a water depth of 15–45cm/6–18in. 'Pygmaea Helvola' is yellow with orange stamens and there is heavy purple and brown mottling on the olive-green pads. The fragrant Laydekeri hybrids include the crimson-flowered 'Laydekeri Fulgens', which has purple-backed leaves.

Rosa 'Königin von Dänemark'

Deciduous shrub (Alba rose) H 1.5m/5ft, S 1.2m/4ft Z4

Full sun Moist but well-drained soil

Every list of notable old roses includes this Alba. The bush can be rather spindly but its blue-green leaves, typical of the group, make a perfect foil for its scented flowers in early summer. When open each elegant carmine-pink bud makes a sumptuous quartered bed of soft pink with carmine-pink depths.

Old roses with quartered flowers from other groups include the fragrant 'Madame Hardy', a green-eyed white Damask that is in season for several weeks in early summer, and the repeat-flowering Bourbon 'Souvenir de la Malmaison', with scented blush-cream flowers that have delicate pink tints. These are all of similar height, although 'Souvenir de la Malmaison' is also available as a climber.

Another climber is 'Gloire de Dijon', variously described as a Noisette and as a Tea Rose. The quartered flowers, creamy buff and scented, first appear in late spring and continue until early autumn.

OTHER GOOD PLANTS

Aquilegia vulgaris var. *stellata* 'Nora Barlow'
A double form of granny's bonnet with pompon flowers in late spring and early summer. Each flower is composed of narrow quilled red and green segments.

Campanula persicifolia 'Fleur de Neige'
A handsome white double, growing to about 75cm/30in, of the peach-leaved bellflower.

Clematis 'Vyvyan Pennell'
Large-flowered clematis with neat fully double flowers about 15cm/6in across in shades of mauve and purple in late spring and early summer. The flowers produced late in the year on the current growth are single.

Hepatica nobilis 'Rubra Plena'
Dwarf perennial for woodland conditions bearing double red-purple flowers in early spring.

Primula 'Miss Indigo'
In effect a double primrose but the flowers are very deep purple with a white frosting at the edges of the petals.

Ranunculus aconitifolius 'Flore Pleno' Fair maids of France, fair maids of Kent, white bachelor's buttons
Dazzling white border perennial loaded in late spring and early summer with tight, long-lasting pompons about 5cm/2in across.

DETAILS

The ornamental value of many flowers is greatly enhanced by a surrounding ruff of handsome bracts. Even where the flowers are insignificant, the bracts can make impresive leaf flowers. In some cases the sexual parts of flowers are very conspicuous and ornamental. Many flowers, including most camellias, have at their centre a prominent boss of stamens. Other details, however, are more like fashionable trims – the deeply cut fringes and strongly ruffled margins of petals, for instance, which are the result of mutations seized on and perpetuated by plant breeders.

The fibrous-rooted perennial anemones revive the garden in late summer and autumn, their wiry branching stems carrying numerous button buds that open to white or pink flowers with a showy boss of stamens. An attractive feature of *Anemone hupehensis* 'Hadspen Abundance' is the shading of the pink segments around the golden boss.

DETAILS

Details of flowers may be like fashion touches, but changing tastes have dictated what plants are in or out of fashion. Many gardeners own up enthusiastically to their delight in novelties. But even those of austere tastes, who in general favour species over 'improved' plants, are to some extent the victims of fashion, if only because their choice is in part dictated by what is available.

LEAF FLOWERS

There is enormous variety in the conspicuous structures, somewhere between leaf and flower, that protect and amplify true flowers and in doing so take on an ornamental value of their own. Perennials include a few members of the carrot family (*Apiaceae*, formerly *Umbelliferae*), which is otherwise poorly represented among ornamentals. Of these, the thistle-like appearance of the sea hollies (*Eryngium*), many of which thrive in sunny dry gardens, is due to the more-or-less jagged bracts that surround the true flowers, which are small, stalkless and packed together in dense cylindrical or hemispherical heads. Branching stems carrying numerous long-lasting ruffs and heads give the sea hollies their exceptional graphic quality but unusual colours, especially metallic blues and silver greens staining stems and ruffs, add to their appeal as ornamentals. Cut stems are easy to preserve and are as dramatic in dried arrangements as they are in the garden (see also p.90). The astrantias, also from the carrot family, are much softer in appearance. The small flowers are gathered in little posies surrounded by papery bracts. These are versatile plants but prefer moister conditions than the sea hollies.

Several spurges (*Euphorbia*) find places elsewhere in this book but this is the right place to explain the long-lasting displays of the shrubs and shrubby perennials from this very large genus that are grown in temperate gardens. The cylindrical heads of *E. characias* subsp. *wulfenii* (see p.155) can remain attractive for several months. What makes the heads so conspicuous and long-lasting are cup-shaped bracts, in the case of this handsome plant and a number of other spurges green to lime-green, which cradle the much reduced male and female parts and later the seeds.

Among the most extraordinary bracts are the dangling handkerchiefs of the dove tree (*Davidia involucrata*), sometimes known as the handkerchief tree, which signal to pollinators the presence of the relatively insignificant flowers. It is a magnificent medium-sized tree for patient gardeners, its allure much heightened by the romantic story of the search for plants after its initial discovery in western China by the French missionary Père David and its introduction to gardens at the beginning of the twentieth century. More generally useful are several dogwoods (*Cornus*). Some of these do best in a Continental climate but *C. kousa* and *C.k.* var. *chinensis* are versatile large shrubs giving magnificent and long displays.

SEX ON SHOW

Sexual reproduction is the essential role of flowers but the male and female organs that make this possible may be hidden or too small to be of ornamental significance in themselves. There are, however, many plants with flowers in which numerous stamens make a bold central tuft or boss. The stalks of these male reproductive organs are usually tipped by bilobed anthers, the parts of the flower that produce pollen. What often makes a cluster of stamens conspicuous is the sometimes strong colour of the anthers. Important ornamentals with showy stamens found in the buttercup family (*Ranunculaceae*) include plants in genera as diverse as *Anemone*, *Clematis* and *Helleborus*. The flowers of peonies, a genus in a family of its own, are generously filled with stamens, which in some of the herbaceous cultivars have turned into what look like shredded petals.

The appeal of many poppies in various genera (including *Meconopsis*, *Papaver* and *Romneya*) owes much to the showy mass of stamens at the centre of the flowers. But another prominent feature, especially in species of *Papaver*, is the ovary. The stigma, the female organ, is not stalked. Instead the ovary is topped by a stigmatic disc marked with radiating lines. The ovary eventually becomes a seedbox of characterful shape. Long after the flowers have gone the seedboxes of Oriental and opium poppies (*P. orientale* and *P. somniferum*), and other species too, remain as stemmed pepperpots, which are attractive in the garden and in dried arrangements.

Another category of plants that could justifiably have been added to this section are those with relatively few but nonetheless conspicuous sexual parts. Most of the fuchsia hybrids have dangling tubular flowers with the style and stamens protruding from the skirt of petals. In the species this arrangement is usually geared to pollination by birds. Ornamentally it gives the flowers a balletic poise, which in many cases is enhanced by colours contrasting with or matching the petals, tube or overskirt of four sepals.

In almost all the lilies, whatever the shape of the flowers, the style and six stamens are very prominent and the pollen on the trembling anthers is often strongly coloured, commonly yellow, orange or red-brown. In the trumpet-shaped *Lilium regale* the yellow anthers are attractive decorations at the mouth; in the lilies of turk's cap shape they are a counterweight to the turned-back petals. Pollen stains are difficult to remove, so cut flowers need to be carefully placed.

In crocuses it is not so much the stamens that are conspicuous but the styles, which in some species are much branched and highly coloured. The autumn-flowering *Crocus sativus* has very long orange-red styles that yield saffron, an important flavouring and food colourant. It is grown commercially in countries such as Turkey but as an ornamental often proves difficult. Other easier crocuses with showy styles include the spring-flowering Dutch crocuses (cultivars of *C. vernus*) and the smaller and earlier-flowering crocuses listed under *C. chrysanthus*.

THE EXTRAVAGANT AND THE CURIOUS

The appeal of several plants in this section lies in the neatness of their flowers. Primroses (*Primula vulgaris*) have petals with gently scalloped margins. Convolvulus flowers are scrupulously pleated. The ray florets of the blue cupidone (*Catananche caerulea*) have tidy fringes while many pinks (*Dianthus*) have finely snipped margins to their petals.

We can appreciate the ornamental qualities of these flowers but it is not always easy to know what precise biological significance there is to a flower's outline. In species, as opposed to cultivars, it is fair to assume that it is something to do with attracting pollinators. Honeybees, for example, show a strong preference for flowers with a cut or ragged edge rather than flowers that are lightly lobed or simply circular.

There are also plants here with flowers of more extravagant appearance. A few are in all important respects the same as plants of the same species found in the wild. Predominantly, however, these extravagances are the result of mutations that have been exploited by plant breeders and gardeners for their ornamental value. The Spencer sweet peas, for example, have larger flowers than the wild *Lathyrus odoratus* and, for that matter, all the early cultivars. The distinctive wavy outline of the upper petals is, however, the result of a mutation that occurred in four different places over the period 1899 to 1902. Breeders have worked on the sweet pea ever since, introducing numerous cultivars with large ruffled flowers but usually inferior in scent to old cultivars.

The Parrot tulips, with multicoloured and fringed flowers, go back much further. They were first noted in the seventeenth century as sports of the capriciously streaked tulips known as bizarres, which owed their unusual colouring to viral disease. Perhaps there will be an increase in the small number of Parrots generally in cultivation (the seventeenth-century Parrots have long gone) as a genetic Parrot (in which the streaked colour is not caused by a virus) has now been produced.

It is the fate of extravagant flowers and other floral curiosities to be either loved or despised. The bearded irises with voluptuously ruffled petals have many devotees but critics point out that the tall kinds generally need staking and the pure beauty of the fleur de lys outline has been lost, particularly in cultivars with falls that spread horizontally rather than hang vertically. As with double flowers, you have to make a judgment case by case, not so much on principle but on the evidence of plants in the garden. I am often pleased to find myself won over by plants that from a description I might anticipate disliking. That is so with the little daffodil 'Rip van Winkle'. Most of the daffodil doubles have disappointed, at best looking blobby and easily wrecked by rough weather; this is especially true of hefty cultivars such as 'Golden Ducat', a sport of the popular nineteenth-century trumpet daffodil 'King Alfred'. 'Rip van Winkle' has the advantage of being dwarf and, although the flowers seem to be no more than gatherings of petal fragments, they have a surprisingly neat and sunny charm.

COLLARS & RUFFS

The bracts that surround some flowers, which may protect the flowers and attract pollinators to them, are often intriguingly shaped or fretted and are sometimes very colourful. To gardeners they have the great advantage of being longer-lasting than fragile petals.

▲ *Eryngium alpinum*

Astrantia major subsp. *involucrata* 'Shaggy'

Perennial H75cm/30in, S 40cm/16in Z4

Sun or partial shade Moist but well-drained soil

The pincushion flower clusters of *Astrantia major*, like those of other astrantias, are surrounded by papery bracts. In the ordinary form the flowers are usually pale green to pink and the green-veined bracts are often tinted pink, beautifully so in var. *rosea*. In the case of subsp. *involucrata* 'Shaggy' the bracts are extravagantly long, green-tipped and suffused with pale pink.

All forms of *A. major* have attractively fingered leaves, which are streaked cream and grey-green in the highly ornamental cultivar 'Sunningdale Variegated'. The bracts surrounding its flowers are pale pink.

Several astrantias have flowers of very deep colouring. Both flowers and bracts of the hybrid *A.* 'Hadspen Blood' are deep red.

Cornus kousa var. *chinensis*

Deciduous shrub or tree H and S 10m/30ft Z5

Full sun Well-drained soil

Cornus kousa is a large shrub with branches that tend to develop horizontally, while the Chinese form is more upright and tree-like. Both flower magnificently in early summer, their display lasting for over a month. The true flowers are clustered in a green knob but surrounding each cluster are four petal-like bracts, which are green at first, then pure or creamy white and then pink before finally turning brown. The 'flowers' of var. *chinensis* are large and almost cover the branches. In a hot summer it may produce curious strawberry-like, but inedible, fruit but this extension of the tree's ornamental qualities is trivial when set against the rich shades of red and crimson that the leaves develop in autumn.

The foliage of *C. kousa* 'Satomi' takes on particularly intense red-purple colouring in autumn and this Japanese cultivar has deep pink bracts in summer.

Another species with showy bracts is the flowering dogwood (*C. florida*), a North American deciduous large shrub or tree that grows best on moist but well-drained lime-free soil. The bracts, borne in late spring, are incurved, slightly twisted and white to pink. 'Cherokee Chief' is a cultivar with deep red-pink bracts. There are also several good hybrids that are best in the conditions that *C. florida* enjoys. *C.* 'Norman Hadden' makes a tree about 7.5m/25ft high that is covered with cream to pink bracts in early summer.

Eryngium alpinum

Perennial H 75cm/30in, S 45cm/18in Z5

Full sun Well-drained soil

Many of the sea hollies are jagged plants with branching stems carrying cones of tiny flowers surrounded by spiky ruffs. The basal and stem leaves of *Eryngium alpinum* are spiny, so it comes as a surprise to find that the exquisite lacy ruffs surrounding the cones of grey-blue flowers are not barbed. The ruffs and the upper parts of the stems are stained steely violet-blue.

A truly spiny plant is *E. × tripartitum*, which has a much-branched wiry framework to about 90cm/3ft supporting numerous small blue cones surrounded by sharp bracts. It is highly effective in mixed borders in the second half of summer. So, too, is *E. bourgatii*, a prickly plant only half its size but with curled and jagged leaves that are conspicuously veined silver. Violet-blue branching stems carry grey-green cones sitting on silvery blue bracts.

A smaller plant still is the true sea holly or eryngo, *E. maritimum*, the roots of which were once candied. Its broad bracts are fiercely spiny but in the free-draining conditions it likes they make a striking study in glaucous blue.

One of the most impressive of all the sea hollies in *E. giganteum*, which goes by the name Miss Willmott's ghost, a reference to a formidable Edwardian gardener. Especially in the form 'Silver Ghost', it is a magnificent garden plant, although one that dies after flowering, with wide-spreading branches carrying white to blue narrow cones sitting on broad and spiky silver-grey ruffs. It dries superbly, as do most of its relatives. See also *E. proteiflorum*, p.90.

Nigella damascena
Devil-in-a-bush, love-in-a-mist

Annual H 40–75cm/16–30in, S 20cm/8in

Full sun Well-drained soil

Love-in-a-mist, to use its most familiar common name, is an easy and appealing annual that goes well with a wide range of other plants that like sunny positions with well-drained soil. It will self-seed freely in ground that is left undisturbed. The foliage, which is bright green and finely cut, provides a good contrast to large and dark leaves. The usual flower colour is blue and the flowers sit prettily on thread-like green ruffs. The flowers pick well, as do the inflated red-brown seed pods. 'Miss Jekyll' is a popular cultivar with semi-double sky-blue flowers floating about 45cm/18in over the wispy foliage. The Persian Jewel Series is a slightly shorter-growing seed strain with flowers in a mixture of blues, pinks and white. 'Oxford Blue' has double flowers of deeper blue on plants that grow to about 75cm/30in. There are also very short-growing cultivars but these are graceless oddities and have little to recommend them.

The best results with all these are usually obtained by sowing plants in autumn where they are to grow and, if necessary, giving them cloche protection in winter.

OTHER GOOD PLANTS

Cobaea scandens: see p.116.

Davidia involucrata Dove tree
In late spring this deciduous tree, also known as ghost or handkerchief tree, dangles unequal pairs of large white bracts as a collar around the round cluster of small flowers. Mature specimens grow to 15m/50ft or more.

Eranthis hyemalis Winter aconite
Tuberous dwarf plant ideal for naturalizing and conspicuous in late winter when its yellow globular flowers sit jauntily on green ruffs.

Euphorbia amygadaloides var. *robbiae*: see p.108.

Euphorbia characias subsp. *wulfenii*: see p.155.

Euphorbia griffithii 'Dixter'
Medium-sized perennial with copper-tinted foliage topped in early summer by clusters consisting of tiny floral parts surrounded by showy and long-lasting orange-red bracts.

Molucella laevis Bells of Ireland
In late summer this annual, also known as shell flower, produces spikes of green bell-like ruffs, up to 60cm/2ft high. In the centre of each ruff is a small scented white flower. Good for cutting and drying.

Morina longifolia Whorlflower
Perennial producing stems to 90cm/3ft high set with tiered whorls of tightly packed long-tubed flowers, first pink, then red, cradled in spiny collars.

Salvia sclarea var. *turkestaniana*: see p.159.

Salvia viridis Annual clary
Annual with insignificant mauve or pink flowers but each whorl is backed by a collar of two colourful bracts, the Claryssa Series including blue, purple, pink or greenish white with darker veins. Good for drying.

▲ *Astrantia major* subsp. *involucrata* 'Shaggy'

▲ *Cornus kousa* var. *chinensis*

▲ *Nigella damascena*

KNOBS & BOSSES

In addition to the numerous members of the daisy family with conspicuous central discs or cones (see pp.54-7), there are many other flowers with an impressive central knob or, even more showy, a boss of stamens, in some cases colourful enough to create a bicoloured effect.

▲ *Camellia* × *williamsii* 'Saint Ewe'

▲ *Papaver orientale* 'Patty's Plum'

▲ *Paeonia lactiflora* 'Bowl of Beauty'

Anemone coronaria De Caen Group

Tuber H 40cm/16in, S 15cm/6in Z8

Full sun Well-drained soil

The cultivars of this Mediterranean species have long been popular as cut flowers and as colourful plants in the garden. Tubers planted in mid- to late autumn will give flowers in spring but blooms can be had at almost any time by delaying or advancing the planting time and, if necessary, giving plants cloche protection. The De Caen Group are singles in a range that includes white, bright reds, pinks, purples and blues, most showing a prominent dark velvety knob surrounded by a circlet of blue-black stamens. The whites, such as 'Die Braut', have a green knob and yellow-green stamens. The fullness of the double flowers in the Saint Bridgid Group rather swamps the knobs and stamens but these are still excellent plants for the garden and for cutting.

Anemone × *fulgens*, a slightly shorter tuberous plant for spring displays and cutting, produces brilliant scarlet flowers with a dramatically dark knob and stamens.

The fibrous-rooted Japanese anemones such as *A.* × *hybrida* 'Honorine Jobert' (see p.99), which freshen the garden in late summer and autumn, also have flowers with prominent central bosses. In a similar style to these are those of another fibrous-rooted perennial, *A. hupehensis* 'Hadspen Abundance' (see illustration on pp.64–5). From mid-summer the branching dark stems up to 90cm/3ft tall carry finely shaded rich pink flowers lit by the circle of yellow stamens.

See also *A. nemorosa*, p.104.

Camellia × *williamsii* 'Saint Ewe'

Evergreen shrub H 4m/13ft, S 3m/10ft Z7

Partial shade Humus-rich, moist but well-drained acid soil; in containers,

an ericaceous compost

The Williamsii camellia hybrids have glossy bright green foliage year-round and flower over a long period, mainly in spring but often beginning in winter or, where the weather is mild, even in late autumn. In 'Saint Ewe' a dense cluster of golden-tipped stamens fits snugly in the trumpet-shaped pink flowers. This fine single is at its peak in early to mid-spring.

The boss of stamens is a winning feature in all the singles and semi-doubles, adding radiance to the various pinks, such as 'J.C. Williams', the first clone of the Williamsii hybrids to be named, and also to whites such as the single 'Francis Hanger'. See also *C.* × *williamsii* 'Donation', p.127.

Paeonia lactiflora 'Bowl of Beauty'

Perennial H 75cm/30in, S 90cm/3ft Z5

Sun or partial shade Humus-rich, moist but well-drained soil

The large, sumptuous and usually scented flowers of the herbaceous peonies are matched by fingered foliage of quality, particularly eye-catching when emerging clenched and red-purple in spring. Many of the so-called Chinese peonies – forms or hybrids of *P. lactiflora* – have incurved petals giving the flowers a globular shape. The more open single or semi-double flowers of the anemone-form or imperial peonies are filled with twisted and tapered petal-like filaments (known as petaloids or staminodes) that are

▲ *Anemone coronaria* De Caen Group

modified stamens. An outstanding example of this group is *P.l.* 'Bowl of Beauty', with rich pink petals cradling cream petaloids.

The less familiar *P.l.* 'Barrymore' is blush white with yellow petaloids. These are beautiful cut flowers but do not last as well as the doubles. See also *P. mlokosewitschii*, p.29.

Papaver orientale 'Patty's Plum'

Perennial H 75cm/30in, S 60cm/2ft Z4

Full sun Well-drained soil

The numerous cultivars of the Oriental poppies, generally recognized as involving two or three closely related species, are hairy plants that in late spring and early summer bear magnificent cup- to bowl-shaped flowers, with a conspicuous central knob surrounded by dark stamens, and then die down somewhat untidily. The knob remains as an attractive seed pod after the collapse of the flower and as the plants die down somewhat untidily. The gap they leave needs to be masked by late-flowering plants.

Numerous cultivars of subtle and unusual colouring provide an alternative to well-established and brightly coloured Oriental poppies: the brilliant scarlet Goliath Group 'Beauty of Livermere', for instance, or 'Patty's Plum', whose large single poppies, rising impressively above hairy grey-green foliage if supported, are ruffled brown-purple with dark centres.

The knobs are even more conspicuous in paler cultivars such as 'Cedric Morris', which has frilled grey-pink petals and purple-black blotches. Even paler is 'Graue Witwe', with no more than a hint of grey-pink on petals with a basal maroon smudge or blotch. In the pale salmon-pink range 'Juliane' has frilly petals but the saucer-shaped bowls of 'Karine' are nearly smooth. This last is a sturdy self-supporting plant.

OTHER GOOD PLANTS

Camellia japonica 'Bob's Tinsie'
The anemone-form cultivars of *C. japonica* all have glossy dark green leaves and usually flower in mid- to late spring. The flower centre is filled with a boss of stamens and filaments. The flowers of this are neat miniatures, with bright red petals cradling the dense paler boss.

Clematis Blue Moon: see p.74.

Clematis montana: see p.164.

Eucryphia × *nymansensis* 'Nymansay'
Dense and fast-growing medium-sized evergreen tree covered in the second half of summer with cup-shaped white flowers, each filled with a handsome puff of stamens.

Geum 'Borisii'
Perennial colourful in early summer at the front of a border or in a large rock garden. Hairy rounded leaves make dense rich green clumps that provide a base for the arresting orange-red single flowers with a boss of yellow stamens.

Helleborus × *hybridus*, see p.25.

Hypericum kouytchense
Small rounded semi-evergreen shrub bearing yellow flowers, bursting with stamens, over a long summer season. They are followed by bright red capsules.

Pulsatilla vulgaris Pasque flower
Compact perennial with filigree leaves of silky hairiness. The nodding cup-shaped flowers, generally a shade of mauve or purple with a conspicuous tuft of yellow anthers, appear in early to mid-spring.

FRINGED & SCALLOPED MARGINS

Small notches in petals can give a flower an attractively scalloped or lobed margin. Short regular cuts create a neatly serrated edge. The petals of some flowers are very deeply incised, giving an extravagantly fringed edge and, where the cutting is irregular, an imprecise outline.

▲ *Catananche caerulea* 'Bicolor'

▲ *Primula vulgaris*

Catananche caerulea
Blue cupidone, cupid's dart
Perennial H 60cm/2ft, S 30cm/1ft Z4
Full sun Well-drained soil

The short-lived cupid's dart is an easy plant for a sunny border and the flowers pick and dry well. In the second half of summer the wiry stems rise through grassy leaves, carrying single flowerheads enclosed in silvery and papery bracts. The ray florets of the open flowerheads are strap-shaped, neatly spaced in layers, and their squared tips are fringed. The normal flower colour is purple-blue. The flowerheads of *Catananche caerulea* 'Major' are large and deep mauve-blue with a darker centre but 'Bicolor', which has purple-centred white flowerheads, is the most eye-catching form.

Papaver orientale 'Curlilocks'
Perennial H 80cm/32in, S 75cm/30in Z4
Full sun Well-drained soil

The numerous cultivars of the Oriental poppies include a small group that have flowers with fringed petals. The single 'Curlilocks' is rich orange-red with conspicuous black blotches. Its petals have a deeply cut edge with pointed threads.

'Türkenlouis' is another single with vivid orange-red flowers blotched at the base. The petals have cut edges with blunt-tipped threads.

The large and more muddled flowers of 'Garden Glory' are orange-pink with a fringe made up of small rounded lobes.

The opium poppy (*Papaver somniferum*), an annual growing to 1.2m/4ft, has several forms with cut petals, sometimes referred to as the Laciniatum Group. 'Swansdown' is a semi-double white but a more appealing plant is 'Danebrog', a single bicolour, blood red with a white base, with deeply cut petals.

Primula vulgaris
Primrose
Perennial H 20cm/8in, S 35cm/14in Z5
Sun or partial shade Moist, humus-rich but well-drained soil

Few 'improved' plants can match the wild European primrose for poise and charm. Its pale yellow flowers rise from a rosette of evergreen or semi-evergreen corrugated leaves, in mild weather often starting as early

▲ *Papaver orientale* 'Curlilocks'

▲ *Tulipa* 'Black Parrot'

as late winter but reaching a peak in early to mid-spring. The lightly fragrant flowers, darker at the centre, have five lobes, each with a well-defined notch at the tip.

The yellow-centred *Primula vulgaris* subsp. *sibthorpii* has pink to purple, or rarely white, flowers. 'Wanda' is long-flowering hybrid of similar character with red-purple flowers and purplish leaves.

Hybrid primulas with heads of notched flowers on short stems include 'Lady Greer', very close in colour to *P. vulgaris*, and 'Guinevere', the flowers of which are mauve-pink and scalloped rather than notched, the foliage bronze. See also *P. denticulata*, p. 168, and *P. japonica*, p.158.

Tulipa 'Black Parrot'

Bulb H 60cm/2ft, S 10cm/4in Z3

Full sun Well-drained soil

The Parrot tulips are hybrids which flower in late spring and produce large single blooms that are often a mixture of several colours and of extravagantly baroque shape, with twisted petals that are cut, fringed and puckered. The stems tend to be weak, so the heavy flowers suffer in the garden, but when cut they are magnificent additions to bouquets in which other flowers give them some support. 'Black Parrot' is fashionably dark purple-maroon with tints of green, bronze and red.

'Blue Parrot', which is sometimes crested green, has a bright violet-blue exterior and a bronze-purple interior. 'Estella Rijnveld' makes a very lively effect with a swirling confection of white and red stripes.

The Fringed tulips constitute another but small division in the modern classification of tulips. They usually have single cup-shaped flowers with the margins fastidiously cut, giving the impression that the petals are magnetic and have been dipped in iron filings. These flowers, curious rather than beautiful, are generally more effective cut than in the garden. Cultivars seem to come and go fairly quickly. To get the best idea of what is available, consult the catalogues of bulb nurseries. 'Hamilton' is an exceptionally rich yellow with a fringe of the same colour. An ivory flame cools the strong pink of 'Fancy Frills', the two colours mixing in the fringe. The fringes of 'Red Wing' are slightly lighter than the vivid red petals.

OTHER GOOD PLANTS

Dianthus 'Loveliness'
Hybrid pink derived from *D. superbus*. Treat as a biennial. The sweetly scented flowers, sometimes green-centred or bicoloured, with deeply cut petals, come in a range that includes white, pink, mauve-pink and crimson.

Dianthus 'Mrs Sinkins': see p. 146.

Dianthus 'Musgrave's Pink': see p.122.

Phlox subulata Moss phlox
Evergreen mat-forming perennial for sunny positions swamped in late spring and early summer by five-lobed flowers, each lobe conspicuously notched. The best-known cultivar 'McDaniel's Cushion' has deep pink flowers.

Rosa 'Pink Grootendorst'
Upright, medium-sized Rugosa rose bearing throughout summer small double pink flowers with frilled petals.

RUFFLES, GATHERS & PLEATS

Neat furling of buds and pleating of petals gives flowers a refined finish. A much less austere refinement is the ruffling of petals. In the most extreme forms, generally the result of chance breaks spotted and then exploited by keen-eyed plant breeders, the finish has a rococo boudoir extravagance.

Clematis Blue Moon ('Evirin')

Deciduous woody climber H 3m/10ft, S 1.2m/4ft Z4

Partial shade or sun with the base in shade Humus-rich, well-drained soil; in

containers soil-based compost (John Innes No. 3)

Blue Moon is one of the most eye-catching of recent introductions among the large-flowered hybrid clematis. Green buds open to silvery mauve-blue flowers with ruffled tepals and a centre of maroon anthers, from which radiate green-tinted rays that become paler as the flowers age. It grows well in shade, in a container as well as in the open garden, and is best protected from strong sun, which will bleach the flowers.

'Gillian Blades' is another single with ruffled petals, white with a hint of mauve and creamy yellow anthers. More strongly coloured than either of these is 'Lord Nevill', with wavy-edged purplish blue sepals and purple anthers. The sepals are sharply tapered and heavily veined very dark purple.

All these clematis flower first in late spring or early summer and then again in late summer or autumn. They do not require pruning but it is good practice to cut out dead stems in early spring, and growths can be cut back to strong buds. Cutting all growths hard back may result in the loss of the first crop of flowers.

Convolvulus cneorum

Evergreen shrub 60cm/2ft, S 75cm/30in Z8

Full sun Well-drained soil

Plants in the bindweed family – even the tiresome weeds – have beautiful trumpet- or funnel-shaped flowers. This one, a shrub, is usually short-lived but worth propagating regularly for its mound of silky grey leaves as well as the yellow-centred white funnels that unfurl from pleated pink buds over many weeks in late spring and summer. It is at its best in a sun-drenched frontal position among other Mediterranean plants.

Although only 15cm/6in or so high, the perennial *Convolvulus sabatius* is trailing and its manner of growth and long flowering season in summer and autumn make it a useful container plant. The pleated buds open to wide funnel-shaped flowers that in the best forms are vivid blue. In the open garden, plant where the roots can get protection under a stone or paving slab.

◀ *Clematis* Blue Moon

Iris 'Edith Wolford'

Perennial H 90cm/3ft, S 20cm/8in Z4

Full sun Well-drained and preferably neutral soil

'Edith Wolford' is one of hundreds of Tall Bearded irises bred in recent years. All have thick rhizomatous roots and produce a fan of sword-like leaves, from which in late spring or early summer rises a stiff flower stem carrying several blooms in a zig-zag arrangement. The ruffled standards and falls give many of these irises a butterfly charm, though in the eyes of purists the frilly elaboration of the large flowers, which are often more than 15cm/6in across, takes away from the natural elegance of their form. The bicoloured flowers have cool yellow standards and blue falls.

Other bearded irises in the same category include 'Lemon Brocade', cream with soft yellow margins that are tightly frilled; 'Loop the Loop', with white standards and falls stippled and edged deep blue; 'Silverado', with sumptuously ruffled standards and falls that are a delicate and silvery mauve-blue; and 'Stepping Out', which has white standards and falls that are stippled and margined violet-purple.

The smaller bearded irises are suitable plants for the front of borders. Some of these irises have markedly ruffled petals. Among the Intermediates, which rarely grow much above 60cm/2ft in height and flower slightly earlier, 'Rare Edition' is outstanding. It has white standards, which are stippled and broadly margined violet-purple, and white falls with a frilled violet edge.

Lathyrus odoratus 'Angela Ann'

Annual climber H 1.8m/6ft, S 60cm/2ft

Full sun Humus-rich, well-manured, moist but well-drained soil

The tall-growing Spencer sweet peas are tendril climbers bearing sprays of large flowers in which the upper petal, the standard, is conspicuously waved. In these cultivars, which are the result of breeding from sports of strongly scented nineteenth-century cultivars, fragrance has to some extent been subordinated to form, freshness and range of colour, and carriage of the flowers on long stems – which mean that these sweet peas make sprays suitable for the show bench and for cutting. There is a constant succession of new cultivars while others disappear. When making a selection, it is worth consulting current catalogues. The ruffled flowers of *Lathyrus odoratus* 'Angela Ann' are rich pink.

Other Spencer sweet peas include 'Anniversary', with white flowers suffused pale pink, especially on the ruffled edge; 'Apple Blossom', a blend of pink and white; the deep wine-red 'Beaujolais'; 'Noel Sutton', which is blue; and the dazzling 'White Supreme'.

All these need a framework of pea sticks, brushwood or even a living plant on which to climb.

There are also short-growing kinds – some with tendrils, such as the Jet Set Group, some without, for example the Explorer Group – which grow 60–120cm/2–4ft high and have more-or-less frilly flowers in a limited colour range.

Cut or deadhead all sweet peas to extend the flowering season. If you have space for a cutting garden, these are the most attractive and productive plants to grow.

OTHER GOOD PLANTS

Incarvillea delavayi
Handsome short perennial producing in the first half of summer pink to purple trumpet flowers with ruffled margins.

Ipomoea purpurea 'Star of Yalta': see p.35.

Nerine bowdenii: see p.98.

Paeonia × lemoinei
'Souvenir de Maxime Cornu'
This tree peony is a medium-sized deciduous shrub, which in late spring or early summer bears large flowers as much as 20cm/8in across and full of yellow petals with ruffled crimson edges.

Pelargonium 'Joy'
The Regal pelargoniums are evergreen subshrubs, usually container grown, that produce clusters of large flowers in summer. 'Joy' has well-proportioned salmon-pink flowers with a white centre and white frilled margins to the petals.

Viola × wittrockiana
Super Chalon Giants Group
Seed strain of large-flowered bicoloured pansies grown for summer as annuals or biennials selected for their ruffled flowers. The flowers, many with whiskered faces, are usually more than 8cm/3in across and come in a wide colour range.

RIGHT, FROM TOP ▶
Convolvulus cneorum
Iris 'Edith Wolford'
Lathyrus odoratus 'Angela Ann'

TATTERS, THREADS & QUILLS

The petals of a few flowers are naturally no more than narrow straps or threads, in the case of the witch hazels forming spidery encrustations on the stems in winter. Other curiosities have been seized on by plant breeders, in particular the tendency of some plants to produce flowerheads composed of tubular ray florets.

Cosmos bipinnatus Sea Shells Group

Annual H 90cm/3ft, S 40cm/16in

Full sun Moist but well-drained soil

In the conventional cosmos the feathery foliage is topped by daisy-like flowerheads. *C. bipinnatus* Sea Shells Group is a seed strain in which the ray florets are quilled, the tubes notched at the mouth and wider than at the base. The colour range includes white and shades of pink and red, some with a contrast of shade between the inside and outside. 'Pied Piper Red' is a separate colour in the same style, the bright yellow centre being surrounded by tubes that are crimson with a paler exterior.

All cosmos pick well and you can prolong the summer season in the garden by deadheading.

Hamamelis × intermedia

Deciduous shrub H and S 4m/13ft Z5

Sun or partial shade Humus-rich, moist but well-drained soil, preferably neutral to acid

The group of hybrid witch hazels grouped under this name have less fragrant flowers than one of their parents, the Chinese witch hazel (*Hamamelis mollis*) but their generous encrustation of curious flowers in winter place them among the most interesting deciduous woody plants for the bleakest part of the year. The foliage of most colours well in autumn. The flowers, which have four narrow and crimped strap-shaped petals, are carried on the twiggy shoots of widespread branches. The pale yellow flowers of 'Pallida' show up well. Richer colours include the bright yellow of 'Arnold Promise', the copper-red of 'Diane' and the orange-red of 'Jelena'.

These and other clones are sold as grafted specimens. All are slow-growing and are excellent shrubs for woodland conditions.

Muscari comosum 'Plumosum'
Tassel grape hyacinth

Bulb H 45cm/18in, S 8cm/3in Z3

Full sun Moist but well-drained soil

The species, which is widely distributed in southern Europe and further east, is itself a curious plant, the flower spike – which rises from the

◀ *Cosmos bipinnatus* Sea Shells Group

strap-shaped leaves in mid- to late spring – having urn-shaped greenish brown fertile flowers topped by violet-blue sterile flowers growing on upright stalks.

In gardens it is represented by the extravagant variety *Muscari comosum* 'Plumosum'. All the flowers are sterile and take the form of purple filaments, which together create feathery tufts. For maximum effect plant several bulbs close together towards the front of a border.

Narcissus 'Rip van Winkle'

Bulb H 15cm/6in, S 5cm/2in Z4

Sun or partial shade Well-drained soil

Many of the double daffodils have coarse heavy heads that are soon knocked about if the weather is rough. This curiosity is a miniature suitable for naturalizing, making a good effect en masse but also appealing seen close to and attractive as a cut flower. The trumpet and surrounding segments are split into narrow tapered straps to make a sunburst of bright yellow.

OTHER GOOD PLANTS

Bellis perennis **Pomponette Series**: see p.60.

Callistephus chinensis 'Florette Champagne'
A selection of the annual China aster growing to 60cm/2ft and producing in the second half of summer large double flowerheads of fancifully swirling cream-pink quills.

Chrysanthemum 'Emperor of China'
Perennial, growing to 1.2m/4ft, that in autumn, when the foliage has already taken on crimson tints, produces silvery pink double flowerheads of quilled petals, crimson at the centre but silvery pink on the outer layers. Good in the garden and for cutting.

Coreopsis tinctoria 'Seashells'
Medium-sized to tall annual with slender foliage and in summer bright golden flowerheads with fluted ray florets. Good for cutting.

Dahlia 'Hillcrest Royal'
Rich purple medium-flowered example of a Cactus dahlia. In this group of these tuberous perennials the double flowers have long and narrow ray florets terminating in a point and recurved for at least half their length. Good for cutting.

Inula orientalis
Hairy rhizomatous perennial growing to 1m/40in and producing in summer woolly buds that open to yellow flowerheads with thread-like ray florets.

Osteospermum 'Whirlygig'
Subshrub suitable for containers or borders bearing numerous white flowerheads with part-quilled ray florets of spoon-like shape showing the slate blue reverse.

CLOCKWISE, FROM TOP LEFT ▶
Hamamelis × *intermedia*
Muscari comosum 'Plumosum'
Narcissus 'Rip van Winkle'

TEXTURES

By the way they catch light or hold shadows, many flowers suggest luxurious fabrics. The sheen of some brings to mind silks and satins. Others have the soft thick texture of velvet. A number of plants, especially various members of the poppy family, have crumpled crêpe-like petals that flutter diaphanously. More curious than these are flowers with fleshy or waxy petals, sometimes bizarrely erupting in warts. Flowers or leaf flowers of some plants suggest durable materials and often prove long-lasting in the garden or when cut.

'Nuits de Young' is a Moss rose dating from the middle of the nineteenth century. It goes by the common name old black rose and has the reputation of being the darkest in colour of all the Moss roses. The velvety maroon-purple flowers are fragrant and open flat.

TEXTURES

Cast a critical eye over your garden and you will see that, even when you have not thought it out, part of its interest lies in contrasts of texture. Try the same exercise at a different time of day and you will realize that the way you see your garden's complex of textures depends very much on the play of light. There are, in truth, many textured elements in the garden that shifting light points up. And week by week, month by month, new elements come to the fore. Leaf surface, in every gradation from corrugated hairiness to waxy glossiness, is important but so too is leaf size, shape and density, not to mention the angle at which leaves are held. Bark and the criss-cross patterns of branches and stems, always present, become conspicuous with leaf fall. In the grand scheme of textures the size, shape and carriage of flowers may make more impact than the texture of petals. But when we see flowers close to it is the unusual qualities of their parts that beguile us.

SUMPTUOUS FABRICS

Textures that immediately bring to mind sumptuous fabrics are far from uncommon in flowers and have a pleasing way of adding distinction to plants that would otherwise be rather humdrum. For example, the woolly grey dusty miller (*Lychnis coronaria*), a short-lived perennial which seeds itself about generously even on poor soils, carries throughout summer velvet patches of vivid magenta widely spaced on its branching stems. There are also easy-to-grow annuals, corn cockle (*Agrostemma githago*), for instance, once a weed of arable land, with silky trumpets, and the cheerfully sheeny and sun-loving California poppies (*Eschscholzia californica*). The list of familiar plants with fabric-like qualities could be greatly extended and should include not only numerous tulips but also many violas and pansies, particularly those of midnight to black colouring.

Refined textures are also found in plants long considered among the most beautiful for temperate gardens. Bearded irises have been grown for centuries but it was in the twentieth century that their breeding really took off. Large numbers of Tall, Intermediate and Dwarf hybrids have been produced but many of these are so quickly deleted from catalogues that it is difficult to find representative examples that are widely available. Thumb through any up-to-date catalogue and you will see what extraordinarily seductive plants these are, their elegant flowers, often ruffled (see also p.67) and suggesting three different kinds of texture in a single flower – standards of silk, falls of velvet and beards of chenille; not uncommonly each flower is in a different colour.

Roses have an even longer history in cultivation and the baby-skin texture of the most refined, such as the exquisite Bourbons 'Madame Pierre Oger' or 'Reine Victoria', provides a benchmark against which other roses can be measured. Many of the Hybrid Teas and Floribundas introduced in the twentieth century have coarser petals than the old roses and as a consequence tend to be longer-lasting on the plant and as cut flowers. In the delicacy and refinement of their colouring, shape and texture the English roses, a modern relatively disease-resistant and mainly repeat-flowering group that has achieved prominence in the last quarter of the twentieth century, hark back to the old roses. The nostalgia for true old roses is, however, strong and in this book this has weighed in favour of an entry on the much-admired Gallica rose 'Tuscany Superb', in which I have also referred to a group of other roses, mainly long-established, that have flowers of rich tones and velvet texture. A drawback of many of the old roses, including 'Tuscany Superb', is that they produce only one flush of flowers in the summer. They are seen at their best in larger gardens, preferably planted in a group of three or four and with stems trained low to encourage generous flowering.

FLESHY FLOWERS

Instead of true petals the flowers of clematis, an important group of ornamentals (mainly climbers but also herbaceous perennials), have showy petal-like sepals. The surface of these can seem almost quilted and in some cases is strongly scored from tip to base. In *C. tibetana* subsp. *vernayi* 'Orange Peel' fleshiness is taken to an extreme, as the cultivar name suggests.

Many other plants have true petals that are fleshy or waxy. Among the most curious are various lilies with waxy petals that have warty protuberances on the inner surface. These mysterious papilliae, as the warts are called, probably serve as touch guides to pollinators. 'Casa Blanca' and other hybrids and species are of such splendour that the eruptions do not register as disfiguring blemishes.

CRUMPLED FLOWERS

Various plants have finely textured flowers that still show evidence of having been tightly packed in bud even when they are fully open. Particularly seductive plants with crumpled flowers belong to several genera of poppies. The common name Iceland poppy is misleading as *Papaver nudicaule*, the plant it is supposed to describe, is an Asiatic species. The seed strains that go under the name *P. nudicaule* are probably hybrids of various closely related species found in mountainous and subarctic to Arctic regions of the northern hemisphere. Serious practitioners of flower arranging often fail to take account of the pleasure that comes from watching the process of buds opening. Iceland poppies cut well, although the stems need to be sealed, and the flowers give a mesmerizing performance as they shake themselves out, like butterflies emerging from their chrysalises.

The poppies are a specially gladdening group of plants and in the genera *Meconopsis* and *Papaver* are many species that warrant superlatives. Few, however, are more splendid than the tree poppies of the Californian genus *Romneya*. There are two, superficially similar, the best known of which is *R. coulteri*. It is subshrubby, annually sending up new shoots from the woody base. Because it can be treated as a perennial, it does surprisingly well even in many areas that are much colder than its native territory. You can forgive its irritating habit of aimless wandering when it produces a succession of large scented white flowers with crumpled petals and a magnificent boss of golden stamens. In its own territory and in areas with a similar climate it flowers in early summer. In a cooler climate spoil yourself and it by establishing plants at the base of a sunny wall, and you may get stems up to 3m/10ft high and flowers over many weeks in the second half of summer.

Also on the tender side are shrubs in the genus *Cistus*. In the first half of summer the white or pink crinkled flowers of various species are a familiar sight along roadsides of countries in the Mediterranean basin and there are some with aromatic foliage that contribute to the distinctive scent of maquis and garrigue, types of shrubby plant communities characteristic of rocky dry areas in southern Europe. Although each flower lasts only a day, the flowers are produced in astonishing quantity for many weeks. Most *Cistus* species and hybrids tend to be short-lived even where the climate is mild enough for them to succeed. It is a good precaution to overwinter semi-ripe cuttings under glass to fill gaps should established plants succumb because of age or exceptionally cold weather.

The rock or sun roses, as the *Cistus* species and hybrids are commonly known, in general look well in large raised beds and rock gardens. The helianthemums, which, in the untidy way of common names, are also known as rock or sun roses, are a genus of smaller shrubs suitable for a wide range of sunny well-drained positions and go well with *Cistus*. The genus is known best by the hybrids derived from species such as *H. nummularium*, all of which produce short-lived tissue-paper flowers in great profusion over many weeks in summer.

LASTING DISPLAYS

A mixed bag of ornamentals produce flowers or flowerheads that are less fragile than the general run of garden plants. The enduring parts of the flowers or flowerheads are usually stiff and rigid, suggesting strong paper, straw and even metal. More often than not the 'flowers' have distinctive bracts that persist after the true flowers have faded and in some cases retain their own bright colour (see also pp.68–9).

Everlastings with bright and glossy straw-like flowerheads have long been popular in dried arrangements. The cloying mixture of commercialism and sentimentality that characterizes so much in current gardening is fully evident in the recent revival of interest in drying, preserving and displaying plant material. However, the fashionable slant that is put on plants and gardens cannot take away from their intrinsic interest or ornamental value.

Everlastings, unlike some plant material, can be preserved very simply. To get the best results, cut the flowers as they are reaching their prime and dry them in tied bunches, hanging flowers down, in a cool and airy place. Grasses are good plants to combine with everlastings in unpretentious arrangements. For satisfactory results these need to be cut before the seedheads ripen and then hung to dry.

SATIN, SILK & VELVET

The most luxurious fabrics have near counterparts in petals of finest texture. Delicate or rich colour enhances the sheen or velvety pile of many flowers and can be appreciated in the open garden, but some plants reveal their full beauty only on close inspection.

▲ *Clematis* 'Rouge Cardinal'

Clematis 'Rouge Cardinal'

Deciduous woody climber H 2.5m/8ft, S 90cm/3ft Z6

Sun or partial shade, with the base in shade Moist but well-drained soil

Among the hundreds of large-flowered clematis hybrids a number stand out because the velvet texture of their flowers adds to the richness of their colouring. 'Rouge Cardinal' is an impressive example, with flowers up to 15cm/6in across. The overlapping blunt-tipped petal-like sepals are a glowing purplish crimson and have at their centre a tuft of beige anthers. It does well in a container as well as in the open garden.

Other large-flowered velvety clematis flowering in the same season include the justly famous rich purple 'Jackmanii'. Earlier flowering than these are 'Niobe', very deep red with yellow anthers, and Royal Velvet ('Evifour'), rich purple with darker rays and red anthers, both of them good in containers and small gardens.

Some of the small-flowered Viticella clematis that flower in late summer and early autumn also have flowers of velvet texture. The very deep red-purple 'Royal Velours' is outstanding.

Iris 'Jane Phillips'

Perennial H 75cm/30in, S 20cm/8in Z4

Full sun Well-drained soil

The fine-textured flowers of the bearded irises inevitably suggest luxurious fabrics, particularly silks and velvets. Irises of a single colour are generally easier to place in the garden than bicolours. Their trembling beauty makes them some of the finest border plants for late spring and early summer. 'Jane Phillips', a study in slightly ruffled blue silk, has beautifully formed flowers without the exaggeration that characterizes some modern cultivars.

Contrasts of texture as well as of colour help to make many of the bicolours among the most ravishing flowers of their season. New cultivars are constantly being introduced, so in making a choice it is as well to look at up-to-date catalogues. The popularity of 'Ringo', a tall cultivar, rests on the contrast between the silky white trembling standards and the red-purple velvet falls, which have a frilled white edge.

Other tall bicolours include 'Sweeter than Wine', with a contrast of very pale pink silky standards and broad plum-purple velvet falls edged mauve-pink, and 'Cabaret Royale' with fine pale blue standards and midnight-blue falls lit by brilliant orange beards. Contrasts of texture can also be found in Dwarf and Intermediate bearded irises. From the latter group 'Oriental Baby', which grows to about 60cm/2ft, combines pale

▲ *Iris 'Jane Phillips'*   ▲ *Lavatera trimestris 'Silver Cup'*   ▲ *Lychnis coronaria*

copper-brown standards and velvet red-brown falls with bright yellow beards. See also *I.* 'Edith Wolford', p.75.

Lavatera trimestris
Annual H 75cm/30in, S 35cm/14in
Full sun Well-drained soil

The annual mallows are easy-to-grow alluring annuals that in summer carry numerous beautifully furled buds that unravel to funnel-shaped flowers of finest satin texture. The taller cultivars are the most versatile, looking at home in mixed borders with shrubs and perennials and providing good material for cutting. *Lavatera trimestris* 'Silver Cup' has prettily shaded pink flowers with darker veining.

'Mont Blanc' is slightly shorter, with dazzling white flowers. Taller than either of these, and growing to 1.2m/4ft high, is 'Loveliness', with deep pink flowers. By comparison, the compact 'White Cherub' makes a dumpy plant but one that can be used effectively in a frontal position.

Lychnis coronaria
Dusty miller, rose campion
Biennial/perennial H 60cm/2ft, S 40cm/16in Z4
Full sun Well-drained soil

Dusty miller makes a clump of silver-grey woolly leaves above which in the second half of summer and early autumn the branching stems carry numerous nicely spaced single velvet flowers of vivid crimson-magenta.

The texture of the petals helps to soften the shock of the colour but if you find it too violent you could try the white 'Alba' and the white but pink-eyed Oculata Group.

In sunny gardens these plants self-seed freely. Unwanted plants are easy to remove.

Meconopsis betonicifolia
Himalayan or Tibetan blue poppy
Perennial H 1.2m/4ft, S 45cm/18in Z5
Dappled shade Humus-rich, moist, neutral to slightly acid soil

The yellow or orange saucer- to cup-shaped flowers of the freely self-seeding Welsh poppy (*Meconopsis cambrica*), admittedly finely textured, are an inadequate preparation for the Himalayan blue poppy. This splendid plant needs a cool moist climate to thrive and is usually short-lived but remains a spectacular reminder of the horticultural riches of its native territory. It has blue-green foliage with rusty hairs and in early summer bears silky poppies up to 10cm/4in across that are saucer-shaped and vivid blue with numerous yellow stamens at the centre.

There are other magnificent blue poppies under names such as *M. grandis* and *M.* × *sheldonii*. Work is currently being done on the confusing nomenclature of these superlative plants, which do best in cool but sheltered conditions.

▲ *Meconopsis betonicifolia*

▲ *Rosa 'Tuscany Superb'*

Rosa 'Tuscany Superb'
Double velvet rose

Deciduous shrub (Gallica rose) H 1.2m/4ft, S 90cm/3ft Z5

Sun Moist but well-drained soil

In roses deep red colouring is often associated with strong scent. The fragrance of 'Tuscany Superb' disappoints but this Gallica, first introduced in the middle of the nineteenth century, holds its place because of the luxurious velvet texture of its blackish crimson double flowers, which are fitfully lit by golden stamens. It blooms in the first half of summer.

So does the Moss rose 'Nuits de Young' (see illustration on pp.78–9), a wiry bush of much the same size. This is sometimes known as the old black rose on account of the very deep velvety maroon of its double flowers. The golden stamens make a striking contrast. The moss on this strongly fragrant rose is dark red-brown to purple.

The Rugosa rose 'Roseraie de l'Haÿ' is a more substantial shrub than either of these and will even make a hedge about 1.8m/6ft high. Its strongly scented double flowers, borne throughout summer and into autumn, are velvety wine red. Unlike some of the Rugosas, this cultivar does not produce hips.

Also repeat-flowering and making a fairly large bush is the Hybrid Perpetual 'Souvenir du Docteur Jamain', with double and velvety maroon-purple blooms. The flowers are of exceptional beauty but are quickly dulled if exposed to hot sun.

Several climbing roses produce sumptuously tactile flowers, the best

known of these being the Hybrid Tea 'Climbing Crimson Glory' and the stiff-stemmed 'Guinée'. Both bear fragrant double velvety flowers, those of 'Guinée' being deep red with black depths. Mask the bare stems of these roses with shrubs or short climbers.

Tulipa 'Queen of Night'

Bulb H 35cm/14in, S 20cm/8in Z4

Full sun Well-drained soil

The satin lustre of the petals of many tulips adds a touch of glamour to them as garden plants and makes them the most sumptuous of spring flowers for cutting. This is most obvious in those of brilliant or deep shades in the red-purple range. The deep maroon 'Queen of Night' is so dark that the cup-shaped flowers need the gloss of the petals to relieve their sombreness.

Much more brilliant are forms or hybrids of *T. fosteriana*. One of the most vivid of these is 'Madame Lefeber', which in early spring bears large and sheeny furnace-red flowers with a yellow base.

Many of the Darwin hybrids, which flower in mid- to late spring, have particularly lustrous flowers. 'Apeldoorn' is a popular example that has stout stems to 60cm/2ft or more carrying globular flowers that are bright scarlet with a mauve sheen on the outside and a yellow-edged black base inside.

Other late tulips with satiny flowers include the bright scarlet 'Red Riding Hood', a Greigii hybrid with the characteristic purple-brown mottling of the foliage.

OTHER GOOD PLANTS

Alcea rosea 'Nigra': see p.110.

Agrostemma githago **Corn cockle**
Tall annual with upward-facing trumpet-shaped flowers, borne on slender downy stems, that open from long pointed buds, within which the silky petals are exquisitely furled. The flowers of 'Milas' are magenta pink and there are white and pink cultivars.

Clarkia amoena **Godetia, satin flower**
Sun-loving annual bearing masses of satiny funnel-shaped flowers in white and shades of red, pink and purple in summer. The taller cultivars, such as the F_1 hybrid Grace Series, about 50cm/20in high, provide excellent cut flowers.

Crocus vernus **'Purpureus Grandiflorus'**
The Dutch crocuses, grown from autumn-planted corms, bear goblet-shaped flowers in spring. Those of 'Purpureus Grandiflorus' are an intense violet-purple made more sumptuous by their satin sheen and orange styles.

Eschscholzia californica **California poppy**
Some say satin, some say silk, but the texture of this easy-to-grow annual's funnel-shaped flowers inevitably suggests luxurious fabrics. The basic colour range of yellow and orange now extends to cream, pinks and reds.

Hemerocallis **hybrids**: see p.33.

Oenothera fruticosa **'Fyrverkeri'**
Medium-sized to tall short-lived perennial which forms a clump of dark foliage out of which rise stiff stems carrying reddish buds that open to yellow silky flowers.

Tulipa 'Queen of Night' ▶

CRÊPE & TISSUE

Despite their apparently fragile crumpled charm, some flowers with crêpe-like petals are surprisingly robust and will last for several days, even more. There are flowers with fine-textured petals that last for no more than a day but in most cases they come in quantity and there is a long-lasting succession.

▲ *Cistus × cyprius*

▲ *Helianthemum* 'Fire Dragon'

▲ *Romneya coulteri*

Cistus × cyprius

Evergreen shrub H and S 1.5m/5ft Z7

Full sun Well-drained soil

Rock roses that give a long display of tissue-paper flowers in the first half of summer vary in their ability to withstand frost and cold winds. This hybrid is one of the hardiest. It makes a rather open bush with olive-green leaves that are clammy to touch and bears white flowers that have five maroon-crimson marks around the showy tuft of yellow stamens.

Another relatively hardy hybrid is *Cistus* 'Grayswood Pink', which makes a dark green mound about 75cm/30in high liberally covered for weeks with fleeting clear pink flowers.

Less hardy rock roses include *C. ladanifer*, one of the parents of *C. × cyprius*. It has larger flowers than the hybrid but otherwise is similar in scale and general appearance, and also has sticky leaves, which on a hot day are lightly aromatic. *C. ladanifer* is also a parent of the rather tender *C. × purpureus*, a slightly smaller shrub, also with sticky leaves and a long-lasting supply of crinkled flowers but in this case rich pink with maroon blotches.

Helianthemum 'Fire Dragon'

Evergreen shrub H 30cm/1ft, S 50cm/20in Z6

Full sun Well-drained, preferably alkaline soil

The numerous hybrid rock or sun roses with their low grey-green foliage and long succession of saucer-shaped flowers in late spring and summer make bright cover in rock gardens, on dry banks and at the front of borders, provided they get plenty of sun. Individual flowers last a day, the shattered tissue-paper petals littering the ground, but the display is constantly replenished. *Helianthemum* 'Fire Dragon' is a particularly vivid hybrid, with orange-red flowers. Another in the strong colour range is 'Ben Afflick', with bronze and copper shades of orange.

Among hybrids in a different colour range is 'Rhodanthe Carneum', with pale pink flowers yellowing towards the centre. A yellow centre is a feature, too, of 'Wisley Primrose' and 'Wisley White'.

Trim all these hard after flowering to keep neat and to encourage a second flowering in late summer.

Papaver nudicaule
Arctic poppy, Iceland poppy

Biennial/Annual H 30–70cm/12–28in, S 15cm/6in Z2

Full sun Well-drained soil

The various seed strains listed under *Papaver nudicaule* are immediately appealing plants which have colourful bowl-shaped flowers with crinkled tissue-paper petals surrounding a boss of yellow stamens. They are deliciously scented. The lobed blue-green leaves are hairy, as are the stems and nodding buds, which become erect before the upward-facing flowers open. Meadow Pastels Group is a tall seed strain, growing up to 70cm/28in high and producing single flowers in a wide range of soft and more assertive colours, from white and cream to orange and red. Spring-sown plants flower over a long season.

The shorter plants of Champagne Bubbles Group, rarely more than 40cm/16in high, produce large flowers in a similar colour range. Summer Breeze Series are F_1 hybrids that grow to about 35cm/14in. Their single flowers are white or in shades of yellow, orange and red, and produced over many weeks.

The long-stemmed Iceland poppies are particularly good for cutting. Cut when the buds are erect but before the petals break, and seal the stems by burning the ends or by dipping them in boiling water.

Romneya coulteri
Matilija poppy, tree poppy
Deciduous subshrub H 1.8m/6ft, S indefinite Z7

Full sun Well-drained soil

The tree poppies from California are whimsical plants with questing underground runners that send up shoots in unexpected places. If you can tolerate this and garden in a mild enough area, the summer reward is a crop of magnificent white fragrant flowers with petals of crumpled silk texture that unfold around a splendid boss of bright yellow stamens. 'White Cloud' is a fine form with flowers up to 20cm/8in across and very grey foliage.

Treat as herbaceous, clearing away all stems between late autumn and early spring.

OTHER GOOD PLANTS

Glaucium flavum
Yellow horned poppy
Short-lived perennial or biennial usually about 60cm/2ft high for well-drained soil bearing yellow or orange crumpled flowers over blue-green foliage during summer.

Meconopsis horridula
Variable Himalayan spine-covered perennial with drooping usually blue flowers in early summer. The flowers are cup-shaped and the petals surrounding the boss of cream anthers are semi-transparent. Plants usually die after flowering. Grow in moist woodland conditions.

***Papaver commutatum* 'Ladybird':** see p.128.

***Papaver rhoeas* Mother of Pearl Group:** see p.107.

Papaver somniferum var. *paeoniiflorum*
Double form of the tall annual opium poppy with crumpled-tissue flowers predominantly in shades of pink, purple and red. Mixed seed is sometimes sold as 'Peony-flowered Mixed'. The large ornamental seedheads dry well.

Papaver nudicaule ▶

WAX & FLESH

Waxy and fleshy textures give flowers an intriguing character. At a first glance, firm smooth and lustrous petals seem to be moulded from waxy plastic. The thick petal-like segments of a few clematis are justifiably compared to orange peel. The most bizarrely human features are the hairy and warty protuberances that partially cover some petals.

Clematis tangutica

Deciduous woody climber H 6m/20ft, S 2.5m/8ft Z5

Sun or partial shade with the base in shade Humus-rich, well-drained soil

Thickening of the petal-like sepals is a feature of many clematis in the Orientalis Group, also known as Tangutica Group. *C. tangutica* has ferny foliage and from mid-summer produces bright yellow lantern flowers with thick sepals tapering to slender tips. The silvery seedheads are highly ornamental.

More extreme fleshiness is found in the flowers of *C. tibetana* subsp. *vernayi* 'Orange Peel'. The foliage of this vigorous clematis is glaucous and finely divided and the nodding yellow flowers are almost bowl-shaped. They are produced freely in late summer and early autumn and there are fluffy seedheads to follow.

Another vigorous late-flowering clematis is the hybrid *C.* 'Bill MacKenzie'. It, too, has nodding yellow flowers with thick-textured sepals surrounding dark red anthers. The fluffy seedheads are large and decorative.

The cut flowers of these clematis make unusual additions to arrangements. The silky seedheads last well and give a light touch when added to other dried material.

Kirengeshoma palmata

Perennial H 1.2m/4ft, S 90cm/3ft Z5

Partial shade Humus-rich, moist, neutral to acid soil

In woodland conditions or even in shade created by house and garden walls, provided that other conditions are right, the mound of vine-like leaves produced by this perennial makes a quiet dignified presence throughout the summer months. In late summer and autumn dark stems arch from the clump, bearing loose clusters of creamy yellow flowers with fleshy overlapping petals.

There is nothing showy in this Japanese native but it deserves to be much more widely grown where conditions are suitable, for it is a plant of exceptional poise and elegance.

Lilium henryi

Bulb H 2.5m/8ft, S 45cm/18in Z5

Sun or partial shade Humus-rich, well-drained soil

In late summer and early autumn the tall arching stems of this lime-tolerant lily carry fifteen to twenty, and sometimes many more, apricot-orange flowers of turk's cap type – that is with segments rolled right back so that they touch the flower stalk. The segments are spotted dark red and towards the centre there are numerous fleshy protuberances. This lily needs staking and should be planted deep as it is stem-rooting.

Less tolerant of lime is the slightly shorter *L. speciosum*, another stem-rooting and summer-flowering species with warty turk's caps. The normal colour is white with pink and crimson markings and crimson shading towards the centre. More commonly grown is the richly coloured var. *rubrum,* which is carmine red with dark red protuberances.

There are also several summer-flowering hybrid lilies with flowers that have fleshy protuberances. These include the white and strongly scented *L.* 'Casa Blanca' and the recently introduced 'La Mancha', which has bright pink flowers with red rays and white edges to the segments. Both these grow 90–120cm/3–4ft high and are excellent as container plants.

Measures to control sucking pests, particularly aphids, will greatly reduce the risk posed by viruses, which cause weak and distorted growth and may lead to the death of plants.

Like most other lilies, these are all strong-stemmed and excellent for cutting.

Pieris japonica

Evergreen shrub H 4m/13ft, S 3m/10ft Z6

Full sun or partial shade Humus-rich, moist but well-drained acid soil

A rounded bush of this evergreen shrub is an attractive sight in winter, when sprays of tinted buds hang among the rather narrow glossy leaves. The young growths are usually bronzed but not as richly coloured as the leaves of several selections of the similar shrub *Pieris formosa* var. *forrestii*, which is mainly grown for its foliage. When the flowers of *P. japonica* open in mid- to late spring they are waxy white and honey-scented.

'Debutante' is a compact cultivar, growing to about 90cm/3ft, and bears upright sprays of white flowers. Also compact but with more drooping sprays of white flowers is 'Purity'. Several clones have become popular because of their stronger flower colour. The buds of 'Blush' are dark pink and open to pale pink flowers that eventually turn white. The flowers of 'Valley Valentine' are dark red.

Remove spent flowers and keep the soil around plants moist during the summer months.

OTHER GOOD PLANTS

Anemonopsis macrophylla
Medium to tall woodland perennial. In late summer dark stems rise above the handsome foliage carrying sprays of nodding waxy mauve-blue flowers.

Caltha palustris
Kingcup, marsh marigold
Waterside perennial with dark green leaves that set off its deep yellow waxy flowers in early spring.

Convallaria majalis: see p.138.

Crinodendron hookerianum
Large evergreen shrub with dark foliage against which the fleshy deep pink or scarlet lantern-like flowers stand out conspicuously in late spring.

Fremontodendron
'California Glory'
This hybrid flannel bush is a large evergreen shrub with lobed leaves that are brown and hairy on the underside, and the young growths are covered with soft brown scales. The waxy saucer-shaped flowers, borne mainly in early summer, are rich yellow and can be more than 5cm/2in across. Hairs and down can irritate skin and eyes.

Hyacinthus orientalis: see p.142.

Lapageria rosea
Chilean bellflower, copihue
Twining evergreen climber bearing, during summer and autumn, fleshy pink to red narrow bells, often with lighter freckling. Needs warmth but also partial shade.

Tricyrtis formosana: see p.129.

CLOCKWISE FROM TOP LEFT ▶
Clematis tangutica
Lilium henryi
Pieris japonica
Kirengeshoma palmata

PAPER, STRAW & METAL

Fleeting flowers have a poignant beauty. Those that are slow to fade keep the garden colourful for many weeks. The flowers of some of those that are long-lasting have textures that suggest paper, straw or metal. Some are suitable for drying and, if properly treated, almost live up to their name 'everlastings'.

▲ *Eryngium proteiflorum*

Eryngium proteiflorum
Perennial H90cm/3ft, S 60cm/2ft Z8

Full sun Well-drained soil

Many of the European sea hollies have stems and bracts of glinting blue that suggest a steely constitution (see *Eryngium alpinum*, p.69). Somewhat different in character to these is this evergreen Mexican species, which develops a rosette of blade-like leaves armed with spines along the edge. In autumn a branching stem carries cones of grey-blue flowers surrounded by stiff bracts that form metallic white 'flowers', suggesting silver or aluminium. These dry well.

Limonium sinuatum
Statice
Annual/perennial H 30–60cm/1–2ft, S 25–35cm/10–14in

Full sun Well-drained soil

Statice is almost invariably grown as an annual for its long display in the second half of summer and autumn and for cutting as an everlasting. The stiff branching stems, which are markedly winged, carry dense sprays of tiny flowers enclosed in showy and persistent papery bracts. These fade only slightly if carefully preserved. In the Forever Series the colour range includes yellow, pink, blue and white.

Statice does well in light soils and is an excellent plant for seaside gardens. It is a usefully versatile plant to grow where space can be devoted to flowers for cutting. Sea lavender (*Limonium platyphyllum*) is a coarse-leaved perennial that requires free-draining soil and, as its common name suggests, thrives in maritime conditions. It produces much-branched wiry stems, which in late summer support a cloud 60cm/2ft or more high of tiny papery flowers. These are generally mauve-blue but those of 'Violetta' are more strongly coloured. They are long-lasting in the garden and also good for drying.

Origanum 'Kent Beauty'

Semi-evergreen subshrub H 10cm/4in, S 20cm/8in Z7

Full sun Well-drained, preferably alkaline soil

This relative of the culinary herb oregano makes a low clump of wiry stems set with pairs of rounded leaves. The long-lasting flowerheads, borne in summer, are hop-like, consisting of whorls of very small pink flowers hiding among tiers of papery bracts. The flowers are insignificant, but the bracts, which vary in colour from pale green to deep pink, are of long-lasting beauty.

A parent of this hybrid, *Origanum rotundifolium*, is similar, with pale pink flowers sheltering among pale yellow-green bracts.

'Kent Beauty' is often grown as an alpine house treasure but both these plants are suitable for rock gardens and raised beds where the soil is free-draining.

A more difficult plant that is intolerant of winter wet is the Cretan dittany (*O. dictamnus*). This aromatic evergreen subshrub has grey felted leaves and also produces hop-like inflorescences. These are composed of purple-pink bracts, from which protrude long-tubed pink flowers. It can be planted in a crevice outdoors with overhead protection to keep off winter rain.

Xerochrysum bracteatum 'Dargan Hill Monarch'

Annual/perennial H90cm/3ft, S 45cm/18in Z8

Full sun Well-drained soil

The straw flowers, short-lived natives of scrub and grasslands in Australia, are still often listed under *Bracteantha* and even under a former generic name, *Helichrysum*. The complications of nomenclature cannot take away from the direct appeal of the lustrous crisp flowerheads, which give a bright display in sunny beds and borders and make superb everlastings.

Perennial cultivars such as *Xerochrysum bracteatum* 'Dargan Hill Monarch', which has bright gold flowerheads on grey-green plants up to 90cm/3ft high, are usually increased from cuttings.

Seed of plants raised as annuals is normally sold as mixtures. The compact Bright Bikinis Series have double flowerheads in orange, yellow, white, pink and red on plants about 30cm/1ft high. Slightly shorter-growing is the more recent Chico Series, in a mixture of five colours.

OTHER GOOD PLANTS

Anaphalis triplinervis 'Sommerschnee'
The common name of plants in the genus *Anaphalus* is pearl everlasting. This compact perennial has grey-green leaves, white and felted on the underside, topped from mid-summer on by domed bunches of brilliant white flowerheads with yellow centres. The flowers dry well.

Armeria maritima Sea thrift
Perennial forming a low mound of grassy leaves above which stiff stems carry compact heads of pink flowers in summer. Even when the petals fade, they remain as papery tufts. 'Düsseldorfer Stolz' is short-stemmed and the flowers wine red.

Carlina acaulis subsp. *simplex*
Perennial or, more commonly, biennial thistle that forms a rosette of divided spiny leaves and in late summer produces a dramatic flowerhead 10cm/4in or more across sitting close to the rosette and consisting of a broad pale disc surrounded by petal-like silvery bracts. The flowerheads dry beautifully.

Echinacea purpurea: see p.55.

Helichrysum bellidioides
Low perennial making a mat of prostrate stems with little grey-green leaves almost hidden in late spring and early summer by numerous brilliant white papery daisies. They are small but make pretty everlastings.

Xeranthemum annuum
Grey-leaved annual producing in summer pink to purple papery flowerheads held on upright stems about 60cm/2ft high. Can be dried.

RIGHT, FROM TOP ▶
Limonium sinuatum
Origanum 'Kent Beauty'
Xerochrysum bracteatum 'Dargan Hill Monarch'

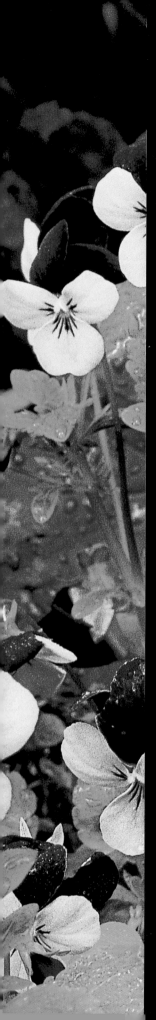

COLOURS

The palette of garden flowers is full of surprises. There are clear bright colours in abundance, although a simple description of a flower as yellow, blue or red does not adequately place it in a spectrum that is infinitely graded. There are cool and hot colours: at one extreme glacial blues, at the other orange-reds of furnace intensity. Some flower petals are so saturated in colour that you are astonished that anything can hold so much pigment. Beside them the palest tints of biscuit, cream, pink and mauve barely register as colour at all. Many flowers are made up of a mixture of colours. Some are startling bicolours, others are more complex mixtures, some of them chameleons with unstable tints that give the flowers in the mass a multicoloured effect. Many are conspicuously marked (see pp.118–33).

The genus *Viola* contains many perennial and short-lived hybrids in a very wide spectrum of colours. Some are selfs – that is of a single colour – but many others, sometimes strikingly marked, combine two or more colours. In the neat flowers of 'Jackanapes' the lower yellow petals, prettily whiskered, seem to spring forward from the very dark purplish brown upper petals.

COLOURS

The colours we observe in flowers are produced by a variety of pigments, the distribution and combinations of which result in an extraordinarily wide range of patterns and tints. The pigments found in the cell sap form two main groups, one responsible for shades of purple and blue as well as most reds, the other for colours that range from near white to deep yellow. In addition pigments are found in cell particles. One of these, chlorophyll, plays a key role as the green leaf pigment responsible for photosynthesis. It also occurs in some flowers, particularly the outer parts. Other pigments in cell particles produce red to brown and orange to yellow colours.

Colours play an important role in signalling the presence of flowers to pollinators, mainly insects but also birds, for which the pollen and nectar in the flowers are a source of food. The colour-vision of these pollinators is often very different from that of humans. For example, ultra-violet light is visible to bees but not red. For humans it is the aesthetic dimension of flower colour that counts. The range of colours and shades available among the many thousands of plants in cultivation provides gardeners with almost limitless opportunities for creating restful harmonies or stimulating contrasts. In exploiting this rich resource you need to be aware that the pigments themselves and the sophisticated anatomical structure of your eyes are not the only factors determining what you perceive as flower colour.

COLOUR AND LIGHT

To complete the equation of sight, light is needed, and the quality of light varies according to geographical position, time of day, season and climate. In the tropics, where intense overhead light creates strong contrasts between sun-drenched colours and heavy shadows, bold colours contrasting vividly with one another sing joyously. The same harsh light drains watercolour tints and subtle combinations so that they simply seem anaemic. Even far from the tropics, in the middle of a bright summer's day bold colours and strong contrasts work well and soft colours can look washed out. However, in these higher latitudes early morning and evening light is diffused as it

angles through the earth's dust-laden atmosphere and is often warmed by it. Light is also diffused by water in the atmosphere. In overcast and misty conditions the eyes adjust to the low light levels and subdued shadows, picking out the subtleties of quiet harmonies composed of pastel colours. The greater the distance from the equator the more marked is the effect of the seasonal cycle on light levels and the degree to which light is diffused.

COLOUR IN THE MIND

There are dimensions to our perception of colour that are not entirely down to pigments and light. For one thing the way we see a colour is much influenced by the proximity of other colours, in particular what we have just looked at. We may not be aware of phantom images but they help account for the way we experience certain colours. For example, when primed by looking on blue the eye registers an exaggerated contrast when the gaze shifts to orange, blue's complementary colour.

In addition to various optical phenomena that seem like tricks played on our perceptions, there are associations with certain colours that many people seem to share. Cool clear blue seems to suggest spacious openness, perhaps because we see it in the infinity of sky. Yellow, the radiant colour of the sun, is full of cheerful promise. Red is daring, sometimes dangerous and even morbid, so strong is our reaction to anything that suggests blood. Many other associations, some more personal, play a part in our complex but exhilarating reactions to colours, including those in flowers.

COLOUR THEMES

Although my own tastes are catholic – I would rather try a plant than wait until I had a colour scheme that suited it – I see that many gardens owe their quality to a degree of discipline in the handling of flower colour. On the face of it, the simplest colour themes are those based on a single colour. The least contrived and relatively short-lived reflect the seasonal dominance of a particular flower – white snowdrops, for example, or yellow daffodils. Longer-lasting in their effect are schemes based on extensive ground cover such as the predominantly pink heaths and heathers. The idea of one-colour schemes is often taken much further, plants of various kinds being brought together to give a sustained display. Among the most pleasing are those based on white and in the most delectable of these the range of flower colour includes not only chalky whiteness but various very pale tints that work harmoniously with one another. Successful one-colour themes are in effect plantings based on close harmonies. Other factors that prevent them from being dull are the various textures and colours of foliage, not to mention the different sizes, densities and textures of flowers.

Many highly successful plantings are based on harmonious colours – that is, those that are close to one another in the spectrum. They do not have to fall within a narrow band as they might in a successful 'white' garden. The harmony could be based on warm to hot colours, ranging from creamy yellow, through shades of apricot and peach to intense oranges and reds. An equally impressive harmonious planting could be based on cool to cold colours, predominantly violet and shades of blue. At their best, these plantings, generally easy on the eye, are exquisitely subtle, particularly in a moist atmosphere when subdued light pastel shades achieve their full potential.

The simplest way of making a colour scheme dramatic is by pairing complementary colours to create lively contrasts. The most common complementary pairings are yellow/violet, orange/blue and red/green. Many different shades and intensities are covered by these broad colour categories, allowing enormous scope for highly individual schemes. These schemes can be large-scale – intense blue delphinium spires, for example, standing at the back of a border in shades of cream and yellow. But schemes can also be small-scale, even playing on colour contrasts within flowers themselves.

More dramatic effects can sometimes be produced by contrasts of tone. The near blacks and other dark colours are fashionably sullen, glowering against silvers and greys. The near whites are of enduring popularity, illuminating shady and dark corners in the garden, standing out in any crowd and still visible as night falls.

FLOWERS AND FOLIAGE

Some very lovely gardens are planted with little if any thought for the way colours are juxtaposed. And it is equally true that the colour schemes of some truly awful gardens are meticulously planned. The massed colour of

bedding schemes and container gardens sometimes demonstrates dramatically the shortcomings of obsessive and congested floral gardening that is made easy by the availability of numerous free-flowering compact cultivars. Gardens that are pleasing are generally airy, the flower colour separated by copious quantities of foliage; making a garden attractive depends on getting a good balance between the two, both with separate plants and on each plant. In some plants the balance is inherent, numerous and well-proportioned flowers being set against a generous background of attractive foliage. The popularity of the hardy geraniums owes much to their typical combination of handsomely lobed leaves and shapely flowers borne freely over a long season. Other ornamentals, owing much more to intensive selection and breeding, have large flowers, usually double and often heavy, that overwhelm the foliage. In the garden and in containers these plants need the companionship of good foliage plants to moderate their floral excess. As well as indispensable foliage plants in a good range of greens, there are those in shades of yellow, blue-green, grey, purple and red. There are, too, numerous variegated foliage plants, some with cool streaks and patterns in ivory or white, others with warm markings in cream and yellow.

COLOUR CHOICES FOR CUT FLOWERS

Planning colour schemes for cut flowers is largely a luxury for those who have space enough for a cutting garden. Most gardeners simply select and cut from beds and borders so that they can take something of the garden's freshness indoors. Discretion is needed if the garden display is not to suffer, and, too, if you are to make up bunches and bouquets that are more than ill-matched handfuls or armfuls. There is little problem with a bunch of a single colour, a straightforward contrast of complementary colours such as violet and yellow or close harmonies, for example in a range of pinks with white. The apparently casual medley can be hugely successful, perhaps because close inspection usually reveals that a deliberate or unconscious process of selection has modified the randomness. It may be that there is a good proportion of foliage, offsetting or enhancing difficult colours. Intermediate shades may help to bridge warring colours. And sometimes it may be that the shock of the unexpected is enough to make us accept a daring association of colours that goes beyond crude confrontation.

COOL, CRYSTALLINE & BRILLIANT

Cool and brilliant flowers, and also those with a crystalline iridescence, help to give the garden a smart, well-turned-out look, even when they are used sparingly as bright fringes or as arresting focal points. They are valuable in any season but particularly useful for reviving the garden in late summer and autumn.

▲ Galanthus nivalis

✲ Gentiana verna

Lithodora diffusa 'Heavenly Blue' ▲

Galanthus nivalis
Common snowdrop

Bulb H 15cm/6in, S 5cm/2in Z4

Partial shade Humus-rich, moist but well-drained soil

The common snowdrop, found wild over much of Europe and an excellent bulb for naturalizing under deciduous trees and shrubs, serves as a standard for judging the qualities of the several species and the numerous cultivars of snowdrops in general cultivation. Most flower in late winter or early spring but a few are autumn-flowering. The common snowdrop, which flowers in late winter, has linear grey leaves, pressed flat together at the base, and the white flowers have green markings at the tip of the inner segments. One variation on this is found in *Galanthus nivalis* 'Viridapice', which has additional green marks on the tips of the outer segments.

Except for a few curiosities in white and pale yellow, all the snowdrops come in a cool mixture of green and white. Some of the finest hybrids, such as G. 'S. Arnott', are like more vigorous and larger-flowered forms of the common snowdrop. Others show differences in the amount of green marking.

Two species to include in any collection are *G. elwesii* and *G. plicatus*. The first of these has broad grey leaves and large honey-scented flowers with a green mark at the base and at the tip of the inner segments. The leaves of *G. plicatus* are deep green with folded-back margins and the flowers have a single green mark at the tip only. *G.p.* subsp. *byzantinus*, an equally good garden plant, has green markings at both the base and the tip of each inner segment.

Gentiana verna
Spring gentian, star gentian

Evergreen perennial H 5cm/2in, S 15cm/6in Z5

Full sun Moist but well-drained, humus-rich gritty soil

In a rock garden or raised bed the spring gentian makes a small but brilliant sensation in late spring or early summer when its mat of leaf rosettes is topped by short-stemmed stars of vivid blue.

Although few other gentians can quite match the sky-blue intensity of this species, many are prized as rock garden plants on account of the vivid blue of their flowers. Another brilliant European species with sky-blue trumpets in late spring or early summer is *G. angustifolia*. See also *G.* × *macaulayi* 'Kingfisher', p.33.

Gladiolus 'The Bride'

Corm H 60cm/2ft, S 10cm/4in Z8

Full sun Well-drained soil

The Nanus Group of gladioli include several hybrids that produce two or three slender spikes per corm, each spike carrying up to seven flowers. They flower in spring or early summer, before the large-flowered hybrids. 'The Bride' is one of the most appealing of the Nanus Group, with pure white flowers about 5cm/2in across. Among others are two with predominantly white flowers but handsomely marked: 'Nymph' has creamy white markings outlined in crimson, and the flowers of 'Prins

▲ *Nerine bowdenii*

Claus' have red-pink tongue-like blotches on the lip segments. All are graceful plants for the garden and the spikes are superb for cutting.

The Grandiflorus Group, with heavy spikes up to 90cm/3ft high and usually ruffled flowers, as well as the somewhat shorter Primulinus Group, with flowers zigzagging up the spikes, are less satisfactory as garden plants but undeniably magnificent as cut flowers. Many of these hybrids have colourful and beautifully marked flowers. 'Florence C' is an example from the Grandiflorus Group with large ruffled white flowers. In these groups old cultivars are constantly displaced by new introductions so to make a choice it is best to consult the catalogues of specialist nurseries.

In areas with a mild climate the corms of the Nanus Group hybrids are best planted out in autumn for an early display. Alternatively plant in early spring, the other groups a few weeks later. To ensure good drainage, plant corms on a bed of sand.

Lithodora diffusa 'Heavenly Blue'

Evergreen shrub H 15cm/6in, S 50cm/20in Z7

Full sun Humus-rich, moist but well-drained acid soil

This species from south-west Europe is almost invariably represented in gardens by one of its clones, most commonly *Lithodora diffusa* 'Heavenly Blue' or the similar 'Grace Ward'. These plants have trailing stems, which are covered with small bristly leaves and can form thick mats in rock gardens or raised beds, even among paving. For several weeks in summer countless funnel-shaped flowers create sheets of intense blue. There is nothing quite like 'Heavenly Blue' and it is not a difficult plant for acid soils.

Trim lightly after flowering to keep plants dense and compact.

▲ *Gladiolus* 'The Bride'

▲ *Polygonatum × hybridum*

Nerine bowdenii

Bulb H 45cm/18in, S 10cm/4in Z9

Full sun Well-drained soil

In gardens in cool temperate areas this is the only species of an attractive genus from southern Africa that is hardy enough to be grown outdoors and even it does best in a warm border, preferably at the base of a sunny wall. Its flowering season is early to late autumn, when the flower stems carry three to nine funnel-shaped pink blooms with segments that have undulating margins and curl back at the tips. A distinctive feature of the petals is their iridescence, which gives the flowers a special sparkle in the garden and is even more apparent under electric light. If you can spare stems from the autumn garden, it is excellent for cutting. The strap-shaped leaves emerge after the flowers, sometimes not until spring. 'Mark Fenwick' is a vigorous clone that may grow to 60cm/2ft or more high.

The bulbs are generally best planted so that they are covered by about 8cm/3in of soil, to give them some protection from frost, and then left undisturbed. Congested bulbs often flower surprisingly freely but if they are pushed to the surface there is a risk of frost damage. If this happens, either apply a winter mulch or lift and replant.

Polygonatum × hybridum
Common Solomon's seal

Perennial H 1.2m/4ft, S 30cm/1ft Z6

Partial shade or sun Humus-rich, moist but well-drained soil

Although not showy, this is a perennial with real presence in late spring. It is ideally planted among ferns and other shade lovers but tolerant of a wide range of conditions and, where the ground is not too scorched and parched, it will form colonies from its spreading rhizomatous roots. Its arching stems are set with alternate strongly veined leaves, below which dangle clusters of two to four waisted and somewhat tubular white bells, tipped green and lightly scented. The leaves of the less vigorous 'Striatum' are striped cream.

Another species, *Polygonatum biflorum*, is like a giant version of the common Solomon's seal. It usually flowers a little later and makes a cool study in white and green as much as 1.8m/6ft high.

The cut stems of all are attractive indoors.

Sanguinaria canadensis f. *multiplex* 'Plena'

Perennial H 15cm/6in, S 30cm/1ft Z3

Shade or partial shade

Humus-rich, moist but well-drained soil

The generic name and the common name bloodroot given to the species refer to the red sap exuded by the plant's rhizomes if they are damaged. The usual single form, with buds clasped by scalloped grey leaves opening to white flowers is a pleasant enough plant but this double form creates a much heightened effect of startling whiteness. The species is a woodland plant from North America. The double form is worth a place in a peat bed or in a damp and shaded corner of a rock garden.

Scilla siberica
Siberian squill

Bulb H 15cm/6in, S 5cm/2in Z5

Sun or partial shade Humus-rich, well-drained soil

In its brilliance the prussian blue of the Siberian squill, particularly of the form 'Spring Beauty', eclipses almost every other blue of the garden in early spring. Each bulb usually produces several stems with up to five nodding flowers that open as the glossy dark green leaves are developing. This dwarf but vivid bulb is easy to grow and naturalizes readily among deciduous shrubs and even in grass.

Although unable to compete in brilliance with the Siberian squill, some of its relatives are excellent small bulbs for early spring. The best of these are *Scilla bifolia*, with lax sprays of rather starry mauve-blue flowers, and *S. mischtschenkoana*, with pale blue, dark striped flowers that open precociously at ground level, as the buds emerge.

▲ *Sanguinaria canadensis* f. *multiplex* 'Plena'

OTHER GOOD PLANTS

Achillea ptarmica 'The Pearl': see p.60.

Anchusa azurea 'Loddon Royalist': see p.44.

Anemone × hybrida 'Honorine Jobert'
The Japanese anemones can be invasive perennials but this is a star of late summer and autumn. The single white flowers that float at about 1.5m/5ft above a base of dark green leaves have a green-tinted central knob surrounded by a ring of yellow stamens.

Begonia 'Olympia White'
A compact white-flowered example of the Semperflorens begonias. These evergreen perennials, often grown as annuals for bedding and containers, have iridescent long-lasting flowers, the Olympia Series including various shades of pink and red as well as white.

Convallaria majalis: see p.138.

Cornus kousa var. *chinensis*: see p.68.

Dianthus 'Musgrave's Pink': see p.122.

Dicentra spectabilis 'Alba': see p.47.

Galtonia candicans: see p.38.

Gentiana × macaulayi 'Kingfisher': see p.33.

Iris 'Joyce'
The dwarf bulbous Reticulata irises are exquisite jewels of the garden in late winter and early spring. This one produces sky-blue flowers with a yellow mark on the falls.

Leucojum aestivum 'Gravetye Giant': see p.38.

Magnolia stellata: see p.22.

Narcissus poeticus var. *recurvus* Pheasant's eye
This bulb, which grows to about 35cm/14in, is one of the last daffodils of spring. It bears sweetly scented flowers, one to a stem, which have glistening pure white segments recurving from a neat yellow cup edged with a wavering red rim. Good for cutting.

Nicotiana sylvestris: see p.139.

Philadelphus 'Beauclerk': see p.144.

Prunus 'Shirotae': see p.164.

Romneya coulteri 'White Cloud', see p.87.

Rosa 'Blanche Double de Coubert'
Medium-sized Rugosa rose making a spiny shrub with bright green foliage and producing a succession of somewhat papery semi-double flowers almost without interruption throughout summer and into autumn. The flowers have a fresh sweet scent but do not last well when picked.

Spiraea 'Arguta': see p. 165.

Trillium grandiflorum: see p.19.

Veronica austriaca subsp. *teucrium* 'Crater Lake Blue': see p.157.

Viburnum opulus 'Roseum', see p.168.

Viola cornuta Alba Group
For many weeks in summer this white version of the horned viola, an evergreen perennial, makes an elegantly dazzling display of alert clean flowers at the front of sunny borders or lights up the shady base of tall perennials and shrubs.

Scilla siberica ▶

INTENSE & INCANDESCENT

Plant breeders have done much to push the spectrum of flower colour towards the luminously shocking. It takes a brave person to gaze unflinchingly on mixed and vibrant plantings that have been thoughtlessly brought together but at their best intense and incandescent colours have the power to excite and refresh the eye.

Impatiens New Guinea hybrids

Perennial/annual H 35cm/14in, S 30cm/1ft

Partial shade Humus-rich, moist but well-drained soil;

in containers soil-less or soil-based compost (John Innes No. 2)

The New Guinea hybrid busy Lizzies, derived from *Impatiens schlechteri*, are subshrubby perennials with seed strains that are grown as annuals for their combination of strongly coloured flowers and handsome foliage, often tinted bronze to red or with yellow variegation. The vivid colouring of the flowers is intensified by their iridescence. All need sheltered positions; many gardeners find the best way of using them is as container plants.

The busy Lizzies listed under *I. walleriana* are another group of perennials grown as annuals, some with flowers of iridescent qualities and very intense colouring. There is a blue tint in many of them but there are also strong oranges in mixtures such as the Accent, Bruno and Tempo Series. These may be difficult to obtain as separate colours and if you want a particular colour, the best course may be to buy plants in flower. The plants are usually less than 25cm/10in in height and provide some of the best-performing annuals for shaded areas, either in containers or in the open ground.

All these varied busy Lizzies need to be placed with care for their strong hues can sap the vivacity of flowers close to them that are more subtly coloured.

▲ An *Impatiens schlechteri* hybrid (New Guinea hybrid)

▲ *Lilium* 'Fire King'   ▲ *Lobelia* 'Queen Victoria'   ▲ *Potentilla* 'Gibson's Scarlet'

Lilium 'Fire King'

Bulb H 1.2m/4ft, S 15cm/6in Z4

Sun, preferably with the base in shade Humus-rich, well-drained soil;

in containers soil-based compost (John Innes No. 2 with added humus and grit)

Lilium 'Fire King' is an Asiatic hybrid with purple-spotted flowers of flaming intensity, borne in mid-summer. The unscented funnel-shaped blooms face outwards, forming an impressive truss at the head of a strong stem. 'Fire King' can be used in strong colour schemes in the border but is especially good as a container plant.

So, too, are several other lily hybrids with hot-coloured flowers. 'Enchantment' flowers slightly earlier than 'Fire King' and the black-spotted orange blooms face upwards on a stem 90cm/3ft high. The shorter-growing 'Orange Pixie' and 'Crimson Pixie' produce clusters of upward-facing blooms in mid-summer, in the first case radiant orange, in the second vibrant red, on stems only 40cm/16in high.

Several lily species have flowers in intense shades of orange and red, notably the somewhat difficult scarlet turk's cap lily (*L. chalcedonicum*) and *L. henryi* (see p.88).

Lobelia 'Queen Victoria'

Perennial H 90cm/3ft, S 30cm/1ft Z6

Sun Reliably moist soil

Very different in character to the popular annual lobelia (*L. erinus*) are upright hybrids of various *Lobelia* species. These include the brilliant scarlet cardinal flower (*L. cardinalis*), with erect stems carrying richly coloured tubular two-lipped flowers in the second half of summer and early autumn. Some of the long-established hybrids tend to be short-

lived but 'Queen Victoria' is such a startling plant, with scarlet flowers and beetroot-coloured stems and leaves, that it remains popular.

'Dark Crusader', one of several newer and hardier (Bowden) hybrids, is maroon in leaf with velvety ruby-red flowers. 'Will Scarlet' from the same range has blood-red flowers.

Potentilla 'Gibson's Scarlet'

Perennial H 45cm/18in, S 60cm/2ft Z5

Full sun Well-drained soil

The Himalayan cinquefoil (*Potentilla atrosanguinea*), a hairy perennial producing sprays of strongly coloured saucer-shaped flowers, is a parent of several vivid hybrids. One of these is 'Gibson's Scarlet', whose single flowers are bright orange-red and make a radiantly eye-catching display towards the front of borders. Another good single with scarlet flowers is 'Flamenco'. Both flower freely in early to mid-summer.

There are also several strongly coloured doubles and semi-doubles, which tend to flower later than the singles. 'William Rollison' has orange-yellow flowers, the petals yellow on the reverse. The more sombre 'Etna' is maroon.

Rhododendron 'Gibraltar'

Deciduous shrub H and S 1.5m/5ft Z6

Partial shade Humus-rich, moist but well-drained acid soil

The deciduous azaleas, which belong to the genus *Rhododendron*, include some very strongly coloured shrubs that are so vibrant that they need to be isolated from more delicately coloured spring flowers.

The Knap Hill-Exbury hybrids are a numerous group, 90–180cm/3–6ft tall, with trusses of large funnel-shaped flowers, often

▲ *Tropaeolum speciosum*

▲ *Rhododendron* 'Gibraltar'

unscented, borne in late spring and early summer. Their relatively late season means that in many areas there is a good chance the flowers will escape frost damage. The foliage of most takes on attractive tints in autumn. The rich crimson-orange buds of *Rhododendron* 'Gibraltar' open to bright orange crinkled flowers with a yellow flash. 'Klondyke', which has copper-tinted young foliage, has red buds that open to red-backed orange-yellow flowers.

Slightly earlier flowering than any of these are the Mollis hybrids, their trusses of funnel-shaped scentless flowers usually opening before the leaves. 'Spek's Orange', which makes a large bush about 1.8m/6ft high, is one of the last of these to flower and bears trusses of orange-yellow funnels.

The Ghent hybrids have scented flowers. One of the oldest cultivars, 'Coccineum Speciosum', grows to about 1.8m/6ft and in early summer bears sprays of fragrant orange-scarlet funnels.

Tropaeolum speciosum
Flame creeper, flame nasturtium

Perennial climber H 3m/10ft, S 90cm/3ft Z8

Sun or partial shade with the base in shade

Moist but well-drained neutral to acid soil

This slender climber makes a sensation in late summer when it festoons a host plant with vivid vermilion-scarlet flowers. The darker the host the better; a classic combination is flame creeper on yew (*Taxus baccata*). The stems make rapid growth once they emerge in late spring and the attractive leaves are composed of five or six rounded leaflets.

▲ *Viola × wittrockiana* 'Padparadja'

The flowers are long-spurred and beautifully formed, with two wedge-shaped upper petals and three larger and rounded lower petals, long stalks keeping the petals well separated. The flowers are followed by deep blue fruits.

Another more tender perennial climber with strongly coloured flowers is *Tropaeolum tricolor*. Its lantern-shaped flowers are variable in colour but predominantly red, with maroon mouth and red spur.

Viola × wittrockiana 'Padparadja'

Annual/biennial H 15cm/6in, S 25cm/10in

Sun or partial shade Humus-rich, moist but well-drained soil; in containers soil-less or soil-based compost (John Innes No. 2 with added leaf mould)

Yellow and warm brown are common colours in pansies, offsetting cool and subtle shades with a bias to blue. The relatively small number with hot colours have a special power to shock. Prime among these is *Viola × wittrockiana* 'Padparadja', an F_2 seed strain producing rounded flowers of intense orange with a tiny yellow eye. It is suitable for bedding and is an excellent container plant.

There are other orange-flowered violas but it is difficult to obtain seed of separate colours. The colour comes up in several mixtures, including the spring-flowering Banner Series and the winter-flowering Ultima Series. If you need a relatively small number of plants, the best option is to buy plants in flower.

All these pansies flower for many weeks if regularly deadheaded and kept moist.

OTHER GOOD PLANTS

Arctotis × hybrida 'Flame'
One of several hybrids grown as perennials or annuals and propagated from cuttings. Vivid orange-red daisy flowerheads on stout stems are borne freely over a long season in sunny gardens.

Canna 'Assaut'
Tall fleshy-rooted perennial commonly used for summer bedding. The large paddle-shaped leaves are purple-brown and the showy flowers, borne in a spike above the foliage, are scarlet.

Crocosmia 'Lucifer': see p.152.

Dahlia 'Zorro'
Giant-flowered Decorative dahlia growing to 1.2m/4ft and bearing in late summer and autumn mophead flowerheads the colour of freshly spilt blood.

Fuchsia 'Thalia': see p.44.

Geranium psilostemon: see p.123.

Pelargonium 'Horizon Deep Scarlet'
The Horizon Series is an F_1 strain of seed-raised pelargoniums that are grown as annuals. These are Zonals with well-marked foliage and domed heads of single flowers giving a long summer display. 'Horizon Deep Scarlet' is glowing furnace red.

Phygelius × rectus 'African Queen'
Dark-leaved shrub producing in summer stems about 90cm/3ft high from which dangle sprays of red to orange tubular flowers.

Tithonia rotundifolia: see p.56.

Tropaeolum majus 'Hermine Grashoff'
Trailing nasturtium propagated annually by stem-tip cuttings and grown, usually as a container plant, for its bright red double flowers.

Tulipa praestans 'Fusilier': see p.153.

WASHES, BRUISES & BLUSHES

Many lightly tinted flowers have a fresh subtlety or complex intermingling of colours, sometimes from different ends of the spectrum, that both makes them interesting in themselves and allows them to be used in quiet mixtures or as foils for more emphatic flowers.

▲ *Anemone nemorosa* 'Robinsoniana'

▲ *Campanula carpatica* 'Blue Moonlight'

▲ *Nectaroscordum siculum* subsp. *bulgaricum*

Anemone nemorosa
Wood anemone
Perennial H 20cm/8in, S 40cm/16in Z5
Partial shade Moist but well-drained soil

The wood anemone is found wild over much of Europe and is common in woodland and hedgerows where the ground is reasonably moist. It is one of the best dwarf plants to naturalize in the wild garden, spreading freely by horizontal rhizomes and producing masses of bobbing white flowers in spring.

Wild populations often contain plants that have a blue to pink flush on the outside and from these several good forms with large flowers that are subtly coloured have been selected. They include 'Allenii', pale mauve-blue on the outside and darker inside, and the silvery mauve-blue 'Robinsoniana'. In general it is a good policy to keep colonies of different clones apart.

Desirable though these plants are, they are too vigorous for rock gardens.

The hybrid *A. lipsiensis* is another low-growing but vigorous perennial, in general appearance very like *A. nemorosa*, which is one of its parents. The flowers, borne in spring, are soft yellow with golden stamens. A particularly good form, 'Pallida', has flowers of delicate creamy yellow that show up well against the foliage.

Campanula carpatica 'Blue Moonlight'
Perennial H 30cm/1ft, S 45cm/18in Z3
Sun or partial shade Moist but well-drained soil

Exquisite shades of blue are found in many campanulas, including the perennial clump-forming *C. carpatica*, an easy rock garden plant about 15cm/6in high that can be given a front-line position in a border or lodged among paving. The trim upturned bells, borne freely for several weeks in summer, are in various shades of blue or white and in the case of 'Blue Moonlight' light grey-blue.

Another species for rock gardens and raised beds is *C. cochlearifolia*, a mat-forming dwarf with running roots that gets its common name fairies' thimbles from the masses of nodding bells in shades of pale mauve it produces in summer. The soft tint of 'Elizabeth Oliver', a double, is particularly fine.

All forms of the peach-leaved bellflower (*C. persicifolia*) are desirable for their elegant cup-shaped flowers in various shades of blue or white carried in extended erect sprays about 90cm/3ft high over a long period in summer. They are easy-going companions for many shrubs as well as other perennials and are also excellent for cutting. 'Telham Beauty' has large flowers rinsed in a delicate blue wash. 'Pride of Exmouth' is a semi-double with cups of soft powder blue.

See also *C.* 'Burghaltii', p.36.

▲ *Erythronium californicum* 'White Beauty'

Erythronium californicum 'White Beauty'

Bulb H 25cm/10in, S 10cm/4in Z5

Partial shade Humus-rich, moist but well-drained soil

The erythroniums are a distinctive group of bulbous plants that in late spring or early summer produce erect stems carrying pendent flowers with recurved segments. One of the most striking, with flowers resembling small and elegant turk's cap lilies, is this clone of a species widely distributed in California. The light green leaves are mottled ivory and the creamy white flowers have central reddish-brown flecks.

Another species from North America similar to *E. californicum* is *E. oreganum*. Its flowers are cream with a yellow centre usually outlined with orange-brown marks.

The European dog's tooth violet (*E. dens-canis*), the only species native to Europe, has dark-mottled leaves and pink or mauve flowers, usually rather pale, with sharply swept-back segments. It gets its common name from its long tooth-like bulb.

All these plants do best in conditions that mimic the woodland habitats from which they come. Plant bulbs as soon as they become available as they deteriorate quickly when dry.

The modest beauty of the erythronium is seen to good effect in simple posies of spring flowers.

Nectaroscordum siculum subsp. *bulgaricum*

Bulb H 90cm/3ft, S 15cm/6in Z7

Full sun Well-drained soil

This tall relative of the alliums betrays its family connection by the strong garlic-like smell of its keeled leaves and stem released if these are crushed while fresh. In late spring or early summer numerous long-stalked bell-shaped flowers splay out from the top of stiff stems. The flowers are straw-coloured with green and purple bruise marks. Once they are over, the bells become knobbly seed pods that turn and point skywards. When dried, the stems and heads are scentless and make distinctive cut decorations to combine with the spherical heads of allium.

Penstemon 'Stapleford Gem'

Penstemon 'Stapleford Gem'

Perennial H 60cm/2ft, S 45cm/18in Z8

Full sun Well-drained soil

Many penstemon hybrids are on the tender side and are propagated annually. Even in many areas that experience winter frosts, this is a reliably hardy hybrid. It has gained a following on account of the delicate opalescence of its broadly tubular flowers, which, arranged in whorls on an upright stem, are suffused pale mauve and pink.

Other hybrids of subtle colouring include the less hardy *Penstemon* 'Mother of Pearl' with broadly tubular flowers that are a pearly blend of mauve-blue and pink, with a white throat darkened by red lines. Both these flower for many weeks from mid-summer, provided they are deadheaded.

Take cuttings as a precaution against losses in winter or cold springs.

Polemonium 'Lambrook Mauve'

Perennial H and S 45cm/18in Z2

Sun or partial shade Moist but well-drained soil

In late spring and early summer the clump of this plant's ferny divided leaves is topped by lax sprays of soft mauve-blue flowers that are yellow at the centre. Their colour is much more subtle than that of the common Jacob's ladder (*Polemonium caeruleum*) but this is an attractive and taller plant with mauve-blue flowers.

The recently introduced hybrid 'Bressingham Purple', which also grows to about 75cm/18in, offers an interesting contrast between dark purple leaves and pale mauve-blue flowers, which are lit by bright yellow anthers.

To keep clumps of all these vigorous, divide every two or three years in spring and plant in fresh soil.

The flower sprays and leaves make pretty additions to small posies.

Rosa 'Great Maiden's Blush'

Deciduous shrub (Alba rose) H 1.5m/5ft, S 1.2m/4ft Z4

Full sun Moist but well-drained soil

The ravishing double flowers of 'Great Maiden's Blush', a rose that has been in cultivation for at least 500 years, are a superb example of refined colouring in the old roses. The blush pink of the muddled petals, likened to the colouring of a nymph's thigh in the French name 'Cuisse de Nymphe', shows well against the healthy blue-grey foliage. A deeper-coloured sport of 'Great Maiden's Blush' goes by the even more fanciful name 'Cuisse de Nymphe Emue', suggesting that its pink tones are the result of strong feeling.

'Céleste' is another old Alba, of uncertain date, with semi-double flowers of soft, melting pink opening from refined buds. 'Fantin-Latour', a Centifolia dating from about 1900, has cupped flowers that open flat to show deeper tints within the blush petals.

All these are of similar height, flower in mid-summer and their fragrant blooms are superb for cutting.

▲ *Polemonium* 'Lambrook Mauve'

▲ *Rosa* 'Cuisse de Nymphe Emue', a sport of *R.* 'Great Maiden's Blush'

OTHER GOOD PLANTS

Abutilon vitifolium
'Veronica Tennant'
Tall and downy deciduous shrub bearing in early summer saucer-shaped flowers that are a delicate shade of mauve and nearly 10cm/4in across.

Bergenia 'Silberlicht': see p.36.

Chaenomeles speciosa
'Moerloosei': see p.24.

Clematis Blue Moon: see p.74.

Gladiolus papilio
Tall-growing corm, spreading by underground runners, which produces sword-like leaves and in summer spikes of hooded flowers that are very variable in colouring but commonly yellow-green with purple suffusions.

Malus floribunda
Japanese crab apple
Deciduous small tree at its most glorious in mid- to late spring when the crimson buds covering the arching branches open to pale pink flowers. The very small yellow crabs sometimes remain on the tree right through the winter.

Papaver rhoeas
Mother of Pearl Group
Several selections of the annual corn or field poppy, including also Fairy Wings Group and Cedric Morris Group, have tissue-paper flowers of diaphanous beauty in delicate shades of smoky pink and grey, sometimes with flecks and paler or darker margins.

Phlox paniculata 'Mother of Pearl'
A cultivar of the perennial phlox, producing domed heads of scented blush-white flowers standing 75m/30in high in the second half of summer. Like others of its kind, good for cutting.

Prunus x *subhirtella*
'Autumnalis Rosea'
Deciduous small tree that splutters into flower intermittently over several months, starting in autumn. The semi-double flowers of 'Autumnalis' show barely a trace of pink but those of 'Autumnalis Rosea' are pink in bud, pale on opening. Cut stems make lovely winter decorations.

Rhododendron 'Cilpinense'
Medium-sized, rounded evergreen rhododendron of great refinement. In early spring bushes are covered with small clusters of pink buds opening to funnel-shaped blush-pink flowers. Best planted with some overhead cover to reduce the risk of frost damage.

SHADES OF GREEN

The miraculous agent chlorophyll, which transforms light into energy, is so omnipresent in the foliage of plants that it may seem difficult to believe that there is a call for green in flowers. Yet people's fascination with green flowers, both in the garden and cut, is real and enduring.

▲ *Euphorbia amygdaloides* var. *robbiae*

▲ *Fritillaria acmopetala*

▲ *Nicotiana langsdorffii*

Euphorbia amygdaloides var. *robbiae*
Mrs Robb's bonnet

Perennial H 60cm/2ft, S indefinite Z7

Partial shade or shade Moist to dry well-drained soil

Mrs Robb's bonnet is evergreen and, though potentially invasive, but extremely useful in dry shade; it also flourishes in moist partial shade. In late spring the dark green leaf rosettes are topped by yellow-green flowerheads, which last through most of summer.

Many other spurges with green or yellow-green flowerheads are plants for well-drained soil in sun. One of the best of these is *Euphorbia characias* subsp. *wulfenii* (see p.155). Others suitable for mixed borders include *E. schillingii*, about 90cm/3ft high, with white-ribbed leaves and branching heads of chartreuse bracts that last through summer and into autumn. Another, effective over much the same period, is *E. seguieriana* subsp. *niciciana*, a slightly shorter and more slender plant with blue-grey fleshy leaves and small lime-green flowers.

For the rock garden or front of a border one of the best is *E. myrsinites*, no more than 15cm/6in high with sprawling stems, clothed with spirals of blue-green fleshy leaves and tipped in early spring with lime-green flowerheads that last for several weeks.

Fritillaria acmopetala

Bulb H 40cm/16in, S 8cm/3in Z7

Full sun Well-drained soil

Some of the fritillaries are demanding bulbs for the specialist but several species with green or green-tinted flowers in mid-spring are good garden plants, suitable for borders and rock gardens. Their flowers are not showy but their gracefulness and unusual colouring have won them many admirers. An attractive example is *F. acmopetala*, a slender plant with blue-green leaves and up to three nodding bells, the tips turned out, suspended from gracefully arching stalks. The flowers are pale green with inner segments shaded purplish brown.

F. pontica is usually slightly shorter. The leaves are grey-green, terminating in a top whorl, below which hang up to three green bells stained purplish brown.

More conspicuous than either of these is *F. pallidiflora*, usually 30–40cm/12–16in in height, with up to six hanging bells to a stem. They are yellow-green and flecked with crimson inside and somewhat square-shouldered on account of the nectaries.

All these make intriguing additions to vases of flowers if they can be spared from the garden.

Helleborus argutifolius
Corsican hellebore

Perennial H and S 90cm/3ft Z7

Partial shade or sun Well-drained soil

In late winter and early spring the foliage and flowers of the Corsican hellebore make a study in sculpted green. This is a rather shrubby plant with stems that bear three-fingered and saw-edged dark leaves and are replaced biennially. In their second year the stems hold up clusters of bowl-shaped pale green nodding flowers, which persist long after the yellow-green stamens have fallen away and while the seeds develop.

More sombre, but an impressive brooding presence even in shady corners, is *Helleborus foetidus*, of which one unflattering common name is stinking hellebore, referring to the smell of the leaves when crushed. It makes a clump about 75cm/30in high, with biennial stems bearing fingered very dark leaves and in winter maroon-rimmed green bells. This is an infallible and long-lasting winter flower. Stems and stalks of the Wester Flisk Group are stained red.

Other hellebores with green flowers include the deciduous *H. viridis*, sometimes called the green hellebore on account of the cool fresh colour of the saucer-shaped flowers it bears in late winter and spring. It is half the size of the stinking hellebore and closely related to the Lenten roses (*H.* × *hybridus*), many of which have green-tinted flowers (see p.25).

Nicotiana langsdorffii

Annual H 1.5m/5ft, S 40cm/16in

Sun or partial shade Moist but well-drained soil

As a garden plant this perennial Brazilian species is almost invariably grown as an annual. In summer and autumn the branching wiry stems, rising from a rosette of basal leaves, carry rather angular sprays of drooping apple-green flowers of curious shape, the tube swelling noticeably before being pinched in just before the flaring lobed mouth. The flowers are unscented but this sticky plant makes a distinctive addition to beds and borders.

Green unscented flowers are also found in the popular hybrid tobacco plants. *Nicotiana* 'Lime Green' grows to a height of 60cm/2ft and its nearly horizontal tubular flowers open to five large lobes, each sharply pleated down the centre.

▲ *Helleborus argutifolius*

OTHER GOOD PLANTS

Alchemilla mollis **Lady's mantle**
The irresistible appeal of this sprawling perennial lies in the combination of velvety rounded leaves and long-lasting sprays of lime-green starry flowers, which are good for cutting. Remove unwanted self-sown seedlings.

Hermodactylus tuberosus: see p.114.

Heuchera cylindrica 'Greenfinch'
The lobed leaves of this perennial form an attractive base for tall stems of small olive-green flowers in summer. Good for cutting.

Kniphofia 'Green Jade'
A perennial, this red hot poker defies its common name, producing tall spikes of green buds that open to cream then white flowers flecked by protruding red-brown anthers.

Ornithogalum nutans
The numerous funnel-shaped flowers of this medium-sized spring-flowering bulb are white but the overall impression is of green on account of the jade stripes on the outside. Good for cutting.

Ribes laurifolium
Small spreading evergreen shrub bearing drooping sprays of yellow-green flowers in late winter and early spring.

Tellima grandiflora 'Purpurteppich'
Perennial flowering in late spring or early summer with attractively lobed and scalloped leaves, veined and tinted maroon, from which rise dark stems 60cm/2ft high carrying pink-rimmed small bells.

Tulipa 'Spring Green'
One of the Viridiflora tulips, late-spring bulbs with cup-shaped flowers marked with a green flush or stripe, in this case combined with white.

Zinnia elegans 'Envy'
Annual for summer displays with semi-double yellow-green flower-heads on stems 75cm/30in high. Good for cutting.

MAROON, MIDNIGHT & BLACK

Although a garden devoted to very deep colours would be penitential, most dark-coloured flowers are not sombre. They have textures and highlights that enhance their near-black depths, making them seem more sumptuous and voluptuous than sinister, especially when viewed at close quarters.

▲ *Alcea rosea* 'Nigra'   ▲ *Buddleja davidii* 'Black Knight'   ▲ *Cosmos atrosanguineus*

Alcea rosea 'Nigra'
Biennial H 2.5m/8ft, S 50cm/20in Z3
Full sun Well-drained soil

Buddleja davidii 'Black Knight'
Deciduous shrub H and S 3m/10ft Z5
Full sun Well-drained soil

There is uncertainty about the origin of hollyhocks, but they are plants that have long been cultivated. Although they are short-lived perennials, to ensure vigour and to reduce the risk of rust disease it is best to grow these cottage-garden favourites as biennials. In sheltered gardens the stiff somewhat woody stems clothed with rough lobed leaves usually need no support. The single or double funnel-shaped flowers, borne in the first half of summer, are almost stalkless, sitting close to the stem.

The single flowers of *Alcea rosea* 'Nigra' are elegantly formed, and of a sumptuous satin texture that complements to perfection their deep maroon, which is lit by a yellow centre.

You can follow the practice of nineteenth-century gardeners, who concealed the bare stems of tall hollyhocks by planting them behind dahlias and other leafy ornamentals.

Self-sown seedlings of the butterfly bush lodged in walls and dry barren ground produce arching stems loaded with cone-shaped spikes of small flowers that give off a heavy scent of slightly musty sweetness. These are an irresistible lure for butterflies and night-flying moths in late summer and early autumn.

Cultivars of superior quality with mauve-blue, red-purple, pink and white flowers do well in sunny dry gardens, especially in coastal areas. Like the interior self-sown plants, they have flowers that attract butterflies and moths and for this reason alone they are worth including in the garden. One of the darkest of these is *Buddleja davidii* 'Black Knight', which has deep violet-purple flowers brightened by small yellow eyes. Less sombre are the large spikes of 'Royal Red', which are packed with rich red-purple flowers.

Hybrids with the white-felted *B. fallowiana*, an attractive foliage plant with very fragrant mauve spikes, are more lax. 'Lochinch' is a downy grey-green shrub with orange-eyed violet-blue flowers.

Left to themselves these shrubs can grow to more than 4.5m/15ft and become leggy. For best results, prune hard in spring, cutting back to a low framework of branches.

Cosmos atrosanguineus

Tuber H 75cm/30in, S 45cm/18in Z8

Full sun Moist but well-drained soil

In a long flowering season, starting in mid-summer and lasting well into autumn, wiry stems of *Cosmos atrosanguineus* rise through its dark green divided leaves, carrying cup-shaped reddish chocolate flowerheads, which, astonishingly, smell of chocolate.

If grown in free-draining soil and protected with a mulch in winter, the tubers of this unusual perennial may survive periods of frost. Where winters are hard, these precautions will not be adequate. The best course is to treat the tubers in the same way as dahlia tubers, starting them into growth, and planting them out when the risk of frost is over and lifting again in autumn.

Fritillaria persica 'Adiyaman'

Bulb H 1.2m/4ft, S10cm/4in Z5

Full sun Well-drained soil

Much of the interest in fritillaries is inspired by the unusual colours of their flowers. This sombre show-stopper flowers in late spring but starts into growth early and, unless protected, risks being damaged by heavy frosts. The bulbs are large and egg-shaped and the stems stout, with narrow grey leaves on the lower part. The upper part of the stem carries as many as thirty bells, almost conical in shape and deep purple-brown, overlaid with a greyish bloom.

The black sarana (*Fritillaria camschatcensis*) is another very dark-flowered species. It tolerates full sun, provided the soil is humus-rich and moist, but grows well in dappled shade, usually reaching a height of 35–45cm/14–18in. In late spring or early summer there are usually three or four black-chocolate flowers hanging from an erect stem above whorls of glossy leaves.

Iris chrysographes

Perennial H 45cm/18in, S 10cm/4in Z4

Full sun Moist but well-drained soil

The dark splendour of this rhizomatous beardless iris owes much to the rich yellow markings on the falls, alluded to in the specific name, which means 'written in gold'. Two or three scented flowers are carried on an unbranched stem above flat and narrow grassy leaves in early summer. The darkest forms, such as 'Black Knight', are a sumptuous near-black velvet with gold scribbling and patches.

Fritillaria persica 'Adiyaman' ▶

▲ *Iris chrysographes*

Pelargonium 'Lord Bute'

Perennial H 50cm/20in, S45cm/18in Z9

Full sun In containers soil-less or soil-based compost (John Innes No. 2)

The darkest of the pelargoniums are found among the Regals, all of them somewhat shrubby and bearing clusters of large flowers in summer that are best appreciated when plants are container-grown in porches and conservatories or, where the climate is mild enough, on sheltered patios.

One of the best known of the dark Regals is 'Lord Bute', which has purple-black petals with wine-red margins. Scarlet and frilled margins illuminate the near-black flowers of 'Rimfire'. Also deep but tinted more to wine red and with variations in shading is 'Morwenna'.

All these are vivacious when set against 'Springfield Black', a Regal with dark red flowers with black depths.

To minimize wind and rain damage, stake the stems of specimens grown outdoors.

Rhodochiton atrosanguineus

Perennial/annual climber H 3m/10ft, S 75cm/30in Z9

Full sun Humus-rich, moist but well-drained soil

When grown as a perennial under glass, this slender climber will flower throughout much of the year but it is easy to grow outdoors as an annual, if the seed is sown in heat in early spring. The curious tubular flowers that dangle among the heart-shaped leaves are deep maroon and open to a five-lobed mouth. Each flower is protected by a cap-shaped bright pink calyx. The cap persists even after the flower proper has fallen.

A wigwam of canes provides an adequate support for the twining leaf and flower stalks.

Viola 'Bowles' Black'

Annual/biennial/perennial H 15cm/6in, S 30cm/1ft Z4

Sun or partial shade

Humus-rich, moist but well-drained soil; in containers soil-less

or soil-based compost (John Innes No. 2 with added leaf mould)

The violas with rich purple and near-black flowers, usually lit by a tiny bright eye, are the least sinister of dark flowers and bloom with great prodigality for weeks in summer if regularly deadheaded. Some are reasonably perennial, others are all the better for being propagated fairly regularly by division or from cuttings. 'Bowles' Black', with small yellow-eyed heartsease flowers, comes reasonably true from seed provided it is not allowed to intermarry with other violas, and it is best grown as an annual or biennial.

Of those that are longer-lived one of the most free-flowering is 'Molly Sanderson', which makes a neat clump of glossy leaves covered with patches of black velvet that have a minute yellow centre.

'Roscastle Black' is also free-flowering and very dark but there is more purple around the yellow eye. 'Huntercombe Purple', not black but wonderfully rich in colour and with a white eye, is one of the most reliably perennial.

OTHER GOOD PLANTS

Angelica gigas
Large biennial with handsome leaves and in the second summer domed flowerheads that are dark beetroot purple. Remove seedheads before seeds fall.

Clematis 'Viola'
Climbing hybrid clematis producing in the second half of summer and early autumn single flowers about 10cm/4in across that are very rich violet-purple with yellow anthers.

Dahlia 'Moor Place': see p.62.

Dianthus barbatus 'Sooty'
Seed strain of the biennial sweet William growing to 60cm/2ft and in late spring and early summer producing heads of maroon to deep blood-red flowers, each with a ring of tiny white dots in the centre. The foliage develops purplish tints and the bracts surrounding the flowers have a whiskery appearance.

Helianthus annuus 'Velvet Queen': see p.56.

Iris 'Langport Wren'
Intermediate Bearded iris about 60cm/2ft high producing in late spring or early summer luxuriously deep black-maroon flowers with a lighter beard.

Penstemon 'Blackbird'
Tall perennial with willowy stems carrying narrowly tubular black-purple flowers in the second half of summer and early autumn. It picks well.

Trillium erectum
Low woodland perennial forming a clump of dark blotched leaves above which stand stalkless maroon flowers in late spring.

Tulipa 'Queen of Night': see p.84.

Veratrum nigrum: see p.159.

▲ *Pelargonium* 'Lord Bute'

▲ *Viola* 'Bowles' Black'

▲ *Rhodochiton atrosanguineus*

TWO-TONE

Smart or spivvy, two-tone or bicoloured flowers have a way of attracting attention that can make them difficult to place among other plants. But they do not have to be isolated. They often look their best when surrounding plants pick up the colours that are brought together in a single flower.

Hermodactylus tuberosus
Widow iris

Tuber H 30cm/1ft, S 5cm/2in Z7

Full sun Well-drained soil

The iris connection is immediately apparent in this intriguingly sombre plant. The single scented flowers, borne on rather weak stems sheathed in linear leaves, are yellow-green with purplish black falls that curve back from angled shafts.

The widow iris, which flowers in the second half of spring, will do well in rather dry chalky soils but demands sun and warmth and needs space for its creeping horizontal tubers to advance.

Lupinus Band of Nobles Series

Perennial H 1.5m/5ft, S 75cm/30in Z3

Full sun Well-drained neutral to acid soil

In early summer there is little in borders that can match the tall spikes dense with the bright flowers of the perennial hybrid lupins rising out of a base of grey-green fingered leaves. These usually bicoloured flowers, the keel and standard petals in different colours, are the result of intensive breeding using various species, notably the yellow-flowered tree lupin (*L. arboreus*) and the blue-flowered *L. polyphyllus*. The Band of Nobles Series is sold as a seed mixture, in a good range of colours, most of the bicolours including white or yellow. Named seed-raised cultivars in the Band of Nobles Series include 'The Chatelaine', pink and white, and 'The Governor', blue and white. More compact seed strains include the Gallery Series, with bicoloured spikes up to 45cm/18in high.

Secondary spikes follow if the first spikes are removed before they set seed.

Nemesia 'Twilight' (syn. 'KLM')

Annual H 20cm/8in, S 15cm/6in

Full sun Moist but well-drained soil; in containers soil-less or soil-based

compost (John Innes No. 2)

Nemesias are annuals that perform best in cool growing conditions; their vivid lipped flowers are quickly over if the growing conditions in summer are hot and dry. Because their season may prove short, it is as well when planting to plan what will succeed them.

Seed is often sold as colourful mixtures that may include or consist entirely of bicolours but there are also several long-established bicolours

▲ *Hermodactylus tuberosus*

▲ *Viola × wittrockiana* 'Jolly Joker'

▲ *Lupinus* 'The Governor'

relaunched at various times under different names. The small flowers of 'Twilight', produced in great quantity, have a white lower lip and blue upper lip, consisting of a fan of four lobes. Bumps at the throat of the lower petal are yellow.

Another bold bicolour is 'National Ensign' (syns. 'Aurora', 'Danish Flag' and 'Mellow Red and White'). The lower lip of the flower is clean white, the upper lip rich red.

Viola × wittrockiana 'Jolly Joker'
Annual/biennial H 15cm/6in, S 30cm/1ft
Sun or partial shade Moist but well-drained soil

Striking colour contrasts are a feature of many large-flowered pansies grown as annuals or biennials, most commonly in the form of a dark mask imposed on the petals. In the *Viola × wittrockiana* Joker Series the whiskered orange mask of 'Jolly Joker' is daringly set against upper petals and a lower rim of deep purple.

In some of the perennial violas the colours are divided between petals. The effect is particularly jaunty in 'Jackanapes' (see illustration on pp.92–3), a viola named after the pet monkey of the influential English garden designer Gertrude Jekyll, who was active in the late nineteenth and early twentieth centuries. The neat flowers, which are produced in great profusion, have red-brown upper petals and yellow lower petals with fine purplish brown rays radiating from the centre. Although an evergreen perennial, it should be propagated frequently. Its tendency to be short-lived probably derives from the heartsease (*V. tricolor*).

'Helen Mount' (syn. 'Johnny Jump Up'), which is very close to this species, is an equally appealing bicolour, with purple upper petals and rayed, sometimes also purple-blotched, yellow lower petals. It is a happy and usually welcome self-seeder.

OTHER GOOD PLANTS

Antirrhinum majus 'La Bella Red and White'
Grown as an annual for its spikes of open-throated flowers that are red with a white base. Long-lasting and good for cutting.

Aquilegia vulgaris 'William Guiness'
Striking cultivar of granny's bonnet, in late spring and early summer bearing spurred flowers that are near-black purple with an outer band of white.

Cerinthe major
Annual or short-lived perennial with fleshy blue-green leaves and tubular nodding flowers that are maroon with a yellow band at the mouth.

Cytisus 'Lena': see p.50.

Fritillaria michailovskyi
Short-growing bulb that in early summer bears nodding purplish brown bells, the tips ringed bright yellow.

Fuchsia 'Lady Thumb'
Compact upright deciduous shrub, often grown as a container plant. Like many fuchsias it bears a profusion of bicoloured tubular flowers that dangle loosely from the stems over many weeks in summer and well into autumn. In this case the tube and sepals are red and the corolla white with red veining.

Iris 'Edith Wolford': see p.75.

Narcissus 'February Silver'
This compact Cyclamineus daffodil, a bulbous plant flowering in early spring, has a lemon-yellow trumpet with slightly reflexed white segments.

Pelargonium 'Splendide'
Compact evergreen subshrub with downy and toothed grey-green leaves. In summer it bears flowers with red-pink upper petals, dark spotted at the base, and three white lower petals.

Rhodochiton atrosanguineus: see p.112.

CHAMELEONS

Most flowers change colour as they age. They usually fade undramatically, gradually transforming into a pale version of themselves in their prime. There are, however, other flowers that go through more interesting shifts of colour, in some cases producing a range of closely related shades but in other cases making a truly multicoloured effect.

▲ *Erysimum* 'John Codrington'

▲ *Cobaea scandens*

▲ *Pulmonaria* 'Lewis Palmer'

Cobaea scandens
Cathedral bell, cup and saucer plant
Perennial/annual climber H 6m/20ft, S 1.8m/6ft Z9
Full sun Moist but well-drained soil

Although a perennial tendril climber capable of growing to more than 15m/50ft, cathedral bell or cup and saucer plant can make a fast-growing sun-loving annual. In late summer and early autumn it bears long-stalked fragrant bells, each with a bright green five-lobed collar at the base. The bell itself opens greenish white but ages to violet-purple, the two colours and intermediate shades adding to this climber's striking appearance. In f. *alba* the flowers are greenish white to cream.

To grow as an annual, sow seed in heat in late winter or early spring. Pinch out the tips of shoots to encourage branching growth.

Erysimum 'John Codrington'
Perennial H 25cm/10in, S 30cm/1ft Z7
Full sun Well-drained neutral or alkaline soil

Several wallflowers, all short-lived perennials, are attractive because the four-petalled flowers, borne in short spikes during spring and early summer, present a range of colours in close proximity. In *Erysimum* 'John

Codrington' yellow blends subtly with varying shades of brown and purplish pink to create a chameleon effect.

A plant in the same vein is 'Jacob's Jacket', with bronze, orange and mauve flowers present at the same time. The flowers of 'Wenlock Beauty', taller than either of these, show tints of biscuit, yellow, bronze and mauve.

To maintain stocks, take softwood cuttings in spring or summer.

Pulmonaria 'Lewis Palmer'
Perennial H 40cm/16in, S 45cm/18in Z4
Partial or full shade Moist but well-drained soil

Interesting foliage, often heavily spotted or silvered, and early flowers in late winter or early spring secure a place for many lungworts as attractive ground cover, particularly useful in shade. A curious feature of some species and cultivars is a colour shift from pink to blue or purple as the flowers open. *Pulmonaria* 'Lewis Palmer' is a hybrid with boldly splashed and spotted hairy leaves, above which erect stems carry clustered funnel-shaped flowers that open pink but turn to bright blue.

Other chameleons among the lungworts include several cultivars of *P. saccharata*, among them 'Frühlingshimmel', which has heavily spotted leaves and clear blue flowers opening from pink buds held in red-brown calyces. 'Mrs Moon' is an old cultivar with flowers that are

▲ *Verbena* 'Peaches and Cream'

pink in bud and mauve-blue on opening. 'Excalibur' is another handsome hybrid. It has silvered leaves and gives a multicoloured effect as coral buds open to pass through various shades of pink before becoming light blue.

Verbena 'Peaches and Cream'

Annual H 30cm/1ft, S 45cm/18in

Full sun Moist but well-drained soil; in containers soil-less or soil-based compost (John Innes No. 2)

The hybrid verbenas are valuable bedding and container plants that carry their domed heads of small flowers over a long season. Variations in flower colour on the one plant make subtle but lively combinations. 'Peaches and Cream', a bushy annual that is particularly effective in hanging baskets and can be raised from seed, has flowers that open coral and fade through salmon and shades of yellow to cream, all colours being present at the same time.

The slightly larger 'Silver Anne' is a perennial hybrid, usually grown as an annual but perpetuated from overwintered cuttings. The lightly scented flowers, carried in dense heads, open pink and then transmute to silvery white, various shades giving a multitoned effect. The spreading stems make a fine skirt to a mixed container planting.

OTHER GOOD PLANTS

Hydrangea paniculata Pink Diamond ('Interhydia')

Large deciduous shrub transformed in late summer when it carries large pyramidal heads of fertile, showy sterile flowers. Ivory white at first, they gradually turn dark pink, and remain attractive when their colour fades to buff.

Ipomoea lobata Spanish flag

Short-lived perennial climber commonly grown as an annual for erect one-sided sprays of slightly curved tubular flowers borne in summer. The flowers open scarlet but change to orange and yellow.

Kniphofia caulescens

Colour contrasts between the unopened buds at the top of the spike and tubular flowers that open at the bottom are common in the red hot pokers. This evergreen species produces a tapered spearhead of green-tinted coral buds that open soft coral red and then fade to greenish yellow.

Nymphaea 'Aurora'

Waterlily suitable for a shallow pool or tub. It has purple-mottled olive-green pads and in summer cream-coloured buds open to yellow flowers, which become orange and then red as they age.

Rosa x *odorata* 'Mutabilis'

Lax shrubby rose, capable of making a short climber if supported. The leaves have a purple tint and the single flowers, borne in summer and early autumn, open light yellow before turning copper-pink and finally deep pink.

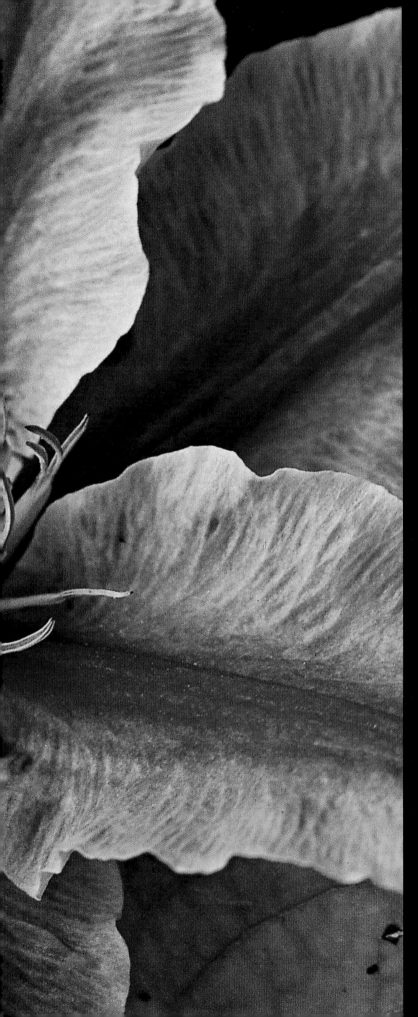

MARKINGS

Very few wild flowers are of unmarked plainness. Most show at least a change of colour at the centre or in the throat, the colour of the eye often contrasting dramatically with that of the petals. This focal point may be one of several guides that direct insects to nectar or pollen in such a way that the visitor effects pollination. Visual guides to nectar are also important for bird pollinators, most of which have a poor sense of smell. Humans see things with different eyes and markings are often very important ornamentally.

The large-flowered hybrid clematis are an important group of climbers with numerous cultivars that are generous with their showy blooms in late spring and early summer. Contrasts of colour give some of these a starred or rayed effect. The single flowers of 'Dr Ruppel' can be up to 15cm/6in across and are composed of broad pink segments with darker central bands.

MARKINGS

The pollinator's view of a flower will in many cases be very different to our own simply because we do not share the same responses to light. Where we may see no spots or lines, pollinators who can see ultra-violet light, such as bees, may catch sight of a lit-up pattern that simplifies landing or positioning and gives an unambiguous indication of where proboscis or tongue should be extended to reach a supply of nectar. In a way we are living in a universe parallel to that of the flower pollinators and fortunately we have our own way of appreciating distinctive features of flowers. Gardeners have long been fascinated by unusual markings and have selected and bred for them. Nothing demonstrates this more clearly than changes in taste that have influenced developments in florist's flowers such as pinks (*Dianthus*).

EYES AND THROATS

The most magnetic of all the floral markings is an eye in a colour that marks it out from the general colour of the flower. Even a small white centre, like a seductive human glance, has an astonishing power to hold the gaze captive, at least momentarily. The eye is commonly a colour contrast at the base of petals or at the opening of a salverform flower – that is one with petal-like lobes surrounding a central tube. However, I have gone beyond a narrow application of the term to include in the entries here descriptions of the Pacific hybrid delphiniums, many of which have flowers with a bee-like cluster of petal-like fragments at the centre. I have also included a daisy, *Osteospermum* 'White Pim', in which the central disc makes a small but distinctive eye. Many other daisies could be featured here; see pp.42–3 and 54–7. There is certainly a strong case for adding a section on flowers in which the colour of the throat is an eye-catching feature. I leave to gardeners the pleasure of noting such plants, as varied as gladioli, penstemons and rhododendrons.

PATTERNS

A wide range of markings on flowers follow more or less regular patterns. Highly distinctive chequered patterns are closely associated with two groups of bulbous plants, the fritillaries and the colchicums. The snake's head fritillary is by far the best known of all the chequered flowers. Its generic and common names both refer to the distinctive pattern, commonly a mixture of chocolate, mauve-pink and red-purple, on its hanging bells. Like other chequered fritillaries its beauty is subtle, even sombre, although forms with green markings on white usually lighten the effect of large colonies.

Many of the autumn-flowering colchicums are worth growing simply for the beautiful goblet shape of their flowers. Those described as tessellated, a reference to the mosaic-like pattern covering their mauve flowers, extend the interest of a genus in which the colour range of the autumn-flowering species is limited. One of the most readily available and easily cultivated of this group is the deep mauve *C. agrippinum*, possibly a hybrid, as it is not known in the wild. *C. bivonae* is another tessellated species with large mauve flowers. It is said to be a good garden plant and one that multiplies freely.

The tracery of veins, which is discernible in very many flowers, is generally much less conspicuous than the chequered patterns on fritillaries and colchicums. If you are looking for a range of good examples in a single genus there is no better group of plants to consider than the hardy geraniums. These plants need no apologist. They have been much praised and as a result planted on account of their versatility and the ground-covering qualities of their attractive foliage as well as for the beauty and long season of their flowers. Gardeners have come to rely on them so heavily that they surely must, despite their virtues, fall out of fashion, at least for a period. Before you jettison them, look closely at the delicate tracery of their veined flowers, in some, such as *Geranium pratense* 'Mrs Kendall Clark', a ghostly pattern, in others, including *G. sanguineum* var. *striatum*, a darker network that is the support of paler petals.

In many flowers larger-scale and more assertive marks are distributed in a pattern around the sexual organs as guides to pollinators. To describe these marks as blotches and splashes suggests that they are clumsy, but they are far from that and in countless cases it is their bold and arresting effect that makes flowers so ornamentally desirable. In many poppies, for instance, they are the clinching detail that marks out a plant of exceptional interest. The contrast of dark blotches on lighter petals sometimes creates a bold pattern in the garden. That is the effect of sowing a drift of the annual *Papaver commutatum* 'Ladybird'. But a blotched pattern can sometimes come as a delightful surprise, discovered only when a plant is inspected closely. A ravishing example of this is *Paeonia rockii*, a shrubby peony worth looking out for in major collections but not described in the entries here because the supply of plants is so limited. The sumptuous flowers have ruffled white petals that part to reveal maroon-black bases around a boss of golden stamens.

Among the boldest flowers are those in which patterns of colour are arranged in bands, stripes or rays. On an initial acquaintance their extrovert character can be enormously appealing. And one welcomes them into the garden because they create an animated party atmosphere. In the end, however, one can feel that there is something forced about their gaiety. In the face of their relentless bonhomie it might be nice to find a quiet corner – or to leave early. It is a shame about the name but I am glad for the wake-up dazzle of *Crocus sieberi* subsp. *sublimis* 'Tricolor', which has a relatively short but early season. Longer-flowering extroverts should be used with discretion.

IRREGULAR MARKINGS

Random speckling, streaking and blotching often also have an immediate appeal and give some flowers a mysterious character. This is certainly true of the best known of the toad lilies, *Tricyrtis formosana*, whose irregular spotting seems to confirm the impression created by the intriguing structure of the flowers. Less mysterious but still subtly intriguing is the curiously speckled violet *Viola sororia* 'Freckles'.

More refined than these are flowers where speckling pays some attention to the form of flowers. This is so with the oriental hellebores (*Helleborus* × *hybridus*), which have crimson spots around the boss of stamens. If you have a colony of these (and why not?) it is well worth making your own selection from self-sown plants, saving in particular the best of the speckled and dark-coloured forms. Even more refined is the spotting on the flowers of *Nomocharis pardanthina*, a tantalizingly exquisite bulb that is one of the great beauties from the mountainous regions

of western China. The marks are concentrated at the centre of the flower and also at the margins of the fringed petals. Unfortunately this species and its lesser-known relatives have proved difficult plants except where the growing season is cool and there is a good supply of moisture.

Heavily splashed and streaked flowers often have an amusing boldness. This is an endearing quality in the monkey flowers (*Mimulus*) but, as so often in company, the joker is rarely an easy companion. They need careful placing, best near plants that pick up one or other of the monkey flowers' colours. Perhaps other gardeners find nothing unsettling in the restless energy of whimsical bicolors such as rosa mundi (*Rosa gallica* 'Versicolor'). It has been a favourite since at least the sixteenth century (if there is truth in its legendary association with Fair Rosamund, mistress of Henry II, it goes back to the twelfth century). Nonetheless, it seems to me at its best when it is kept apart, for example as a low hedge, preferably not on a main axis of the garden, as it is frequently attacked by mildew in the second half of summer.

OUTLINES

A fascination with flowers that have petals or other segments outlined in a colour different from the main colour of the flower is a recurrent theme in fashionable gardening. The best evidence of this can be found in the fluctuating fortunes of the various *Dianthus* hybrids, which in western gardens have been enormously popular since the sixteenth century. In the classification of carnations (hybrids derived from *D. caryophyllus*), the picotees are those with petals outlined in a contrasting colour. The term is sometimes used loosely in seed catalogues to describe other plants, for example tuberous begonias, where this characteristic is an ornamental feature.

Although in the past of lesser status than carnations, pinks (mainly derived from *D. plumarius*) have endured better as garden plants. Laced hybrids – that is, those with petals banded and blotched at the base in a colour contrasting with the ground colour – became enormously popular in the late eighteenth and nineteenth centuries. Some old-fashioned laced pinks, such as 'Dad's Favourite', certainly go back a long way. They are pleasingly authentic and spicily scented old garden flowers. It is worth growing also modern laced pinks, which have a longer flowering season and require less frequent propagation.

BRIGHT & DARK EYES

Eye contact is astonishingly hard to resist. We are strongly drawn not only to human eyes but also even to the vegetable eye, whether dark and sultry, vivid and cheerful, or even just a pinprick of gold at the centre of sombre petals. We respond to the magnetic power of this focus, just as flower pollinators do.

▲ *Delphinium* Black Knight Group

▲ *Dianthus* 'Musgrave's Pink'

Delphinium Black Knight Group
Annual/biennial H 1.5m/5ft, S 75cm/30in Z3
Full sun Moist but well-drained soil

Like the Elatum Group delphiniums (see *D.* 'Fanfare', p.155), the Pacific hybrids produce impressive spikes in early and mid-summer stacked with spurred flowers that have a central eye or 'bee', usually of contrasting colour. These hybrids are, however, short-lived and are raised from seed to be grown as annuals or biennials for planting out in borders and for cutting. The flowers of the Black Knight Group are deep purple with black eyes.

Other Pacific hybrids include the white-eyed pink-purple Guinevere Group and the Percival Group, which has white flowers with a black eye.

For best results add generous quantities of well-rotted compost to the soil before planting, stake early and take measures to control slugs and snails.

Dianthus 'Musgrave's Pink'
Perennial H 10cm/4in, S 20cm/8in Z4
Full sun Well-drained neutral to alkaline soil

The old-fashioned pinks are a group of complex parentage, much valued in the past for their clove-scented flowers in early summer. Many are double and heavily marked (see *Dianthus* 'Dad's Favourite', p.132) but there are also charmingly simple singles such as the green-eyed 'Musgrave's Pink', which was introduced before 1750, has pure white, fringed petals.

A number of compact hybrid pinks, the result of crossing small mainly alpine species, make mounds about 10cm/4in high, suitable for rock gardens and raised beds. The flowers, usually well scented, are borne above the tufts of grey or grey-green leaves in early summer. 'Dewdrop' is like a miniaturized 'Musgrave's Pink'. 'Little Jock' is semi-double and its pale pink, deeply fringed, fragrant flowers have a crimson eye.

Geranium psilostemon
Armenian cranesbill

Perennial H 90cm/3ft, S 1.2m/4ft Z5

Sun or partial shade Moist but well-drained soil

Like many geraniums, the Armenian cranesbill is a very good foliage plant, the clump of deeply divided leaves often colouring well in autumn. In early summer, though, all eyes are on the flowers. They are bowl-shaped, brilliant magenta, with an arresting black centre and produced with great freedom over several weeks. Without support plants tend to flop.

This species is a parent of the remarkable hybrid G. 'Ann Folkard'. When they first appear, its deeply cut leaves are yellow-green and this colour persists in the end leaves of shoots right through summer. The trailing stems will travel sideways but are also capable of working their way into the lower branches of shrubs. The flowers, magenta-purple and black-centred, begin to appear in early summer and there is no break until the autumn. This hybrid has an advantage over many geraniums in that it does not set seed but is easily propagated by division and from cuttings.

Another dramatic plant is G. subcaulescens, which is stunning in a rock garden and good anywhere in sun where the soil is well-drained, making an impression out of all proportion to its size. The black-eyed bright magenta flowers are borne freely over a long period in summer on a low plant with a spread of about 30cm/1ft.

The flowers of G. wallichianum 'Buxton's Variety', from a very different part of the spectrum, are rich blue with darker veining and a white eye. The plant is rarely more than 30cm/1ft high but the stems trail, working themselves among other plants and presenting bright flowers in unexpected places throughout late summer and autumn. It can bring to life mixed borders in which shrubs have long finished flowering.

Osteospermum 'White Pim'

Evergreen subshrub/annual H 25cm/10in, S 60cm/2ft Z9

Full sun Well-drained soil

Under whatever botanical name it is given, and it has been cursed with many, this aromatic and sprawling evergreen daisy is immediately appealing on sunny days in summer. On dull days the slim mauve-blue buds remain shut but when triggered by sunshine open brilliant white with navy-blue centres.

A more upright but similar plant growing to 60cm/2ft is Osteospermum ecklonis and the hybrid 'Silver Sparkler' is like a variegated form of this. 'Whirlygig' keeps to the same colour scheme but is altogether more fanciful, the petal-like ray florets being folded together for part of their length, giving them a spoon shape.

These daisies are often grown as annuals. Even where the climate is mild enough for them to be grown as perennials, it is a wise precaution to overwinter rooted cuttings under glass.

Geranium psilostemon ▲
Osteospermum 'White Pim' ▶

Phlox divaricata subsp. *laphamii* 'Chattahoochee'

Perennial H 20cm/8in, S 30cm/1ft Z4

Partial shade Humus-rich, moist but well-drained soil

In late spring and the first half of summer this phlox is one of the most arresting plants for a shaded corner in a rock garden, and it is adaptable enough to plant in other slightly shaded and reasonably moist positions. It has rather lax stems and at its peak the narrow dark green leaves are almost hidden by flowers about 2.5cm/1in across, which are mauve-blue and crimson-eyed. The flowers pale with age, with the result that there is a pleasing mixture of tones on the one plant at the same time.

More tolerant of drier conditions are the various forms of the evergreen *P. douglasii*. Its linear leaves are covered in late spring and early summer with rounded flowers, principally in shades of mauve and pink, making mounds abut 20cm/8in high. The flowers of 'Boothman's Variety' are cool mauve-pink with a purplish eye.

The moss phlox (*P. subulata*) is another evergreen species that does well in conditions similar to those that suit *P. douglasii*. In late spring and early summer the cushions of leaves are covered by numerous flowers with notched petal lobes. The named forms cover a wide colour range, in most instances the flowers having a contrasting eye. 'Amazing Grace' has white flowers with a pink centre; the flowers of 'McDaniel's Cushion' are bright pink with a crimson eye.

Thunbergia alata
Black-eyed Susan

Annual climber H 2.5m/8ft, 75cm/30in Z8

Full sun Moist but well-drained soil

In a warm sheltered position outdoors this tropical twining climber will produce a succession of showy flowers in summer and early autumn. It can be used as a trailer, for example in hanging baskets, as well as on vertical supports. As generally seen, the flowers have a dark purple tube with five orange-yellow lobes opening flat at the mouth around a chocolate-brown centre.

There are also various colour variations in shades of white, ivory and salmon. The newly introduced F_1 hybrid *Thunbergia alata* 'Blushing Susie' has flowers in shades of red, pink and cream.

Veronica peduncularis 'Georgia Blue'

Perennial H 10cm/4in, S 60cm/2ft Z6

Full sun Well-drained soil

For many weeks in spring and summer the glossy evergreen foliage of this mat-forming speedwell is covered with numerous white-centred deep blue flowers. As a long-flowering plant for rock gardens and raised beds it presents no special problems and is adaptable enough to plant in paving and at the front of borders. Unlike the beautiful weed *Veronica filiformis*, it is not invasive.

▲ *Phlox divaricata* subsp. *laphamii* 'Chattahoochee'

▲ *Thunbergia alata*

▲ *Veronica peduncularis* 'Georgia Blue'

OTHER GOOD PLANTS

Anchusa azurea
'Loddon Royalist': see p.44.

Chionodoxa luciliae
Gigantea Group: see p.22.

Convolvulus cneorum: see p.74.

Euphorbia characias subsp.
wulfenii: see p.155.

Lavatera x *clementii* 'Barnsley':
see p.34.

Lobelia erinus 'Sapphire'
Trailing seed strain of the
common lobelia with white-
eyed brilliant blue flowers. This
perennial, grown as an annual,
provides a lively effect in hanging
baskets and other containers for
several months.

Myosotis sylvatica 'Royal Blue'
Relatively tall forget-me-not,
growing to about 40cm/16in and
producing numerous sprays of
yellow-eyed blue flowers in spring
and early summer. This biennial
goes well with tulips.

Petunia Surfinia Purple: see p.35.

Phlox paniculata 'Blue Ice'
The fragrant flowers of many
perennial border phloxes have
contrasting eyes, which are
known as 'pips'. These heighten
the dramatic impact of their
domed or pyramidal heads in
the garden and in flower
arrangements. *Phlox paniculata*
'Blue Ice' is an unusual cultivar
which has pink buds that open to
blue-tinted arctic-white flowers
with a small pink eye.

Primula japonica: see p.158.

Saxifraga x *irvingii* 'Jenkinsiae'
Miniature alpine perennial with
tight rosettes of lime-encrusted
leaves almost hidden in early
spring by numerous out-of-scale
pale pink flowers with darker
centres.

Verbascum (Cotswold Group)
'Cotswold Queen'
The Cotswold Group of hybrid
mulleins are short-lived perennials
whose spikes of saucer-shaped
flowers make splendid verticals in
borders and wild gardens in early
summer. The yellow flowers of
'Cotswold Queen' have a
conspicuous purple eye.

Viola 'Bowles' Black', see p.112.

CHEQUERS & VEINS

Among the most intriguing markings on flowers are the mosaic-like chequered patterns found on some of the fritillaries and colchicums. When heavy, these patterns give flowers a sombre richness. The tracery of veins is usually much lighter. The beauty of the pattern on the petals of many modest flowers is revealed only on close inspection.

▲ *Fritillaria meleagris*

▲ *Geranium pratense* 'Mrs Kendall Clark'

▲ *Iris* 'Caesar'

Fritillaria meleagris
Snake's head fritillary
Bulb H 30cm/1ft, S 10cm/4in Z4

Full sun Humus-rich, moist soil

The snake's head fritillary, which flowers in mid-spring, is a slender plant with narrow grey-green leaves arranged up the stem, from the arching tip of which dangle one or two bell-shaped flowers. They are usually in a shade of purple and strongly chequered in deeper purple or chocolate. The botanical name alludes to a dice box, and hence a chequerboard, as well as to the guinea fowl, a speckled bird. In any colony there is likely to be considerable variation and some plants will have white as the base colour. Among the most beautiful are those subtly chequered with a green pattern. This irresistible form is cumbersomely listed as *F. meleagris* var. *unicolor* subvar. *alba*.

   The snake's head fritillary is the most commonly and easily grown of all the chequered fritillaries, doing well in a variety of positions in the garden, provided the ground is reasonably moist, nowhere looking better than when naturalized in grass.

Geranium pratense 'Mrs Kendall Clark'
Perennial H 75cm/30in, S 60cm/2ft Z5

Sun or partial shade Well-drained soil

Veining adds depth to the flowers of many cranesbills and in some creates patterns of ethereal beauty. The widely distributed meadow cranesbill (*Geranium pratense*) is a superb plant, with lobed leaves and, in the first half of summer, numerous saucer-shaped flowers, usually blue or violet with some degree of veining. 'Mrs Kendall Clark' is a form with large sky-blue flowers, which are covered by embossed white veining. Another tall cranesbill suitable for a wide range of positions in sun or partial shade is the early-flowering *G. clarkei* 'Kashmir White', with large white flowers warmed by grey-pink tracery. It can be cut back hard after its first flush and will come again in late summer.

   One of the easiest and most pleasing of the compact sun-loving cranesbills is *G. sanguineum* var. *striatum*. The deeply divided leaves, which colour red in autumn, make a low mound that is brightened over many weeks in summer by slightly crumpled pale pink flowers intensified by crimson veining.

Another compact cranesbill is *G. renardii*, which does best in full sun on rather poor soils. It is a first-class foliage plant, making a mound about 20cm/8in high of velvety grey-green leaves, and its flowers in early summer are opalescent palest mauve saucers veined dark violet.

Iris 'Caesar'

Perennial H 90cm/3ft, S 75cm/30in Z4

Sun or partial shade Moist but well-drained soil

Although they are tough and long-lived perennials that thrive in a wide range of conditions, the Siberian irises, which are beardless and rhizomatous, do best where the soil is reliably moist. In early summer the erect clumps of grassy leaves are topped by sprays of up to five flowers. The neat flowers of *Iris sibirica* are violet-blue with dark veining on the falls. The flowers are followed by neat brown seed pods. Veining is conspicuous in many fine hybrids. The falls of 'Caesar' have dark reticulation superimposed on gold, white and purplish blue.

The reverse applies in 'Vi Luihn', where the lines are pale, the ground colour midnight blue. 'Sparkling Rosé' has mauve-pink flowers, the falls, yellow at the base, overlaid with dark purple veins. In a different colour range 'Dreaming Yellow' has ivory petals with a network of olive-green lines.

All are suitable for cutting.

Platycodon grandiflorus
Balloon flower

Perennial H 60cm/2ft, S 35cm/14in Z4

Full sun Moist but well-drained soil

The balloon flower is a long-lived perennial but dislikes being disturbed. Because its blue-green leaves are late developing it is as well to mark the position of plants. The common name refers to the curious inflated buds. These appear in late summer and open to five-petalled flowers that are usually a shade of purplish blue intensified by a tracery of darker raised veins. 'Mariesii' is a compact cultivar and 'Albus' has white flowers with blue veins.

All are suitable for cutting.

▲ *Platycodon grandiflorus*

OTHER GOOD PLANTS

Camellia x *williamsii* 'Donation'
Evergreen shrub bearing semi-double pink flowers with darker veining in late winter and spring. The flowers are rather coarse but produced with great freedom over several weeks. The spent flowers drop before turning brown.

Clematis 'Venosa Violacea'
Small-flowered (Viticella) hybrid clematis that flowers in late summer and autumn. The flowers, up to 10cm/4in across, are white with red-purple veining, densest at the margins, and the anthers are black-purple. Magnificent in the garden and for cutting.

Codonopsis clematidea
Slender perennial climber carrying in late summer pale blue nodding bells that are finely veined. The orange and maroon markings inside are surprisingly vivid. The flowers have a foxy smell.

Digitalis ferruginea: see p.155.

Enkianthus campanulatus: see p.36.

Lavatera trimestris 'Silver Cup': see p.83.

Colchicum agrippinum
In autumn the corms produce several flowers, almost white but heavily overlaid with a chequered pattern in reddish purple. They stand about 10cm/4in high. The leaves follow in spring.

Oenothera speciosa 'Siskiyou'
Compact perennial capable of spreading but effective in a container. White saucer-shaped flowers with yellow bases and pink veining borne in summer.

Petunia Daddy Series
Grandiflora petunias grown as annuals with large funnel-shaped and heavily veined flowers in a wide range of colours. 'Sugar Daddy' has purple flowers with darker veining. Long flowering season in summer and early autumn.

Salpiglossis Casino Series
Medium-sized annual bearing richly coloured funnel-shaped flowers in summer. Many flowers are multicoloured and they are textured as well as heavily veined. Good for cutting.

SPECKLED, SPOTTED & BLOTCHED

Dark blotches at the base of petals give many flowers their visual weight, but there are many other interesting patterns of markings, some in an overall scheme, some at the tips of petals and some, as in the case of snowdrops, slight but significant in their variation if you are trying to distinguish one plant from another.

▲ *Papaver commutatum* 'Ladybird'

▲ *Tigridia pavonia*

▲ *Viola sororia* 'Freckles'

Papaver commutatum 'Ladybird'
Annual H 45cm/18in, S 15cm/6in
Full sun Well-drained soil

A close relative of the field poppy (*Papaver rhoeas*), *P. commutatum* is a bristly annual found wild in rough and arid conditions or as a weed of cultivated land in Crete, Turkey and further east. The selected form 'Ladybird' has brilliant red bowl-shaped flowers, the centre of each petal marked with a large black blotch. Sow in patches or drifts to suggest this poppy's wild character. In favourable conditions it will self-seed.

Many other poppies have flowers with blotched petals. These include the opium poppy (*P. somniferum*), a tall annual with grey-green leaves that grows to 1.2m/4ft or more. It is the source of valuable as well as harmful drugs but is also an attractive ornamental, the single forms with pink, mauve, red or white flowers usually having dark marks at the base of the petals. The large seed pods are handsome and worth saving for dried decorations.

Dark blotches at the base of the petals also add to the magnificence of many Oriental poppies (*P. orientale*), which grow to about 75cm/30in and rank among the most splendid border perennials of late spring and early summer. 'Black and White', large, single and clean

white, has crimson-black blotches just above the base of the slightly ruffled petals and the marks are strong enough to show through on the outer side. Other handsomely blotched Oriental poppies, all with single flowers, include the orange-red 'Allegro', and the delectable pink 'Watermelon'.

See also *P.o.* 'Curlilocks', p.72 and *P.o.* 'Patty's Plum', p.71.

Tigridia pavonia
Peacock flower, tiger flower
Corm H 60cm/2ft, S 10cm/4in Z8
Full sun Well-drained, preferably light, soil

The various forms of this member of the *Iris* family are some of the showiest harlequins of the summer garden. The three large outer segments are orange-scarlet, yellow, pink or white, usually contrasting vividly with the centre and with the short inner segments, which are commonly heavily speckled. The flowers are too fugitive for cutting but although individual blooms last only a day, each stem, rising from a fan of narrow leaves, bears six to eight flowers in succession.

Treat as large-flowered gladioli hybrids, planting in mid-spring and lifting in autumn.

Tricyrtis formosana

Perennial H 75cm/30in, S 40cm/16in Z7

Partial shade Humus-rich, moist but well-drained soil

The toad lilies are not showy but they make up for this by the intriguing form and colour of their flowers, which in most cases are borne in autumn. The foliage of this species, a native of Taiwan, is glossy dark green and the slender wiry stems, which branch in a somewhat zigzag way, carry sprays of upward-facing waxy flowers that are pale purple with darker purple freckling.

Plant in woodland conditions or in a shady border near a path so that the flowers can be appreciated. A few stems make a fascinating arrangement indoors.

Viola sororia 'Freckles'

Perennial H 10cm/4in, S 20cm/8in Z4

Sun or partial shade Moist but well-drained soil

The sister violet, also known as the woolly blue violet, is a native of North America. Its short-spurred flowers, borne in late spring and early summer, can be unmarked deep violet-blue but commonly this colour appears as heavy speckling on a white ground. *Viola sororia* 'Freckles' is a particularly good clone in which the dark speckling is fairly evenly distributed.

Several perennial viola hybrids have flowers that are prettily and unconventionally marked. Those of *V.* 'Columbine', rounded and near white, are veined and dappled with violet-purple. The finely scented flowers of 'Rebecca' are creamy white and liberally covered with dark mauve-blue splashes.

▲ *Tricyrtis formosana*

OTHER GOOD PLANTS

Cistus × cyprius: see p.86.

Clematis cirrhosa 'Freckles'
Evergreen winter-flowering climber producing nodding cream flowers that are heavily speckled red-pink on the inside. Silky seedheads follow. It needs no pruning.

Erythronium californicum 'White Beauty': see p.105.

Helleborus × hybridus: see p.25.

Iris 'Green Spot'
Dwarf Bearded iris in an unusual combination of ivory and green, with prominent green blotches on the falls. Perennial, flowering in late spring.

Lilium 'Fire King': see p.101.

Lilium henryi: see p.88.

Mimulus 'Viva'
Compact annual monkey flower that likes moist partially shaded conditions. The yellow two-lipped flowers, with red-brown spots in the throat, have five lobes that are heavily blotched and spotted chocolate.

Nemophila maculata Five-spot
Low annual bearing in summer upturned saucer-shaped flowers, white with mauve-blue veining, with conspicuous blue to purple spots at the tips of each petal.

Nomocharis pardanthina
Elegant bulb flowering in early summer but only suitable for cool woodland conditions on acid soils. Wiry stems up to 90cm/3ft high carry nodding white or pale pink flowers spotted red-purple. The markings are densest on the inner segments, which are fringed.

Paeonia lactiflora 'Festiva Maxima'
Herbaceous perennial with scented double flowers, the white petals loosely arranged and marked with random crimson flecks. Splendid for cutting.

Pelargonium 'Fair Ellen'
Compact scented-leaved pelargonium with dark green sticky foliage marked purple. The flowers, borne in summer, have notched mauve-pink petals arranged with exquisite neatness and all dabbed with a darker shade, especially the upper petals, which also have finely feathered markings.

Rhododendron 'Sappho'
Large evergreen rhododendron carrying in early summer numerous trusses of white flowers that are handsomely blotched red-purple with a black overlay.

Saxifraga 'Southside Seedling'
Rock garden saxifrage producing in late spring or early summer sprays up to 30cm/1ft high of white flowers liberally covered with heavy red spots.

BANDS, STRIPES & RAYS

The particoloured harlequins, with various colours arranged in bands, stripes and rays, are often gaudy but appealing flowers. These are attention-seekers, looking good when they can show off against a quiet background; less assertive mixed colours do not come off well in competition with them.

▲ *Arisaema candidissimum*

▲ *Ismelia carinata* 'Court Jesters'

▲ *Clematis* 'The Vagabond'

Arisaema candidissimum

Tuber H 40cm/16in, S 20cm/8in Z6

Partial shade Humus-rich, moist but well-drained

neutral to acid soil

The intriguing flower-like spathes of this species emerge before the leaves but not until late spring so it is as well to mark where the tubers are planted. The spathes, which are narrowly funnel-shaped with an expanded hood that narrows to a tail, are white, usually suffused or striped pink and pale green, and the pencil-like spadix inside, on which the true flowers are clustered, is green. The sweet scent comes as a surprise. The leaves that develop after the spathes are three-lobed.

More eye-catching is *Arisaema sikokianum*, which has brown-purple spathes that develop with the leaves in spring and a hood that has pale stripes. The inside of the spathe and the club-shaped spadix are white.

Clematis 'The Vagabond'

Deciduous woody climber H 1.8m/6ft, S 75cm/30in Z4

Sun or partial shade with the base in shade Humus rich, moist but well-drained soil; in containers soil-based compost (John Innes No. 3)

A number of the most popular large-flowered clematis hybrids are more or less bicoloured, with a bar running down the centre of each segment in a colour that is deeper or brighter than that of the segment. 'The Vagabond' is a relatively recent and darkly handsome introduction flowering over a long summer season. It is compact and suitable for growing in containers. The flowers, often more than 10cm/4in across, are deep purple with a red-purple bar and creamy yellow anthers.

'Pastel Princess' is another relatively recent and slightly taller introduction suitable for a container. The flowers, usually more than 15cm/6in across and borne in early summer and again in autumn, are pearly blue with light mauve-pink bar and tips to the segments. The central filaments are white, tipped with maroon anthers.

Other well-established cultivars flowering early and again late are 'Bees' Jubilee', mauve-pink with a deeper bar, 'Doctor Ruppel' (see illustration on 118–9), deep pink with carmine-pink bar, and 'Souvenir du Capitaine Thuilleaux', with ruffled soft pink segments, deeper pink bar and dark red anthers. All are under 3m/10ft in height and suitable for containers. 'Bees' Jubilee' and 'Doctor Ruppel' are particularly good for cutting.

Crocus sieberi subsp. *sublimis* 'Tricolor'

Corm H 8cm/3in, S 2.5cm/1in Z7

Full sun Gritty, well-drained soil

All forms of *Crocus sieberi*, a species to brighten rock gardens and raised beds in late winter or early spring, have globular flowers with rich yellow throats, usually contrasting with mauve or purple. In this arresting tricoloured form a white band separates gold and purple.

▲ *Crocus sieberi* subsp. *sublimis* 'Tricolor'

Many crocuses, including cultivars of *C. chrysanthus* (see p.132), have beautifully feathered markings. In some cases the markings are more emphatic stripes. The spring-flowering and rather variable *C. biflorus*, which is usually pale mauve-blue or white, sometimes has strong purple or purplish brown stripes on the outer segments. Slightly earlier in flower is *C. imperati* subsp. *imperati* 'De Jager'. The inner violet-purple segments are cradled by larger buff segments with strong violet lines and feathering.

Ismelia carinata 'Court Jesters'

Annual H 60cm/2ft, S 30cm/1ft

Full sun Well-drained soil

The painted daisy is a stiffly upright annual of Mediterranean origin with somewhat fleshy leaves that suggest the plant's adaptation to dry conditions. In gardens it is generally represented by a small range of long-flowering cultivars with flowerheads that are boldly zoned. The most eye-catching of these is *Ismelia carinata* 'Court Jesters' with flowerheads in white and shades of pink, yellow, orange and red, most with bands of brownish red and yellow around the dark yellow-spotted central disc.

Less dramatic but easier to mix with other flowers are 'German Flag', with scarlet flowers lit by a radiant yellow band around the red-brown disc, and 'Polar Star', also with a red-brown disc surrounded by a yellow band contrasting with white.

Autumn-sown plants usually need cloche protection in winter.

OTHER GOOD PLANTS

Camellia japonica 'Lavinia Maggi': see p.60.

Convolvulus tricolor 'Royal Ensign' Dwarf morning glory grown as an annual to flower in early summer. The funnel-shaped flowers are rich blue and have a ragged white band surrounding the yellow centre.

Cuphea ignea Cigar plant
Evergreen shrubby plant usually grown as an annual for the numerous narrowly tubular flowers it carries over several months, deep red, white at the rim and with tiny deep purple petals.

Lilium auratum Golden-rayed lily
Tall lily producing numerous bowl-shaped scented flowers in late summer or early autumn. Each of the white segments, which are turned back at the tips, has a conspicuous yellow band down the centre and is sometimes speckled crimson.

Primula auricula 'Butterwick'
This alpine auricula is an evergreen perennial suitable for an alpine house or for growing outdoors. In spring it produces heads of flowers that have a strong near-black zone and an outer orange-brown zone around a gold centre.

Rosa gallica 'Versicolor'
Rosa mundi
In a single summer flush this compact rose bears a heavy crop of pale pink semi-double flowers that are striped deep pink.

Sparaxis tricolor Harlequin flower
Corm producing fans of blade-like leaves and in late spring or early summer sprays of funnel-shaped flowers, red, purple, orange or white, with a yellow centre outlined in black. Good for cutting.

FLAMED, FEATHERED & LACED

In the competitive showing of flowers, which has a long history, special terms have been used for distinctive markings. Some of those formerly applied to different classes of tulip are now obsolete. Other terms, including 'flamed', 'feathered' and 'laced', remain current, although they are used rather loosely.

Crocus chrysanthus 'Zwanenburg Bronze'

Corm H 8cm/3in, S 5cm/2in Z4

Full sun Well-drained gritty soil; in containers soil-based compost (John Innes No. 1 with added humus and grit)

The dwarf crocuses listed under this species rank with the Reticulata irises as some of the most endearing bulbous plants of late winter or early spring. The small honey-scented flowers are goblet-shaped, opening wide when warmed by winter sun. The subtle and bright colours are in some cases enhanced by exquisite feathering and the bright yellow or scarlet of the tri-lobed style. *C. chrysanthus* 'Zwanenburg Bronze', one of the most richly coloured, has orange-yellow flowers heavily feathered purplish mahogany on the outside. 'Gipsy Girl' is also strongly coloured. The flowers are rich yellow with chocolate feathering and markings on the outside. 'Advance' is a paler yellow with dark mauve streaks and feathering on the outer petals.

All the cultivars of *C. chrysanthus* are suitable for planting in rock gardens and raised beds or even along the edge of paths. They are also good plants for containers and pans of them make beautiful displays in an alpine house.

Dianthus 'Dad's Favourite'

Perennial. H 30cm/1ft, S 25cm/10in Z4

Full sun Well-drained neutral to alkaline soil

This old-fashioned pink, flowering in early summer, is a well-scented example that probably dates from the eighteenth century. The semi-double flowers have a white ground with red-purple centres and slightly paler margins to the petals. A nineteenth-century example, *Dianthus* 'Murray's Laced Pink', is a white semi-double with maroon-purple centre and lacing.

The best of the modern pinks are also plants of great charm, producing clove-scented flowers in two or three flushes between early summer and early autumn. In the first rank is the double strong-stemmed 'Becky Robinson', with pink flowers laced ruby-red. Others include the short-stemmed 'Gran's Favourite', a white double with mauve-purple centre and lacing in dark and lighter shades, and 'London Delight', a pink semi-double with purple eye and mauve-pink lacing.

◀ CLOCKWISE FROM TOP
Crocus chrysanthus 'Zwanenburg Bronze'
Tulipa 'Prinses Irene'
Dianthus 'Dad's Favourite'

Primula Gold-laced Group

Perennial/biennial H and S 25cm/10in Z4

Sun or partial shade Moist but well-drained soil; in containers soil-based

compost (John Innes No. 2 with added leaf mould)

The polyanthus-type primula hybrids, which are often grown as biennials, bear flowers bunched at the top of a stalk. In the late eighteenth and early nineteenth centuries the gold-laced forms of polyanthus were enormously popular plants. The many cultivars that were grown then have been lost but new cultivars give a good idea of their quaint appeal. The plants are evergreen or semi-evergreen and in spring bear small trusses of yellow-centred flowers that are deep mahogany, even almost black, but with each petal outlined in gold.

Primrose-type primula hybrids usually bear flowers among the leaves but in some cases also produce flowers bunched on a stalk. Primula 'Miss India is a double primrose that has deep purple flowers with a frosty edge. It usually comes into flower in early spring but in a favourable season the tight buds may open precociously in winter. It is a compact plant about 20cm/4in high that makes a good contrast to white and pale yellow primroses. Divide this perennial after flowering.

Tulipa 'Prinses Irene'

Bulb H 35cm/14in, S 10cm/4in Z4

Full sun Well-drained soil

The 'broken' tulips with sharply defined feathered and flamed patterns that were the sensation in seventeenth-century Holland, and elsewhere, too, have failed to survive but a number of attractively marked modern tulips are commonly described as feathered and flamed. One such is 'Prinses Irene', which produces single cup-shaped flowers in mid-spring, and combines a base colour of orange with flame-like red-purple marks.

Other attractively marked tulips include 'Sorbet', with single off-white flowers with deep pink feathers and flames, and, late in the tulip season, 'Marilyn', hybrid of the Lily-flowered Group, with light red flames warming the ivory petals.

In some of the Viridiflora tulips, which are all to some extent marked green, this colour appears as a flame on the base colour. In 'Esperanto' the green flame runs up reddish pink petals. The green frame makes a strong accent on the pink petals of 'Groenland' (see illustration on p.2). See also *T.* 'Spring Green', p.109. The unusual markings on all these tulips adds to their value as cut flowers.

OTHER GOOD PLANTS

Begonia 'Can-can'
Upright tuberous begonia bearing in summer large double yellow flowers with petals that have a frilled red margin.

Eucomis bicolor
Bulbous perennial with a base of strap-shaped leaves from which rises in late summer a tufted stout stem about 45cm/18in crowded with pale green flowers, each segment outlined in purple.

Nemophila menziesii var. *discoidalis* (syn. 'Penny Black')
Low annual producing in summer saucers of darkest purple relieved by a scalloped white edge that gives these brooding flowers a sparkling finish.

Pelargonium 'Copthorne'
A scented-leaved pelargonium, this shrubby perennial has strongly aromatic foliage and bears clusters of relatively large flowers that are mauve-pink with heavy purple feathering on the upper petals. An excellent pelargonium for planting out in large containers.

Petunia Picotee Series
Large-flowered petunias grown as annuals that flower over a long summer and autumn season. The somewhat floppy funnel-shaped flowers are in shades of red, pink, blue and purple with wavy white margins.

Rosa Sue Lawley ('Macspash')
Floribunda rose bearing throughout summer and early autumn sprays of double red flowers with white centres and margins to lightly ruffled petals.

Rosa 'Roger Lambelin'
Hybrid Perpetual rose making a shrub 1m/3ft high. The fragrant flowers have scalloped dark red petals with white margins. Repeats after its first flush.

Viola 'Etain'
Compact perennial viola producing in late spring and summer numerous well-scented yellow flowers with a violet edge.

Primula Gold-laced Group ▶

SCENTS

The most successful gardens go far beyond a pleasing arrangement of colour and shapes: they exploit all the qualities of plants, including the unseen but enormously important dimension of scent. Elusive and formless though it is, the fragrance of flowers has a haunting power that captivates and holds not merely by direct appeal but also through associations. These may be so powerful that we make connections quickly, but just as often a delicate insinuating perfume leaves us in a state of suspended and blissful puzzlement.

Far from all the flowers worth growing are scented, but many are; and there are some that have little visual appeal but deserve a place in the garden simply on account of their delicious fragrance.

Hyacinthus orientalis 'Ostara' and other modern cultivars of the common hyacinth are the result of several centuries of breeding, starting in Turkey before the species was first introduced to western Europe in the sixteenth century. The spikes have become stiff and dense but the waxy flowers have retained their powerful scent.

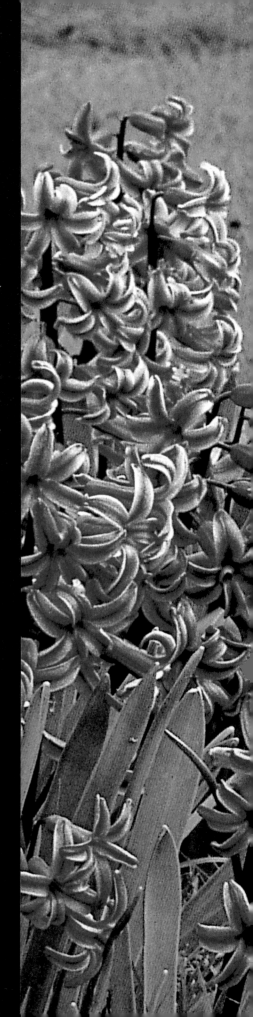

SCENTS

Scent is one of the most powerful allures plants have to attract pollinators, in order to achieve their business of ensuring the production of viable seed to perpetuate the species. Through scent the message goes out, carried on the air, sometimes to a specific accomplice, more often to a broad band of pollinators, that the flower has nectar or other delights to offer. It is incidental that humans are drawn to and ravished by many of the varied and often complex scents in the floral repertoire – though not, as it happens, by all: some scents we may not even detect; some are sickly, rank or pungent, while others, fetid as the stench of rotting flesh, are utterly repellent to us.

CATEGORIZING SCENTS

Our appreciation of floral scents is highly personal. Some people have a very sharp and focused sense of smell; others can hardly detect a whiff even in plants that are generally regarded as highly scented. Even those with a good sense of smell may be impervious to certain fragrances. A great disappointment to many is their mysterious inability to detect the delicious perfume of freesias.

Sometimes one suspects that the keenness of one's own sense of smell is not consistent. But it is not easy to be confident about this because flora scents are themselves variable in intensity and sweetness. Atmospheric conditions play an important part in the way that we experience them. We often find that our most vivid memories of scents are of evenings that were warm, humid and still. The age of the flower counts, as the freshness of scents deteriorates quickly as flowers age, especially once they have been pollinated. Even when flowers are fresh, time of day or night is significant. Many flowers seem to release their scent in pulsating waves, some most powerfully in warm sunny conditions; others, like the common jasmine (*J. officinale*), are at their strongest in the evening.

Another difficulty when categorizing pleasing scents is the inadequacy of words to describe them. There are no accepted scales of sweetness or intensity, let alone widely used terms to convey complex layers and shadings of scent. Sometimes in an attempt to be specific writers use one flower as a standard for others – lily-of-the-valley (*Convallaria majalis*) is a favourite – or invent a scent palette, using perversely the fragrance of the almost mythic myrrh, for example, as a reference.

It has seemed to me most helpful to distinguish, although not too rigidly, between three broad categories of floral scents. In the first category are plants with refined sweet scents that are generally best appreciated when the flower is brought close to the nose. The second category includes flowers with heavier sweet scents or sweet fragrances that carry well. The last group includes flowers with less conventional but pleasant scents.

SCENTED FLOWERS IN AUTUMN AND WINTER

Hyacinths, honeysuckles, lilacs, lilies and roses are among the numerous fragrant flowers that add immeasurably to the quality of gardens in spring and summer. One might expect the period between autumn and early spring to be almost scentless; but for those prepared to venture out, the garden proves to be surprisingly rich in well-scented plants, even in this period. The most valuable scented plants in the garden are those with a scent that travels well.

Elaeagnus × *ebbingei*, a useful evergreen shrub for informal hedges, bears inconspicuous flowers in late autumn that would go unnoticed were it not for their lovely scent, which carries far. One of the most refined fragrances of the winter garden is that of *Mahonia japonica*, an evergreen with bold divided foliage and sprays of small yellow flowers gathered in whorls at the ends of stems and a striking plant at any season. It is best in partial shade near but not right on a path, where its jagged leaves might seem threatening. One of the shrubby honeysuckles, *Lonicera* × *purpusii* 'Winter Beauty', on the other hand, is enjoyable for the sweetness of its pale flowers in winter but not of great interest in summer, so drape a small-flowered clematis over it or plant it with a foreground that will make a beautiful distraction in spring or summer. My favourite of the winter shrubs that scent the air around them are the various species of sweet box (*Sarcococca*). These short-growing evergreens do well in shade under trees. Their curious petalless flowers exhale a scent enticing enough to draw you to its mysterious source.

WELL-PLACED PLANTS

Thoughtful placing goes a long way to giving you the best value from scented plants. Ornamental plants that have rank scents, such as the martagon lily (*Lilium martagon*), are best planted in prominent positions but away from paths and seating areas. Plants with scents that can only be fully appreciated if they are sniffed should be planted so that you do not have to clamber through beds and borders to get to them. This is particularly the case if you open your garden to the public. Once one admirer has beaten his or her way to an exquisitely scented plant, other tramplers will follow.

Unless your winters are very mild, from autumn to early spring you are not likely to spend long sitting in the open garden, so there is not much to be gained by planting plants that flower in that season near seats. At this time of the year scented flowers make more impact if planted near doors and close to the main paths in the garden, particularly where a gate or step slows down pedestrian traffic. For the relaxed enjoyment of your garden from late spring to early autumn plan a succession of plants that will create a scented zone around areas where you regularly pause and rest. The scented bower, using climbers such as honeysuckle (*Lonicera*) or common jasmine as well as plants near ground level, has a timeless appeal. Fine scents rarely clash. By planting climbers that shed their scent from above as well as shrubs and lower-growing annuals, bulbs and perennials you can create a delectable web of scents.

Among the most valuable of all the fragrant plants are those that produce masses of flowerx and scent the air over a wide area. Classic plants for this purpose are various species and cultivars of lime (*Tilia*). I do not describe any of these here as they make large specimens. They can be kept to a moderate scale by pleaching, but this removes most of the flowering wood. Other plants that achieve this overarching fragrant effect are the Rambler roses. Many of these are very vigorous and need a substantial support, either living or constructed, to carry their pliant stems. Most flower in a single summer flush, producing quantities of flowers in large clusters, and the best of them are deliciously scented.

SCENTED PLANTS AT A HIGHER LEVEL

The fragrance of low-growing plants with delicate scents often goes unnoticed or can be appreciated only if you get down on all fours. One way to make it easier to appreciate their scent is to grow the plants in raised beds – a suitable way of growing the compact alpine pinks (*Dianthus*). Another solution is to grow plants in containers. A lovely group of plants that come off well when used in this way are scented violas such as 'Maggie Mott'. Their beautifully shaped and marked flowers, produced for months if conscientiously deadheaded, deserve to be appreciated at close quarters.

Even if you have only windowboxes or a balcony you can have a delightfully fragrant garden by putting together mixtures that include a few well-scented plants. For those warm days in spring when the windows can be thrown open, put in well-scented bulbs such as hyacinths (*Hyacinthus orientalis*) and compact wallflowers (*Erysimum cheiri*). Good fragrant choices for these small-scale gardens in summer include cherry pie (*Heliotropium*) and more lightly scented flowers such as various verbenas and, of course, violas. Where there is more room on a balcony or patio the range of container-grown plants can be greatly extended to take in fragrant lilies, of which the regal lily (*Lilium regale*) remains my first choice, various kinds of stock (*Matthiola*) and lavenders (*Lavandula*).

Container-grown plants are also useful for adding scent to patios and terraces that you use for sitting and dining outdoors. And forced bulbs, for example of daffodils or hyacinths, are an attractive fragrant alternative to cut flowers for conservatories and rooms.

SCENTED FLOWERS FOR CUTTING

Many favourite flowers for cutting owe a great deal of their popularity to their scent: daffodils (*Narcissus*) in early and mid-spring, peonies (*Paeonia*) in late spring and early summer, lilies (*Lilium*) and sweet peas (*Lathyrus odoratus*) in high summer, and late roses and phloxes in the second half of summer and early autumn. Many smaller scented flowers are only easily appreciated when they are picked. Lily-of-the-valley is one of these. Others for even smaller posies include common snowdrops (*Galanthus nivalis*) and *Iris reticulata*. The enclosed and warm atmosphere of a room can bring out a scent. The flowers of wintersweet (*Chimonanthus praecox*) have a fragrance that can be fugitive outdoors on a cold day but opens out generously if you dare cut stems and bring them indoors. A light and sweet or slightly spicy fragrance is almost always welcome. Heavier scents, for example of hyacinths and some lilies, can be overpowering and are best avoided in sick rooms, where other flowers would be welcomed enthusiastically.

SUBTLE & EXQUISITE BOUQUETS

Some of the finest scents in the garden belong to plants that have been much hybridized, such as numerous roses. Loss of scent is, however, common in plants that have been highly bred. Many of the most delicate and refined perfumes belong to unshowy flowers that owe their prestige as garden plants largely to their fragrance.

◀ *Aquilegia viridiflora*

Aquilegia viridiflora
Perennial H 30cm/1ft, S 20cm/8in Z3

Sun or partial shade Moist but well-drained soil

Its sombre colouring and exquisite scent make this short-lived species one of the most unusual columbines. In late spring and early summer the divided leaves are topped by nodding and spurred chocolate-purple flowers clasped by dark green sepals. A light touch is provided by yellow anthers.

There are other columbines noted for their scent, including *Aquilegia fragrans*. Its dark stems carry nodding pale flowers that often show a blue tint.

Convallaria majalis
Lily-of-the-valley
Perennial H 25cm/10in, S 30cm/1ft Z3

Full or partial shade Humus-rich, moist but well-drained soil

Lily-of-the-valley is not always pleased with the moist lightly shaded conditions that seem ideal but, where it settles down, its thong-like rhizomes spread freely. It is well suited to a wild garden, where it does not have to keep to precise boundaries. Paired oval leaves shelter the sprays of waxy white drooping bells in late spring, the foliage giving good cover until late summer. A large bed in flower will perfume the air and provide material for cutting. However, although lily-of-the-valley is a favourite token of spring because of its ravishing scent, the flowers do not last long in water.

There is an early-flowering mauve-pink form, *Convallaria majalis* var. *rosea*, and a large-flowered white, 'Fortin's Giant'.

Iris unguicularis
Perennial H 25cm/10in, S 40cm/16in Z8

Full sun Well-drained soil

Although native to parts of North Africa and the eastern Mediterranean, this beardless iris is surprisingly hardy but to flower freely it needs sharp

▲ *Iris unguicularis*

▲ *Lathyrus odoratus* 'Matucana'

▲ *Convallaria majalis*

drainage and a summer baking. The ideal position for it is at the base of a warm wall. The finely scented flowers seem fragile but survive rough weather in winter and early spring. The main colour range extends from pale mauve to deep purple, the falls marked by a yellow band and dark veining. *Iris unguicularis* 'Mary Barnard' is rich violet-purple, 'Walter Butt', with larger flowers, silvery pale. The creamy white 'Alba' is said to be more tender.

I. unguicularis is a lovely flower indoors at a time of the year when there is little to choose from, but it is not long-lasting.

Remove the narrow evergreen leaves when they turn brown so that the rhizomes are well exposed to sun.

Lathyrus odoratus 'Matucana'

Climbing annual H 1.8m/6ft, S 60cm/2ft

Full sun Humus-rich, well-manured, moist but well-drained soil

Although many of the modern sweet peas (see *Lathyrus odoratus* 'Angela Ann', p.75) have a refreshing scent, their fragrance is outclassed by that of several old cultivars close to the original species, a tendril climber introduced to northern Europe from Sicily in the late seventeenth century. One of these is 'Matucana', with sprays of relatively small flowers that are deep blue with purple wings. Their scent is strong but refined. Similar to 'Matucana' is 'Cupani', named after the monk who sent the original seed from Sicily.

Another powerfully scented old cultivar is 'Painted Lady', which has pink and white flowers. It dates from the eighteenth century and represents an important stage in the development of a broader colour range.

Alternatives to these are various mixtures of 'old-fashioned' or 'antique' sweet peas that are often specially featured in seed catalogues. They are smaller in flower than the modern cultivars and in a limited colour range but are strongly fragrant.

All these sweet peas require supports and need to be cut or deadheaded regularly to give a prolonged season.

Nicotiana sylvestris

Biennial/annual H 1.5m/5ft, S 60cm/2ft

Sun or partial shade Moist but well-drained soil

Of the ornamental tobacco plants with fragrant flowers, this species, which is usually grown as an annual, is the most impressive. It is a sticky plant with large basal leaves and a stout stem, usually branching, with heads of sweetly fragrant white flowers in summer. These have narrow long tubes and they shoot out at different angles as though competing fiercely for pollinators.

The short-lived perennial *Nicotiana alata*, of similar size, is also treated as an annual. It is a parent of the shorter-growing hybrids, most of which are unscented or only lightly fragrant. The species has white tubular flowers that release their elegant perfume in the evening.

▲ *Osmanthus delavayi*

▲ *Nicotiana sylvestris*

Osmanthus delavayi

Evergreen shrub H 4m/13ft, S 4.5m/15ft Z7

Sun or partial shade Well-drained soil

In mid- to late spring the arching stems of *Osmanthus delavayi*, set with small glossy leaves, carry numerous tubular white flowers in small clusters. Their exquisite sweet scent carries well. Cutting small sprays for indoors will not damage plants.

Of other shrubs in the genus with scented flowers the most suitable for general garden use is *O. × burkwoodii*. It is a somewhat smaller and coarser shrub than *O. delavayi* and its flowers are less finely scented.

Both these plants are suitable for hedging or broad topiary shapes, although heavy pruning will result in fewer flowers. Trim as soon as flowering has finished.

The holly-like *O. heterophyllus* and its various forms are fine foliage shrubs that also have well-scented flowers, which are borne in autumn.

Rosa 'Madame Isaac Pereire'

Deciduous shrub (Bourbon rose) H and S 1.8m/6ft Z5

Full sun Moist but well-drained soil

In all categories of roses there are scented examples and the best have a refined fragrance matched by few other flowers. The Bourbon 'Madame Isaac Pereire' is a fine example, which can be grown as a shrub or trained as a short climber. The quartered double flowers are large, sometimes malformed in the first flush, but at their best magnificent and deep purplish pink. A fresh bloom exhales a splendid scent.

Many other roses match it and the following are only intended as starting points. Another Bourbon, usually grown as a climber to a height of about 5m/16ft is 'Blairi Number Two'. The double pink flowers, paler at the edges, are produced only in early summer but they are richly scented and well formed. A well-scented Portland, 'Madame Knorr' (still sometimes listed as 'Comte de Chambord'), makes a bush about 1.2m/4ft high and produces throughout summer very double flowers, with muddled petals that are bright pink, paling at the petal edges.

The combination of beautiful form, colour and scent makes many modern roses in the old style superb garden plants that perform over a long season and provide sumptuous cut flowers. Gertrude Jekyll ('Ausbord'), growing to about 1.5m/5ft, and producing deep pink double flowers, is a good example.

In many instances the classic bush roses of the twentieth century, the Hybrid Teas, usually with double flowers of conical form, are strongly scented. 'Deep Secret', with rich crimson flowers, and the salmon-pink Paul Shirville ('Harqueterwife') are two examples. In general the cluster-flowered bush roses, the Floribundas, are at best lightly scented but there are plenty of exceptions. Among these are the pale pink 'English Miss' and the bright yellow 'Korresia'.

See also *R.* 'Bobbie James', p.145, *R.* Constance Spry, p.29, *R.* 'Great Maiden's Blush', p.106, and *R.* 'Königin von Dänemark', p.63.

Viola 'Maggie Mott'

Perennial H 15cm/6in, S 30cm/1ft Z4

Sun or partial shade Humus-rich, moist but well-drained soil; in containers

soil-less or soil-based compost (John Innes No. 2 with added leaf mould)

'Maggie Mott' has remained one of the most popular of the numerous violas raised in the late nineteenth and early twentieth centuries. The highly scented flowers are about 5cm/2in across and in colour are a delicate silvery mauve.

Other fragrant violas include 'Cleo', its cream flowers tinted with a blue wash, 'Etain' (see p.133) the violet-blue 'Inverurie Beauty' and 'Rebecca' (see p.129).

All these violas are lovely at the front of beds and borders, going well with roses, and are excellent in containers. They flower over a long period in summer provided they are kept moist and regularly deadheaded or picked to make small posies.

A plant with a much longer history in cultivation is *V. odorata*, sometimes called the English or sweet violet. Many of the cultivars and hybrids grown commercially in the nineteenth and early twentieth centuries for cut flowers have been lost. The species, with spurred and sweetly fragrant blue or white flowers, remains an attractive plant that will self-seed freely in a wild garden.

OTHER GOOD PLANTS

Camellia sasanqua 'Narumigata'
Medium-sized to tall evergreen shrub bearing in autumn and winter subtly fragrant single flowers that are white with a red-pink margin. Other fine cultivars are also scented.

Clematis flammula
Semi-evergreen or evergreen tangled climber carrying in summer and autumn showers of small starry white flowers that are deliciously scented. Excellent on a fence or low screen.

Coronilla valentina subsp. glauca: see p.50.

Crinum × powellii: see p.35.

Gladiolus murielae: see p.49.

Iris 'Florentina'
Bearded iris, the dried roots of which are the source of orris root. In late spring stems about 60cm/2ft high carry finely scented pale grey flowers. Good for the front of a border.

Jasminum officinale
Common jasmine
Vigorous woody and usually deciduous climber carrying for weeks in summer and early autumn sprays of small white flowers renowned for their refined sweet fragrance.

Lonicera × purpusii 'Winter Beauty'
Deciduous shrub bearing small white two-lipped flowers in winter and early spring. Their scent is clear and sweet.

Mahonia japonica
Medium-sized to large evergreen shrub with large jagged leaves composed of numerous spiny leaflets. The small yellow flowers, carried in arching sprays, have a fresh sweet fragrance.

Narcissus 'Trevithian'
A hybrid of the famously scented wild jonquil (*N. jonquilla*). 'Trevithian' is a relatively tall and elegant example for early spring with small-cupped rounded flowers, usually two to a stem, that are soft yellow and sweetly fragrant.

Prunus 'Jô-nioi'
Flowering cherry making a spreading deciduous tree laden in mid-spring with clusters of fragrant white flowers that open from pink buds.

Reseda odorata Mignonette
Upright branching annual bearing in summer tiny buff or greenish white flowers with conspicuous orange stamens. Sweetly scented.

Smilacina racemosa: see p.161.

Rosa 'Madame Isaac Pereire' ▲
Viola 'Maggie Mott' ▲

HEADY & PENETRATING PERFUMES

There is no adequate vocabulary with which to describe the powerful and evocative perfumes of these plants. They are often strong enough to provide a delicious but invisible dimension to the garden, in favourable conditions their scent spreading over a wide area. A few cut stems are enough to perfume a room.

▲ *Daphne cneorum* 'Eximia'

▲ *Hyacinthus orientalis* 'L'Innocence'

Daphne cneorum 'Eximia'
Garland flower

Evergreen shrub H 20cm/8in, S 1.5m/5ft Z4

Full sun Moist but well-drained soil

The daphnes are a group of mainly small shrubs, many of which have deliciously scented flowers, usually with a crystalline iridescence. The sprawling evergreen mat of *D. cneorum* 'Eximia' looks well in a rock garden or at the front of a border and in early summer its numerous small deep pink flowers fill the air with a lightly spiced perfume.

Another evergreen species is *D. odora*, which grows to about 1.5m/5ft. In winter and early spring the bush is studded with heads of small white flowers that open from red-purple buds and broadcast a sweet and penetrating scent. The variegated form 'Aureomarginata' is said to be hardier than the type.

The larger evergreen *D. bholua* 'Jacqueline Postill' is another well-scented shrub of winter and early spring. The flowers are white

inside with a red-purple exterior and their concentrated fragrance spreads far.

The mezereon (*D. mezereum*), the best known of the deciduous species and growing to about 1.2m/4ft, also flowers in late winter and early spring, when its rather stiff stems are wreathed in small red-purple flowers, which are followed by red fruit. 'Bowles' Variety' has white flowers and the fruits are yellow.

Hyacinthus orientalis
Hyacinth

Bulb H 25cm/10in, S 10cm/4in Z4

Full sun Well-drained soil; in containers soil-less or soil-based compost (John Innes No. 2); forced bulbs can be grown in bulb fibre

Modern hyacinths are the result of a long history of breeding. Individual cultivars are of very uniform growth and produce columns of densely packed, waxy fragrant flowers that are reliable, although somewhat stiff,

▲ *Lilium regale*

▲ *Lonicera periclymenum*

performers in containers and in the open garden. Prepared bulbs that have been heat-treated can be forced to provide flowers indoors in the depths of winter.

An advantage of *H. orientalis* 'L'Innocence' is that its pure white bells are less congested than those of many cultivars. It flowers in early to mid-spring, as does 'Ostara' (see illustration on pp.134–5), violet-blue with darker bands down the centre of the petals, and the pale pink 'Anna Marie', one of the best for forcing. The soft yellow 'City of Haarlem' flowers in mid- to late spring.

Forced hyacinths in containers and cut flowers will fill a room with their scent.

Lilium regale
Regal lily

Bulb H 1.2m/4ft, S 20cm/8in Z5

Sun or partial shade Humus-rich, well-drained soil; in containers soil-based

compost (John Innes No. 2 with added leaf mould and grit)

Since its introduction from China in the early twentieth century, the regal lily has established itself as one of the finest garden plants. It is tolerant of a wide range of soils and easy to grow but as it is stem-rooting it needs to be planted deep. In early to mid-summer its wiry stems carry up to ten magnificently poised trumpets that are white and yellow-throated with purplish red staining on the outside. The flowers have a strong sweet scent that carries well in the garden and in a room. The

trumpets of *Lilium regale* 'Album' are dazzling white with a radiant gold throat, those of the equally beautiful cultivar 'Royal Gold' yellow with a purplish brown exterior.

The capricious Madonna lily (*L. candidum*) has a much longer history in cultivation for it was grown even in classical times. It seems to do best in full sun and well-drained slightly alkaline soil planted just below the surface. Stiff stems up to 1.5m/5ft high carry as many fifteen outward-facing trumpets that open pure white, but are lit by golden anthers, from green-tinted buds. They are strongly and sweetly scented. A rosette of overwintering leaves develops in early autumn. As is indicated by countless depictions of it in paintings of the Virgin, this is a cut flower of great distinction.

For other scented lilies see *L.* Golden Splendor Group, p.34.

Lonicera periclymenum
Common honeysuckle, woodbine

Deciduous woody climber H 6m/20ft, S 3m/10ft Z4

Partial shade Moist but well-drained soil

This woody twining climber has a wide natural distribution and can be found growing wild in woodland and hedgerows, bearing sprays of sweetly scented tubular two-lipped flowers that change from cream to yellow as they age. It is usually represented in gardens by one or other of its cultivars. In late spring early Dutch honeysuckle (*Lonicera periclymenum* 'Belgica') bears reddish purple flowers that fade to white

▲ *Philadelphus 'Beauclerk'*

▲ *Sarcococca hookeriana var. digyna 'Purple Stem'*

and yellow. Late Dutch honeysuckle ('Serotina'), with similar red-streaked flowers, is in bloom from mid-summer to mid-autumn. 'Graham Thomas', which flowers throughout summer, is white in bud, yellow when open.

Two other scented honeysuckles, both deciduous and summer-flowering, are *L. × americana*, with yellow flowers tinged purple, and the Italian honeysuckle (*L. caprifolium*), with white to yellow flowers that are flushed pink.

All these plants need supports and benefit from periodic cutting out of old growths after flowering.

Sprays of scented honeysuckles help to sweeten bunches of summer flowers.

Philadelphus 'Beauclerk'

Deciduous shrub H and S 2.5m/8ft Z5

Sun or partial shade Well-drained soil

Although somewhat dull out of flower, the numerous hybrid mock oranges are worth growing as they are easy-going plants that fill the garden with their sweet heavy scent in early to mid-summer. Small sprays are enough to scent a room.

Purists demand white flowers without a trace of colour but if you can tolerate a hint of pink at the centre of the cupped flowers *Philadelphus* 'Beauclerk' is a first-rate shrub with arching stems loaded with single richly scented flowers. 'Belle Etoile' is of similar size, slightly earlier coming into flower, and the white cups have a pale purple centre. Even more strongly marked are the flowers of 'Sybille', a shrub about 1.2m/4ft high but spreading.

For pure white flowers choose the tall 'Virginal' with double flowers, or the compact 'Mont Blanc', which grows to about 1m/3ft and has less powerfully scented single flowers. 'Manteau d'Ermine', even shorter but about 1.5m/5ft across, has double ivory-tinted flowers.

Sarcococca hookeriana var. digyna

Evergreen shrub H1.2m./4ft, S 90cm/3ft Z6

Partial or deep shade Moist but well-drained soil

The Christmas or sweet boxes are small self-effacing shrubs, useful for filling awkward shady corners and springing a surprise in late winter when their little tassel-like flowers exhale a scent that carries well. The leaves of *Sarcococca hookeriana* var. *digyna* are narrow and the strongly scented white flowers are followed by black berries. The young wood of the form 'Purple Stem' is flushed purple.

Other sweet boxes showing a marked family resemblance are *S.h.* var. *humilis*, with pinkish flowers, and the very fragrant *S. confusa*.

Syringa vulgaris
Common lilac

Deciduous shrub H and S 6m/20ft Z5

Full sun Well-drained soil

The popularity of the numerous cultivars of the common lilac lies partly in the way their richly fragrant flowers, forming dense cones at the ends of stems, come in time to bridge the gap between spring and summer. In 'lilac time' one can be delighted by the delicious scent and forget that the

▲ *Syringa vulgaris* 'Andenken an Ludwig Späth'

▲ *Viburnum carlesii*

shrubs are rather coarse, with a tendency to sucker. The stems are splendid for cutting.

The flowers of the doubles tend to be longer-lasting than the singles. Those of *Syringa vulgaris* 'Charles Joly' are dark red-purple. Other doubles are 'Katherine Havemeyer', purple fading to mauve-pink, and 'Madame Lemoine', which has white flowers opening from ivory buds.

A good example of the singles dating from the late nineteenth century is 'Andenken an Ludwig Späth', which has wine-red flowers.

There are other lilacs with fragrant flowers, although their scent is less powerful than that of the common lilac cultivars. Far more refined than these is *S. pubescens* subsp. *microphylla* 'Superba'. It is small-leaved, grows to about 3m/10ft, sometimes more, and bears sprays of sweet-scented pink flowers in late spring and then intermittently until autumn.

All these lilacs do well in a wide range of well-drained soils.

Viburnum carlesii

Deciduous shrub H and S 1.8m/6ft

Full sun or partial shade Moist but well-drained soil

Several viburnums that have attractive domed heads of small flowers in mid- to late spring are powerfully and sweetly scented. Prime among these for scent is *V. carlesii*, which is pink in bud and then glistening white. The buds of 'Aurora', more strongly coloured and set against coppery foliage, open pink, and 'Diana' has even deeper colouring.

Another slightly smaller deciduous shrub is *V. × juddii*, with near spherical heads of pink buds opening to scented white flowers.

Very close in style to *V. carlesii* is the hybrid *V. × burkwoodii* 'Anne Russell'. It is more or less evergreen and the flowers are richly scented.

OTHER GOOD PLANTS

Buddleja davidii 'Black Knight': see p.110.

Cardiocrinum giganteum: see p.32.

Elaeagnus × ebbingei
Evergreen shrub useful as an informal hedging plant with somewhat silvery scaly foliage. The flowers, borne in autumn, would escape notice if they did not release a sweet scent that hangs on the air.

Erysimum cheiri Wallflower
Evergreen biennial or short-lived perennial producing in spring short spikes of velvety four-petalled flowers with a strong sweet scent. Colours include yellow, orange (e.g. 'Fire King'), cream and deep red (e.g. 'Blood Red').

Euphorbia mellifera Honey spurge
Dense and rounded evergreen shrub of medium size with blue-green leaves. In late spring numerous domed heads of red-brown flowers exhale a honeyed scent.

Heliotropium arborescens
Cherry pie, heliotrope
Short-lived shrub commonly grown as an annual. Dark crinkled leaves are topped in summer and early autumn by heads of small heavily scented flowers, mainly in shades of mauve and violet.

Malcomia maritima **Virginian stock**
Self-seeding annual bearing in summer small four-petalled flowers, white or in shades of pink, purple and mauve. Self-seeds freely.

Rhododendron luteum
Deciduous azalea making an open bush about 4m/12ft high carrying in late spring and early summer numerous trusses of strongly scented yellow flowers.

Rosa 'Bobbie James'
Scented Rambler roses produce masses of flowers over several weeks in summer, perfuming the air over a large area. This vigorous one trails many large clusters of semi-double creamy white flowers.

CURIOUS & PIQUANT SCENTS

The complex scents of flowers are full of surprises. They often stray from the purely floral, their bouquet including aromatic and fruity hints. Some of the best-loved scents of the flower garden are markedly spicy, the clove scent of many old-fashioned and modern pinks being a classic example.

▲ *Chimonanthus praecox* 'Grandiflorus'

▲ *Dianthus* 'Mrs Sinkins'

▲ *Lavandula angustifolia* 'Hidcote'

Chimonanthus praecox
Wintersweet

Deciduous shrub H 4m/13ft, S 3m/10ft Z7

Full sun Well-drained soil

Only one species in this genus is widely grown and when it is out of flower it is difficult to see why it is a favourite in temperate gardens. In late winter *Chimonanthus praecox* is another matter. Then small nodding flowers cluster stemless on the twiggy stems. The maroon inner segments are surrounded by pale, almost translucent outer segments. Their sweet scent has an underlying spiciness, invigorating even in a cold garden and expanding generously in a warm room. The flowers of 'Grandiflorus' are yellow stained red and those of var. *luteus* a purer yellow.

When a specimen is trained against a warm wall the wood ripens more fully and it produces flowers more freely. Prune immediately after flowering.

Dianthus 'Mrs Sinkins'

Perennial H 35cm/14in, S 30cm/1ft Z4

Full sun Well-drained, preferably neutral to alkaline soil

The scent of the old-fashioned pinks, usually with a strong suggestion of cloves, remains a standard by which the fragrance of all modern pinks is

judged. Their season is relatively short and they require frequent propagation but they remain a rewarding field for those interested in collecting plants of intrinsic value and historical interest. While *Dianthus* 'Mrs Sinkins' has shortcomings – the fringed double white flowers are untidy and the petals tend to spill out of the split calyces – its scent is simply ravishing.

Other powerfully scented old-fashioned pinks include 'Inchmery', a pink double, and 'Sam Barlow', a double white with deep purple centres.

These are all fine plants for raised beds or for edging paths. And they are very desirable as cut flowers. Planting with longer-flowering modern pinks such as 'Becky Robinson', with dark lacing on light pink, helps to extend the season.

See also *D.* 'Dad's Favourite', p.132, and *D.* 'Musgrave's Pink', p.122.

Lavandula angustifolia 'Hidcote'

Evergreen shrub H 60cm/2ft, S 75cm/30in Z6

Full sun Well-drained soil; in containers soil-based compost (John Innes No. 2)

The lavenders, shrubs of dry and sunny habitats, have grey-green aromatic foliage and short spikes of spicily scented two-lipped flowers, which are rich in nectar and are assiduously worked by bees. They make attractive low informal hedges and look thoroughly at home in mixed borders planted among other sun-loving Mediterranean plants. They normally flower in mid- to late summer. The dried flowers, best gathered

▲ *Viburnum × bodnantense* 'Dawn'

before they are fully open, are traditionally used to scent linen and in pot-pourri.

Old names have had to give way in recent revisions. Several good plants are now listed under *L. angustifolia*, the compact 'Hidcote', with grey foliage and deep purple flowers being one of the best. 'Twickel Purple', which also has deep-coloured flowers, is a match for it.

Other good lavenders are listed under *L. × intermedia*, including the broad-leaved Dutch Group, which can grow to 1.2m/4ft and has mauve-blue flowers over grey foliage.

Trim lavenders in early spring, cutting back close to the old growth.

Viburnum × bodnantense 'Dawn'

Deciduous shrub H 3m/10ft, S 1.8m/6ft Z7

Sun and partial shade Moist but well-drained soil

The very long flowering season of this shrub, extending from late autumn to spring, puts it in a special category. The outline of the bare branches can be rather graceless but the densely packed clusters of pale pink flowers brighten winter days and small sprays are attractive as cut flowers. The rich scent is sweet but with an underlying and bracing hint of bitter almond. Other clones are equally good: 'Charles Lamont', also pink, and 'Deben', pink in bud and white in flower.

If it is necessary to cut back growth, trim these deciduous viburnums lightly immediately after they have flowered.

OTHER GOOD PLANTS

Azara microphylla
Evergreen shrub or small tree with glossy neat leaves. Small petal-less yellow flowers borne in early spring are vanilla-scented.

Cosmos atrosanguineus: see p.111.

Cytisus battandieri Pineapple broom
Large deciduous shrub with hairy and silvery leaves. In summer bushes are covered with numerous dense spikes of yellow flowers that smell of pineapple.

Erysimum × marshallii (syn. *E. × allionii*) Siberian wallflower
Evergreen biennial growing to about 60cm/2ft and producing in spring heads of four-petalled bright orange flowers that give off a spicy scent.

Hamamelis × intermedia: see p.76.

Lupinus arboreus Tree lupin
Usually evergreen shrub or subshrub with fingered grey-green leaves and in late spring to summer spikes of yellow, white or blue pea flowers that have a sweetly earthy scent.

Matthiola incana Ten Week Mixed
Perennial grown as an annual for its spikes of usually double flowers, which are white and cream or, more commonly, red, pink and purple. There is more than a hint of clove in their sweet scent.

Papaver nudicaule: see p.86.

Tulipa 'Generaal de Wet'
The complex scent of 'Generaal de Wet' and several other hybrid tulips comes as a surprise. From the Single Early Group, it bears cups in shades of orange during the first half of spring.

Wisteria sinensis: see p.163.

NATURAL ARRANGEMENTS

Garden plants that bear solitary flowers are the exception rather than the rule. The much more common arrangement of a few or many flowers to a stem is highly characteristic of particular plants. The nature of the inflorescence, as the arrangement is called, is not merely a key to identification but goes a long way to determining how plants can be used effectively in the garden. Some arrangements are in open and airy bunches or sprays. These can make a telling contrast against dramatic ornamentals that carry numerous flowers densely packed on upright stems, or in flat to rounded heads. Arrangements in broad columns, tall spikes, branched candelabra and large domes are impressive if dominating components of the garden. More graceful are plumed stems and drooping chains of flowers.

The rusty foxglove (*Digitalis ferruginea*) makes an attractive rosette of basal leaves from which rises a spire of curiously veined yellow flowers. It is a generous self-seeder, best treated as a biennial, and it is suitable for naturalizing in woodland and lightly shaded areas of a wild garden.

NATURAL ARRANGEMENTS

Botanists are generally agreed that the arrangement of more than one flower to a stem has evolved from the solitary flower. They distinguish between various kinds of inflorescence: in particular, on the one hand, those in which each growing point ends in a flower and, on the other, those where the flowers arise at junctions on the axis of the stem and there is usually no flower at the tip. The various technical terms used to describe particular kinds of inflorescence are undoubtedly essential for botanists but for the ordinary gardener can confuse rather than clarify the ornamental qualities that make plants worth growing. This, at least, is my defence for using impressionist language to describe various arrangements.

GATHERED FLOWERS
A number of plants have flowers grouped in neat bunches or sprays that in some way convey the impression that they have been gathered by a superior being with an eye for flower arranging. Sometimes it comes as a surprise that some plants produce more than one flower to a stem. Tulips are a case in point. Most of the countless hybrids raised since the introduction into Europe of plants from Turkey in the sixteenth century produce one flower per bulb but several species and a few hybrids, including *T. praestans* 'Fusilier', are multiflowered. Although many of the daffodil (*Narcissus*) hybrids bear only one flower to a stem, there are also many well-known bunch-flowered kinds belonging to various groups, including the Tazettas and the Jonquillas, the latter famous for their scent.

It is not surprising that plants with attractively gathered flowers such as cornflowers (*Centaurea cyanus*) and sweet peas (*Lathyrus odoratus*) are popular for picking, although the florist trade rejects the many roses that present their flowers in large clusters in favour of single blooms to a stem. As an illustration of cluster-flowered roses I describe 'Cornelia' and a group of Hybrid Musk roses that show a clear family resemblance. The cluster-flowered characteristic in roses might just as easily have been illustrated using the deep orange Fellowship 'Harwelcome' or one of the many other Floribunda roses (a group sometimes referred to as Cluster-flowered bush roses). There are many good things one could say about the Floribundas, in particular the way they produce flowers almost continuously from early summer into autumn, making them the roses best suited to use in bedding. I have opted, however, for the older, more graceful and more delicately coloured group which, despite excellent qualities, tends to be neglected.

STRONG UPRIGHTS
The large number of plants that have flowers arranged on a more or less vertical axis are enormously varied in scale. The biennials and perennials include giants that can exceed 2.5m/8ft in height, the dwarfs can be under 15cm/6in high and there are plants at every height in between. There is considerable variation, too, in the size of individual flowers and the degree to which they stand free from their upright support. In the true spike the flowers are stalkless and not only hug the stem but usually are also tightly stacked, as in the curious autumn-flowering *Liriope muscari*. Many more have stalked flowers but the racemes, as these are called, of many delphiniums and other plants conform to a generalized idea of a spike. Other uprights include plants such as the Candelabra primulas that have their flowers arranged in series of tiered whorls. Long-stalked flowers or a series of upturned branchlets thickly set with small flowers produce looser arrangements. In the case of *Perovskia* 'Blue Spire', the grey stems show as verticals through a violet-blue haze. More vigorously branching uprights, as are found in some of the verbascums, suggest massive candelabra.

Tall uprights, for example those of well-grown delphiniums, assembled at the back of a border, help to create an impression of policed order. But tall plants that need staking, as the delphiniums certainly do, are just the sort of border components that you may feel have to be sacrificed because they are too labour intensive. Fortunately you do not need tall verticals to give a border a spruce appearance. In fact it is far more effective to distribute blocks of verticals of different heights at irregular intervals, placing some short-growing ones right at the front and also bringing forward some of middle height to avoid a strictly graduated assembly of plants. Useful contrasts to stiff verticals are fluffy plumes and tapered tails.

AIRY AND TRAILING ARRANGEMENTS

Trees, large shrubs and climbers are key components for establishing the scale of a garden's three dimensions. Several shrubs and trees make vertical accents with flowers hanging in ropes or tassels. By and large these are graceful arrangements that are flexible enough to sway loosely in a breeze. Some, such as the male catkins of *Garrya elliptica* and hazels (*Corylus*), depend on wind to disperse their pollen, which they produce in prodigious quantity.

At their peak, the Japanese ornamental cherries (*Prunus*), with their frothing cloud-like blossom, are a perfect expression of the buoyancy of spring. A criticism frequently levelled against them is that their flowering season is too short. Most of those that are worth growing are wide-spreading, which in itself makes them unsuitable for small gardens, where more compact plants, such as spiraeas, can at least produce an effect of massed blossom. But the splendour of the flowering cherries' short-lived season is of such an order that they are serious contenders for space in any large garden.

Twining and weaving climbers are versatile plants, many of them suitable for training on a variety of supports. The most vigorous, including some Rambler roses and several clematis, do well trained into large sturdy trees or over built structures, such as pergolas. In a new garden, climbers on built supports offer a quick way of getting foliage and flowers at a height sufficient to lift the garden into the third dimension. It is important to choose plants of appropriate vigour, for pruning to control size greatly reduces the ornamental value of many. Wisterias, however, respond well to a regime of summer and winter pruning that maintains these spirited climbers at moderate size and encourages the development of flowering spurs. Young plants pruned systematically are likely to start flowering at a much earlier stage than those that are left unchecked.

DENSELY PACKED HEADS

Ornamentals with flowers arranged in dense spherical, domed and plate-like arrangements can be very assertive and they are not all easy to use well in the garden. The problem is highlighted by rhododendrons, a particularly important group of shrubs and trees for those who garden on acid soils, although many of the numerous species and hybrids can be container-grown satisfactorily in a lime-free compost whatever the underlying chemistry of the soil. A great many of these rhododendrons bear their flowers in dense more or less domed trusses. In late spring and early summer, when most of these trees and shrubs flower, a single plant covered with numerous upright trusses can make a spectacular effect. The smaller cultivars are well established as shrubs for town gardens but there are also many woodland gardens with extensive plantings of rhododendrons under a light protective tree canopy provided by deciduous trees. Although these gardens can be ravishing in late spring and early summer, they often demonstrate the difficulty of creating close communities of plants that present flowers, in many cases vividly coloured, condensed in large blobs. The overall effect is too congested and too contrived for a setting where the ideal is an impression of complete naturalness.

The mophead hydrangeas – the numerous cultivars with large domed heads of sterile flowers, sometimes called florets – are another group of plants that undermine the credibility of woodland as 'natural', but they are magnificent shrubs for a more formal setting and for growing in containers. Hydrangeas with lacecap heads, the fertile central flowers surrounded by larger infertile flowers, are more versatile and create a lighter effect among other plants.

Much easier to use are several border plants. Although some gardeners grumble at the strong yellow of *Achillea filipendulina* 'Gold Plate', it remains a mainstay of summer borders, its large plate-like flowerheads creating a series of near horizontal lines to contrast with powerful verticals. The Galaxy Hybrids and *A.* 'Taygetea' are more subtle in their colouring but make less emphatic horizontals at a lower level. The ornamental onions (*Allium*), which have gained enormously in popularity over recent years, include many species and hybrids with conspicuous spherical heads. The most valuable as garden plants are the handsome drumstick kinds that are well adapted to hot dry conditions. The large bulbs tide them over from one growing season to the next and in late spring or early summer the rounded heads, packed with starry flowers, make a grand show before the main border plants are in flower. My preference is for the taller alliums, which, when planted in groups or allowed to self-seed, usually provide an airy display of spheres at a nicely staggered range of heights. The foliage of most of these begins to wither before the flowers open and you need plants that come into leaf or flower later to mask the awkward phase or gap.

BUNCHES, POSIES & SPRAYS

The large numbers of plants that produce several flowers to a stem usually make more impact in the garden than those bearing a single flower to a stem. Sometimes the flowers are thickly bunched and sometimes they form neat posies or elegant sprays that enhance the effect of individual flowers.

Crocosmia 'Lucifer'

Corm H 1.2m/4ft, S 30cm/1ft Z5

Sun or partial shade Humus-rich, moist but well-drained soil

In the second half of summer stiff branching stems thrust up through the grassy or sword-like leaves of the montbretias, carrying sprays of funnel-shaped flowers in warm, even intense colours. Those of the vigorous *Crocosmia* 'Lucifer' are furnace red and stand upright from the arching stems.

Many other good montbretias are listed under *C. × crocosmiiflora*, most growing 60–90cm/2–3ft high. 'Emily McKenzie' has drooping rich orange flowers magnificently blotched maroon. Both 'Gerbe d'Or' and 'Solfatare' have bronzed foliage, the flowers of the former pale orange and of the latter soft apricot-yellow. These and others are splendid border plants and the stems are excellent for cutting.

Dierama pulcherrimum
Angel's fishing rod, wandflower

Corm H 1.5m/5ft, S 60cm/2ft Z7

Full sun Moist but well-drained soil

The wandflower is an exceptionally graceful perennial with a pliant beauty that is full of movement. In summer the slender stems, which rise from a base of grassy evergreen leaves, carry sprays of silvery buds that open at the arching tips to nodding bells. The normal colour is red-pink but *Dierama pulcherrimum* var. *album* is white and 'Blackbird' is violet-purple.

There are several other species as well as hybrids, including the Slieve Donard hybrids. They are all remarkable plants but none can quite match the pliant beauty of the wandflower.

Rosa 'Cornelia'

Deciduous shrub (Hybrid Musk rose) H and S 1.8m/6ft Z5

Full sun Moist but well-drained soil

Many roses make their impact by the freedom with which they carry generous sprays of single or double flowers. The Hybrid Musks are a relatively small group of vigorous lax-stemmed roses that carry large sprays of flowers with prodigious freedom in mid-summer and then, after a lull, produce a good second flush, especially if bushes are deadheaded after the first flowering. 'Cornelia' is one of the most reliable of these, with copper-tinted pink flowers. Another is 'Felicia', with light pink flowers that have

▲ *Crocosmia* 'Lucifer'
◀ *Tulipa praestans* 'Fusilier'

salmon-pink shading at the centre. Both these are well scented. 'Buff Beauty' is less fragrant but the unusual colour of the flowers – apricot-yellow fading to creamy buff – makes a valuable plant for sophisticated colour schemes. All these roses provide good material for cutting.

Where there is room these roses can be allowed to make large arching specimens but they will also make a broad hedge or can be trained on wires running between strainers as highly decorative screens.

Tulipa praestans 'Fusilier'

Bulb H 30cm/1ft, S 8cm/3in Z5

Full sun Well-drained soil

An easy plant that makes a bright show in a rock garden, *Tulipa praestans* 'Fusilier' may carry a bunched cluster of up to five in early to mid-spring. The flowers are vivid scarlet with no basal blotch. The flowers of *T.p.* 'Unicum' are similar but this cultivar has grey-green leaves with broad creamy yellow margins, a combination that makes it a striking bulb for low bedding. The hybrid *T.* 'Toronto' is in the same general style as these, although slightly shorter. Its flowers, borne in mid-spring, are coral-pink, redder inside and with a yellow base.

OTHER GOOD PLANTS

Anchusa azurea
'Loddon Royalist': see p.44.

Aster 'Little Carlow'
Like many of the asters this autumn-flowering perennial carries its heads of violet-blue daisies in bunch-like panicles.

Bergenia 'Silberlicht': see p.36.

Chrysanthemum 'Mary Stoker'
The Rubellum chrysanthemum hybrids are bushy perennials covered in late summer and autumn with twiggy sprays of daisies, long-lasting in the garden and when cut. The single flowerheads of 'Mary Stoker' are amber with bronze shading around a centre that changes from green to yellow.

Centaurea cyanus Blue-bottle, cornflower
Easy-to-grow annual with tall cultivars up to 90cm/3ft high, suitable as fillers in beds and borders and as a supply of bunch-like sprays of pretty tufted flowers for the house in summer. The flowerheads, as the common name conveys, have deep blue florets around a violet-blue centre.

Lathyrus odoratus 'Angela Ann': see p.75.

Lilium 'Côte d'Azur'
In early and mid-summer this compact lily presents pink upward-facing flowers gathered in a bunch. Suitable for containers.

Myosotis sylvatica 'Royal Blue': see p.125.

Narcissus 'Minnow'
In early to mid-spring this Tazetta hybrid has up to four refined little flowers to a stem, with yellow cups at the centre of rounded segments, each of which is finished with a fine tip.

Primula vulgaris: see p.72.

Ribes sanguineum
Flowering currant
Deciduous shrub of medium size bearing numerous sprays of tubular red-pink flowers in spring.

Saxifraga fortunei: see p.23.

Dierama pulcherrimum ▲
Rosa 'Cornelia' ▶

COLUMNS, SPIKES & SPIRES

The dramatic uprights of the garden include several weighty perennials and biennials. The tallest are impressive plants that make substantial and firm verticals for the back of borders. Just as useful are short-growing plants that provide ranks of foot soldiers for the middle ground or even frontal positions.

Delphinium 'Fanfare'

Perennial H 1.8m/6ft, S 90cm/3ft Z2

Full sun Moist but well-drained soil

The tall perennial delphinium hybrids are sometimes referred to as the Elatum Group. Their impressive spikes, which attain their full height in the first half of summer, are thickly set with single, semi-double or double flowers, usually with a conspicuous eye or 'bee' of inner petals, often dark but in some instances white or pale. The flowers open from the bottom up, above the base of fingered leaves. If the first spikes are cut back as soon as they have finished, lesser spikes will follow and extend the season. In addition to those growing to a height of 1.8m/6ft or more, there are medium-sized and short hybrids but even those in this last group can grow to a height of 1.5m/5ft. The colours include white, cream, yellow, pink, red and purple as well as an exceptional range, from mauve-grey to navy and deep midnight blue. 'Fanfare' is one of the tallest and its semi-double flowers are silver-mauve with white eyes. More intense is 'Faust', the semi-double flowers vivid blue with purple shading and an indigo eye.

'Blue Nile' is a white-eyed and vivid mid-blue hybrid in the medium range. Short-growing hybrids include 'Sandpiper', a pure white semi-double with black eyes; 'Sungleam', a semi-double in shades of cream and yellow; and 'Mighty Atom', a semi-double with mauve-purple flowers and a brownish eye.

Even short-growing hybrids may need staking. To maintain vigorous stock it is best to propagate all these frequently from basal cuttings taken in early spring.

All are handsome as cut flowers, and the tall hybrids invaluable for large displays.

See also *D.* Black Knight Group, p.122.

Digitalis ferruginea
Rusty foxglove

Biennial or perennial H 1.2m/4ft, S 45cm/18in Z4

Sun or partial shade Well-drained soil

The rusty foxglove (see illustration on pp.148–9), like many of its close relatives, forms a basal rosette of leaves from which it sends up a tall stem crowded with somewhat tubular- to trumpet-shaped flowers. These are amber yellow with curious red-brown veining. This species is not a reliable perennial but self-seeds freely and makes an impressive mid-summer stand in a glade-like setting.

The extended lower lip of some foxgloves gives the tubular to bell-shaped flowers the appearance of backless slippers. *Digitalis* × *mertonensis*, which comes true from seed, has strongly veined almost lance-shaped leaves and in late spring or early summer produces spikes up to 90cm/3ft high laden with deep buff-pink slippers hanging by their toes.

◄ CLOCKWISE FROM TOP LEFT
Delphinium 'Fanfare'
Digitalis × *mertonensis*
Euphorbia characias subsp. *wulfenii*

The slippers or thimbles of the common foxglove (*D. purpurea*), borne in towering one-sided spires 1.8m/6ft or more tall, are narrower. This freely self-seeding biennial or short-lived perennial is a lovely plant among shrubs and in a wild garden. The flowers, predominantly purple or pink with darker spotting inside, are most refined in the white f. *albiflora*, which can be maintained by roguing out young plants with purplish leaf stems, for these will have purple-pink flowers. In the Excelsior Group the flowers are arranged evenly around the stems and are almost horizontal, so that they show the attractive pattern of spots inside.

Euphorbia characias subsp. wulfenii

Evergreen shrub H and S 1.2m/4ft Z7

Full sun Well-drained soil

This shrubby spurge forms an impressive clump of upright stems densely set with narrow blue-grey leaves and culminating in massive columnar heads of lime-green flowers. These heads remain in good condition for many weeks because of the long-lasting cup-shaped bracts surrounding the small floral parts.

The cultivar *Euphorbia characias* subsp. *wulfenii* 'John Tomlinson' has more spherical heads that are brighter yellow-green. *E. characias* itself has purplish brown glands that give the bracts a dark eye.

When the bracts begin to fade, cut the old stems to the base, avoiding contact with the milky sap, which can irritate skin.

Kniphofia 'Bees' Sunset'

Perennial H 90cm/3ft, S 60cm/2ft Z5

Full sun Humus-rich, moist but well-drained soil

Like the species, the *Kniphofia* hybrids produce densely packed tubular flowers on erect stems. There is a wide choice in a warm colour range among those of medium size that flower in early and mid-summer. The sturdy bronze stems of 'Bees' Sunset' carry spikes of amber-yellow flowers to a height of 90cm/3ft throughout summer. It is often beaten into flower by the slender 'Goldelse' and 'Sunningdale Yellow', both yellow, the latter with hints of ochre. 'Apricot Souffle' is another slender hybrid in an unusual shade of soft apricot.

Follow these with 'Prince Igor', one of the giants among the kniphofia hybrids. It lives up to the common name red hot poker with glowing spikes of scarlet flowers that make searing hot verticals up to 1.8m/6ft high in the autumn garden.

See also *K. caulescens*, p.117.

Ligularia 'The Rocket'

Perennial H 1.8m/6ft, S 90cm/3ft Z4

Full sun Reliably moist soil

In late summer the teetering black stems of *Ligularia* 'The Rocket' seem to be on the point of launching themselves from a base of large fingered leaves as small orange-yellow flowerheads open with a splutter from the bottom of long spires.

▲ *Kniphofia* 'Bees' Sunset'

A plant of similar dimensions and character but with flowerheads more yellow than orange is *L. przewalskii*. Another tall moisture-lover like these but a coarser plant is *L.* 'Gregynog Gold'. It has large heart-shaped leaves and pyramidal spikes of brown-centred orange flowerheads that are up to 10cm/4in across.

Perovskia 'Blue Spire'

Subshrub H 1.2m/4ft, S 75cm/30in Z6

Full sun Well-drained soil

Russian sage (*Perovskia atriplicifolia*) and the hybrids that are very close to it, such as *P.* 'Blue Spire', are useful plants for sunny and rather dry gardens. The plants are stiff-stemmed with aromatic grey-green leaves topped by airy spires of small tubular flowers. 'Blue Spire', which has deeply cut leaves, is very free-flowering and from late summer to autumn a group of several plants makes a pleasing haze of violet-blue and grey just below eye level. It is an excellent plant for filling out the border in late summer and its diffused colour makes it a good companion for more vivid sun-lovers.

To maintain vigorous plants, cut back to just above ground level in early spring.

Salvia × superba

Perennial H 90cm/3ft, S 45cm/18in Z5

Full sun Well-drained soil

There is a strong family resemblance between several hardy salvias that in the second half of summer produce closely ranked erect spikes densely packed with small flowers of intense colour. The leaves of *S. × superba* are rich green and the spikes violet-blue, their colour intensified by red-purple bracts that persist even when the flowers have fallen.

The cultivar 'Rubin' grows to about 60cm/2ft and produces spikes of purplish pink flowers with narrow bracts.

Very similar to *S. × superba* in character and in the violet-purple colouring of their flowers are two cultivars of *S. nemorosa*: 'Lubecca' grows to 45cm/18in, 'Ostfriesland' to 75cm/30in. Slightly taller than the latter is the mauve-purple 'Amethyst'.

S. × sylvestris also has short-growing cultivars suitable for frontal positions. The flowers of 'Mainacht' are deep indigo blue, those of 'Blauhügel' a rich but purer blue.

Wide spacing of tightly packed whorls of purple flowers on the spikes of *S. verticillata* 'Purple Rain' gives this plant a different character but it is an excellent mid-border perennial.

▲ *Ligularia* 'The Rocket' ▲ *Perovskia* 'Blue Spire' TOP RIGHT *Salvia × superba* 'Rubin' ⬍ ▲ *Veronica austriaca* subsp. *teucrium* 'Crater Lake Blue'

Quite different from all these is the less hardy and moisture-loving *S. uliginosa*, which for weeks in late summer and autumn carries loose spikes of clear blue flowers on stems up to 1.5m/5ft high.

Veronica austriaca subsp. *teucrium* 'Crater Lake Blue'

Perennial H 30cm/1ft, S 40cm/16in Z6

Full sun Well-drained soil

Many speedwells are low-growing plants that in summer send up spikes of small densely packed flowers, notably in shades of blue. *Veronica austriaca* subsp. *teucrium* 'Crater Lake Blue' makes a patch of gentian brilliance at the front of a border. A similar clone, 'Kapitän', is slightly taller and darker.

The pale blue slender spires of *V. gentianoides*, rising to 45cm/18in over glossy leaves, make a good contrast.

Another mat-forming species is *V. spicata*, with several red- and pink-flowered cultivars suitable for growing in rock gardens as well as at the front of borders. The short spikes of 'Heidekind' are 30cm/1ft high and vivid red-pink. A more subtle plant is the silver speedwell (*V.s.* subsp. *incana*), which has a base of grey-green foliage topped by spikes of purple-blue flowers.

OTHER GOOD PLANTS

Alcea rosea 'Nigra': see p.110.

Aconitum × cammarum 'Bicolor': see p.48.

Baptisia australis: see p.50.

Cardiocrinum giganteum: see p.32.

Cleome hassleriana Spider flower
Tall annual with a base of fingered leaves and columns of four-petalled scented flowers with prominent stamens. The colour range includes white, pink and purple.

Gladiolus 'The Bride': see p.97.

Hyacinthus orientalis: see p.142.

Lavandula angustifolia 'Hidcote', see p.146.

Liriope muscari
Short tuberous perennial with evergreen strap-shaped leaves, among which rise autumn spikes of densely set violet flowers.

Lupinus Band of Nobles Series: see p.114.

Lysimachia clethroides
Perennial with creeping rhizomes throwing up tall erect stems terminating in sinuous, tapered spikes of small white flowers.

Penstemon 'Stapleford Gem': see p.106.

Persicaria bistorta 'Superba'
Ground-covering perennial for moist soils producing in summer bottlebrush tall spikes of deep pink flowers on stems 90cm/3ft high.

WHORLS, TIERS & CANDELABRA

Some attractive ornamentals have flowers grouped in a circular arrangement, either at the tips of stems or in a series of tiers, as in the Candelabra primulas. Much more like the familiar candelabrum shape are several bold perennials and biennials with flowers arranged on branching stems.

◀ *Primula japonica*

Monarda 'Cambridge Scarlet'
Perennial H 90cm/3ft, S 45cm/18in Z4
Sun or partial shade Moist but well-drained soil

The bergamots get their common name from the scent of their foliage, which is said to resemble the bergamot orange. *Monarda didyma*, one of the parents of the hybrids, is sometimes known as Oswego tea and is used to make an infusion. The hybrids, which flower in the second half of summer, develop a base of aromatic pointed leaves, from which rise square stems carrying terminal whorls of hooded sage-like flowers. M. 'Cambridge Scarlet' is an old cultivar with flowers that are intense red, their colour intensified by purple-red calyces.

One of the darkest of them all is the mauve-purple 'Prärienacht', with green bracts tinted red. 'Beauty of Cobham' is a soft pink.

Primula japonica
Japanese primrose
Perennial H 60cm/2ft, S 45cm/18in Z5
Partial shade or sun Humus-rich, reliably moist, preferably neutral to acid soil

The Candelabra primulas are perennial species and hybrids characterized by the way they carry their flowers in a series of whorls on upright stems. They are moisture-loving plants that thrive in bog gardens but also flourish under trees and shrubs where the ground does not dry out.

The first of the Candelabra primulas to flower is *P. japonica*. In mid- to late spring stout stems rising from large pale green leaves carry as many as six whorls of magenta, pink or white flowers. A particularly fine form is 'Postford White', white but red-eyed.

P. pulverulenta, which follows in late spring and early summer, is of similar height but has more slender stems covered with white meal and ringed with several whorls of wine-red flowers. The Bartley hybrids derived from it are pale pink with red eyes.

In another colour range are Candelabra primulas such as the orange-flowered *P. bulleyana*, with a season in early summer, and the yellow-flowered and evergreen *P. prolifera* which follows it.

The Candelabra primulas are most effective in naturalistic plantings, ideally with different colour groups kept well apart.

▲ *Monarda* 'Prärienacht'

▲ *Salvia sclarea* var. *turkestaniana*

▲ *Verbascum olympicum*

Salvia sclarea var. *turkestaniana*
Biennial clary

Perennial/biennial H 1.2m/4ft Z5

Full sun Well-drained soil

Although this coarsely hairy and aromatic evergreen may persist for a few years, as a garden plant it is best treated as a biennial. In their first year plants develop a compact rosette of basal leaves. In the second year the rosette becomes a clump, from which rises a branched candelabrum carrying numerous hooded flowers that are white and mauve-purple, with purplish pink bracts. Flowering occurs in mid-summer but the bracts remain colourful after the flowers fade.

Biennial clary thrives in sunny and rather dry gardens, usually producing numerous seedlings. Those that are unwanted are easily removed.

Verbascum olympicum

Biennial H 2.2m/7ft, S 90cm/3ft Z6

Full sun Well-drained soil

In its first year this giant mullein produces a grey felted rosette 90cm/3ft or more across. In its second year a stout woolly stem surges skywards to form with lesser side shoots a candelabrum that is lit in summer by yellow flowers. Plants usually die after flowering even if this is delayed until the third year.

Many other mulleins produce markedly dominant spikes but in several of the hybrids there are sharply angled secondary stems below the strong vertical and their flowers open after those on the main stem. *Verbascum* 'Gainsborough', from the Cotswold Group, is in this mould and gives a season of saucer-shaped yellow flowers through most of summer. It is not long-lived. *V.* 'Helen Johnson' is evergreen and perennial with branched spikes up to 90cm/3ft high of unusual pink-brown flowers.

OTHER GOOD PLANTS

Leonotis leonurus Lion's ear
Medium-sized semi-evergreen or deciduous shrub producing in autumn and early winter erect stems carrying whorls of orange tubular and two-lipped flowers arranged in whorls.

Morina longifolia Whorlflower
Tall perennial making a rosette of aromatic spiny leaves and producing spikes of waxy flowers arranged in several tiers of whorls. The flowers are at first white but age to pink and red.

Onopordum acanthium
Giant biennial thistle making a large rosette of felted spiny leaves in the first year and in the second a white-felted candelabrum about 2.5m/8ft high holding mauve flowerheads. Self-seeds prolifically.

Phlomis russeliana: see p.49.

Sisyrinchium striatum 'Aunt May'
Evergreen perennial with stiff blade-like leaves variegated cream. In the first half of summer stiff stems up to 90cm/3ft tall carry clusters of cream stalkless flowers arranged in zigzagging tiers.

Veratrum nigrum
Majestic and long-lived perennial producing a fan of broad strongly pleated leaves from which rises in the second half of summer a branched plume about 1.2m/4ft high composed of numerous maroon or near-black starry flowers. Their smell is somewhat rank.

PLUMES & TAILS

The most theatrical of natural arrangements are those on upright stems that suggest plumes and bushy tails. Some of the perennials amongst these are very tall and make powerful accents in the garden but they have a grace and looseness that suggest free spirits rather than fixed sentinels.

▲ *Eremurus × isabellinus* 'Cleopatra'

▲ *Macleaya microcarpa* 'Kelway's Coral Plume'

▲ *Smilacina racemosa*

Astilbe 'Straussenfeder'
Perennial H 1.2m/4ft, S 90cm/3ft Z4
Sun or partial shade Humus-rich, moist, even boggy soil

The numerous astilbe hybrids show a strong family likeness but the way the tiny flowers are gathered together makes for several different styles of plume and there is considerable variation in scale. The colour range includes various shades of red and pink as well as cream and white. 'Straussenfeder' is one of the largest, a superlative example for late summer and early autumn with rich pink open plumes, the small flowers carried in arching sprays. This is a good foliage plant at any time and especially in spring, when the leaves are bronze-tinted.

A tall counterpart for mid-summer is 'Professor van der Wielen'. The mid-green foliage makes an attractive base for elegantly arching and open white plumes. Other tall *A. × arendsii* cultivars for early summer are the mauve-pink 'Amethyst' and the feathery and soft pink 'Venus'.

Early-flowering cultivars of medium size, rarely more than 60cm/2ft in height, include *A. × a.* 'Irrlicht', with stiff and dense white plumes, the rich crimson *A. × a.* 'Fanal', and *A.* 'Sprite', which has soft pink plumes that are spare and arching.

There are also short hybrids 20cm/8in or less in height. The summer-flowering *A. × crispa* 'Perkeo' has very dark foliage tinted bronze when young and narrow stiff plumes that are deep pink.

Eremurus × isabellinus 'Cleopatra'
Perennial H 3m/10ft, S 1.2m/4ft Z5
Full sun Well-drained soil

The foxtail lilies or desert candles are remarkable plants, found in the wild in near-desert conditions. They die down after their floral display in early to mid-summer, leaving awkward gaps, a problem compounded by the space needed for the starfish-shaped crown of fleshy roots. The more compact and shorter-growing species and hybrids are attractive alternatives to the tallest species. A number of hybrids are listed under *Eremurus × isabellinus*, most of which grow no more than 1.5m/5ft high. The plume of 'Cleopatra' is packed with yellow flowers, which open from the bottom up.

A species of medium height is *E. stenophyllus*. It grows to 90cm/3ft and has dark yellow flowers that turn orange-brown as they age.

There is no denying that, where the conditions are right and there is space, the giant among the species, *E. robustus*, makes a sensational impact. This native of the Tien Shan and Pamir mountains needs a cold winter period to flower well. A fine specimen can stand 3m/10ft tall and the foxtail flowerhead itself, densely packed with starry pink flowers, is as much as 1.2m/4ft long.

The plumes of the foxtail lilies are splendid as cut flowers.

Macleaya microcarpa 'Kelway's Coral Plume'
Perennial H 2.5m/8ft, S 90cm/3ft Z5

Full sun Moist but well-drained soil

Despite its impressive dimensions, this is a refined and graceful plant with very attractive large and lobed leaves that are grey-white on the underside. The roots tend to run so it needs plenty of space but rewards in early to mid-summer with large airy plumes of petal-less flowers that are apricot-pink in bud, buff-pink on opening.

Macleaya cordata is a similar species but does not spread so quickly at the roots. Its handsome leaves are grey-green and the plumes are creamy buff. A plant in the same vein is *M.* × *kewensis* 'Flamingo', which has pink plumes.

These giants are best planted in sheltered positions, as staking takes away from their elegance.

Smilacina racemosa
False spikenard
Perennial H 90cm/3ft, S 60cm/2ft Z4

Partial or deep shade Humus-rich, moist but well-drained neutral to acid soil

This is a handsome and unduly neglected plant for a cool corner or shady border. The strongly veined leaves are carried on arching stems and make a fresh green prelude to fluffy plumes of tiny creamy white flowers in the later half of spring or early summer. The flowers are sweetly scented. As they age they develop pink-brown tints. There are usually a few red berries to follow, provided different clones are grown in close proximity.

▲ *Astilbe* 'Straussenfeder'

OTHER GOOD PLANTS

Aruncus dioicus 'Kneiffii'
Compact version of the perennial goatsbeard with finely divided, almost shredded, leaves that form a lacy base to plumes of creamy flowers in mid-summer.

Celosia argentea Plumosa Group
Cultivars of a tropical annual grown as a bedding plant for their long-lasting pyramidal flowerheads, which are feathery and usually brightly coloured.

Cortaderia selloana Pampas grass
Perennial grass making large mounds of arching linear leaves (with cutting edges), through which, in late summer, tall flower stems rise to hold aloft large feathery plumes, those of 'Sunningdale Silver' being silvery white.

Cotinus coggyria Rubrifolius Group
These forms of the smoke bush make large deciduous shrubs that colour well in autumn and in summer produce frothy plumes of purplish pink flowers.

Liatris spicata Gayfeather
Perennial with grassy leaves and tall stems terminating in purplish pink plumes composed of numerous flowerheads, which open from the top down. 'Kobold' is compact and strongly coloured.

Miscanthus sinensis 'Silberfeder'
Perennial grass with elegant ribbon-like leaves and in autumn silver to beige-pink splayed plumes.

Pennisetum alopecuroides 'Hameln'
A form of the perennial fountain grass. From mid-summer wiry stems rise through the narrow leaves and arch over with cylindrical fuzzy bottlebrushes, at first greenish white with dark hairs but fading to grey-brown.

Rheum palmatum 'Atrosanguineum'
The large lobed and toothed leaves of this perennial open crinkled and red-purple and retain their vivid colour on the underside. In early summer stout branching stems carry large plumes of small purple-pink flowers.

Rodgersia aesculifolia
Large perennial with magnificent fingered leaves above which tower plumes of white to pink small flowers in mid-summer.

Sanguisorba obtusa
Japanese burnet
Medium-sized perennial with grey-green divided leaves and from mid-summer to early autumn pink bottlebrushes of small fluffy flowers.

CHAINS & TASSELS

Flowers arranged in hanging chains and tassels are sometimes curious but more often elegant additions to the garden. The magnificent chains of wisteria, the flowers arranged spirally on a trailing stem, need to be seen hanging free, and no climbers are more deserving of a large-scale pergola.

▲ *Garrya elliptica* 'James Roof'

▲ *Itea ilicifolia*

▲ *Wisteria sinensis*

Garrya elliptica 'James Roof'
Silk tassel tree

Evergreen shrub or tree H 4.5m/15ft, S 3m/10ft Z8

Sun or partial shade Well-drained soil

Because of its tenderness this fast-growing native of California and Oregon is often trained as a wall shrub in areas that experience winter frosts. Its wavy-edged leaves are sombrely handsome throughout the year but it is for the silver-grey and silky winter catkins of male plants that it is worth wall space.

The catkins start to develop in late summer and by early winter in the clone *Garrya elliptica* 'James Roof' can be about 30cm/1ft long. On a still day they hang elegantly but sway gracefully when stirred by a breeze. The less interesting catkins of female plants are followed by bunches of purplish berries.

Prune wall-trained specimens after flowering to control growth and to remove frost-damaged shoots.

Itea ilicifolia

Evergreen shrub H 3.7m/12ft, S 3m/10ft Z7

Full sun Moist but well-drained soil

The small genus *Itea* is most commonly represented in gardens by this species, which is a native of western China. Where the conditions are mild enough it makes a handsome evergreen that, at a quick glance you might take for a holly on account of its glossy dark green leaves edged with spines.

In the second half of summer catkin-like streamers up to 30cm/1ft long dangle from the arching stems. Densely clustered along the streamers are tiny greenish white flowers that exhale a honeyed scent. On the plant they remain attractive for many weeks. The streamers make an unusual addition to cut flowers.

This can be grown as a free-standing shrub but in frost-prone areas it needs a sheltered position and is best lightly trained against a wall. Avoid excessive pruning but in early spring trim back any growths that have suffered frost damage.

Laburnum × watereri 'Vossii'

Deciduous tree H and S 7.5m/25ft Z6

Full sun Well-drained soil

The common name golden rain, often given to the two species of laburnums and their hybrid, refers to the dangling chains of yellow pea flowers produced by these deciduous trees in late spring or early summer. 'Vossii' is a free-flowering form of the hybrid L. × watereri noted for its trailing sprays, which can be as much as 50cm/20in long. It can be grown as a specimen tree or trained on an arbour or pergola so that the flower chains dangle freely.

Spur-prune plants trained on supports to encourage flowering by cutting back to within a few buds of older wood in early winter.

Laburnums are not suitable for gardens where there are young children because all parts, especially the seeds, are highly poisonous.

Wisteria sinensis
Chinese wisteria

Deciduous climber H 9m/30ft, S 6m/20ft Z5

Sun or partial shade Moist but well-drained soil

The vigorous twining Asiatic wisterias trail magnificent streamer-like racemes of pea flowers in late spring and early summer. The most widely grown species is the Chinese wisteria, with stems that twine anti-clockwise and large leaves composed of numerous leaflets. The fragrant flowers, usually purplish blue but white in W. sinensis 'Alba', hang in racemes that are up to 30cm/1ft long, all the flowers in a spray opening almost simultaneously. There are usually a few more sprays in late summer and in some years the flowers are followed by velvety seed pods.

W. floribunda is similar but twines clockwise, and flowers slightly later, and in each raceme the flowers open in succession, those at the tip last. The most spectacular cultivar is 'Multijuga' with purplish blue flowers in streamers that can be 90cm/3ft or more long. The racemes of 'Alba' are usually about 60cm/2ft long, their white flowers sometimes lightly tinted mauve.

Train in the stems of young wisterias to form a framework and thereafter prune regularly in summer and again in winter to encourage the development of short flowering spurs.

▲ Laburnum × watereri 'Vossii'

OTHER GOOD PLANTS

Amaranthus caudatus
Love-lies-bleeding
Large bushy perennial grown as annual for the curious chenille-like tassels, up to 60cm/2ft long, that dangle from the stems in summer and early autumn. These are composed of tiny crimson-purple flowers. The tassels of 'Viridis' are green then chartreuse-cream. Suitable for cutting and drying.

Chiastophyllum oppositifolium
Succulent evergreen perennial suitable for part shade in a rock garden, bearing tassels of yellow flowers in late spring/early summer.

Corylopsis sinensis var. *sinensis* **'Spring Purple'**
Deciduous shrub for woodland conditions growing to 3m/10ft and carrying tassels of scented yellow flowers in spring, followed by purplish copper young leaves.

Corylus avellana 'Contorta'
Corkscrew hazel,
Harry Lauder's walking stick
Large deciduous shrub with twisted branches and twigs from which dangle yellow catkins in late winter and early spring. Valued for cutting.

Leycesteria formosa
Himalayan honeysuckle
Deciduous shrub making a thicket of stiff stems, attractively blue-green when young. In summer and early autumn white flowers hang among dangling chains of long-lasting red-purple bracts.

Lotus berthelotii: see p.53.

Stachyurus praecox **'Magpie'**
Medium-sized deciduous shrub with stiff tassels of yellow bells which appear in early spring before the prettily variegated leaves develop.

CLOUDS, GARLANDS & CASCADES

The weightless mass of spring blossom, particularly that of flowering cherries, ranks among the most generous displays the garden can produce. Lax plants loaded with flowers garland man-made and living supports. Some plants that flower generously seem more earthbound, the flowers lying in sheets or falling in tiered cascades.

▲ *Prunus 'Shirotae'*

Clematis montana

Deciduous woody climber H 10m/30ft, S 6m/20ft Z6

Sun or partial shade with the base in shade

Humus-rich, moist but well-drained soil

In late spring or early summer this vigorous clematis garlands walls, fences, pergolas, arbours and large trees with clusters of flowers bursting from every joint. It is worth obtaining a named cultivar as the flowers of seedlings are sometimes of indifferent quality. The flowers are usually 5–10cm/2–4in across, white or pink and sometimes scented. One of the most vigorous is *C. montana* f. *grandiflora*, which has dark foliage and white flowers with cream anthers.

The various forms of var. *rubens* have purple-tinted leaves and pink flowers, those of 'Tetrarose' being scented, and conspicuous bosses of yellow anthers.

The evergreen *C. armandii*, which flowers even earlier in spring, is also vigorous and covers its support with scented white stars. The leaves of the cultivar 'Apple Blossom' are tinged bronze when young and its white flowers open from pink buds. This species and its cultivars need a sunny sheltered position.

Prunus 'Shirotae'

Deciduous tree H 6m/20ft, S 7.5m/25ft Z5

Full sun Moist but well-drained soil

The clouds of blossom produced by the ornamental cherries provide a relatively brief but spectacular billowing spring display. The single or semi-double lightly fragrant flowers of *Prunus* 'Shirotae' (often listed as 'Mount Fuji') is a wide-spreading small tree with somewhat drooping branches carrying masses of snowy single or semi-double fragrant flowers in mid-spring. Their whiteness is freshened by the light green of young leaves.

'Shôgetsu', which flowers slightly later, has pink-budded semi-double flowers that open white. Among the last to flower is 'Kiku-shidare-zakura', a small weeping tree with bright pink double flowers among bronzed leaves.

The foliage of these ornamental cherries often takes on rich colours in autumn.

See also *P.* 'Jô-nioi', p.141.

▲ *Clematis montana* var. *rubens*

▲ *Rosa* 'Félicité Perpétue'

▲ *Spiraea* 'Arguta'

Rosa 'Félicité Perpétue'

Deciduous woody climber (Rambler rose) H 6m/20ft, S 3m/10ft Z6

Full sun Moist but well-drained soil

The long flexible canes of the Rambler roses weave among the stems of other climbers or work their way through the branches of living supports. Although most do not repeat, their cascading profusion of flowers is a glorious feature in early and mid-summer. Some are not too vigorous for gardens of moderate size, suitable for a pergola or for training into an old apple tree. The almost evergreen 'Félicité Perpétue' produces masses of lightly scented small double flowers that are stained crimson in bud and are almost pompon-shaped when open.

Another Rambler of moderate size is 'The Garland'. Its scented semi-double flowers fade from blush to white and are followed by small red hips.

Many other Ramblers are more vigorous, among them the ultimate giant *R. filipes* 'Kiftsgate', with masses of small and creamy white flowers that perfume the garden. Its explosive energy is almost matched by that of *R.* 'Paul's Himalayan Musk': this demands a sturdy large tree for support, which it will festoon with fragrant blush-pink double flowers.

Prune these Ramblers as soon as flowering has finished, removing some of the old canes.

See also *R.* 'Bobbie James', p.145.

Spiraea 'Arguta'
Bridal wreath, foam of May

Deciduous shrub H and S 2.5m/8ft Z4

Full sun Moist but well-drained soil

The common names say it all. In mid- to late spring the arching wiry stems of this easy-to-grow shrub bear tiny white flowers clustered all along their length. Light green narrow leaves keep the plant looking fresh throughout the summer. Other spiraeas that bear masses of small white flowers in spring or early summer include *S. nipponica*, *S. thunbergii* and *S.* × *vanhouttei*. Prune immediately after flowering.

OTHER GOOD PLANTS

Buddleja alternifolia
Deciduous shrub best trained as a short weeping standard on a stem about 1.8m/6ft high. In early summer its long trailing stems are wreathed with clusters of tiny mauve-purple flowers the whole of their length, making a scented cascade.

Ceanothus 'Cascade'
Large evergreen shrub suitable for wall training. In late spring or early summer the arching branches are loaded with long-stalked clusters of tiny bright blue flowers.

Exocorda × *macrantha* 'The Bride'
Lax deciduous shrub, its arching branches garlanded with white flowers in late spring.

Fuchsia 'Riccartonii'
Deciduous shrub, suitable for a hedge where the climate is mild enough. Its pointed leaves are dark green, sometimes bronze-tinted, and from early summer to autumn the arching stems carry showers of small dangling flowers that are crimson with a purple skirt.

Gypsophila paniculata
Baby's breath
Once the indispensable cut flower to add to summer arrangements of carnations, sweet peas and their like, its airy mass of small white flowers makes a pretty and weightless filler in the garden or in a vase. 'Bristol Fairy' has quaint double flowers that are long-lasting.

Kolkwitzia amabilis 'Pink Cloud'
Deciduous shrub growing to about 3m/10ft with gracefully arching stems loaded with yellow-throated pink flowers in late spring and early summer.

Pieris japonica: see p.88.

Solanum laxum 'Album'
Vigorous evergreen or semi-evergreen climber that will ramble through and over a large shrub or tree, showering sprays of pure white flowers over an exceptionally long period in summer and autumn.

Tropaeolum speciosum: see p.102.

Viburnum plicatum f. *tomentosum* 'Mariesii'
Deciduous shrub growing to about 3m/10ft with spreading horizontal branches. In late spring lacy flower clusters, composed of a mixture of sterile and fertile florets, look like layers of creamy snow caught in the tiers.

SPHERES, DOMES & PLATES

At their best these densely packed arrangements of flowers are powerful, well-defined shapes and blocks of colour that stand out conspicuously from a background of foliage and looser masses of flower. Many have the advantage of being long-lasting.

▲ *Achillea filipendulina* 'Gold Plate'

▲ *Allium* 'Globemaster'

Achillea filipendulina 'Gold Plate'
Perennial H 1.2m/4ft, S 45cm/18in Z3
Full sun Moist but well-drained soil

Many perennials in the yarrow family produce almost flat plates or domes composed of numerous daisy flowerheads. They are long-lasting in the garden, cut well and in many cases hold their colour if carefully dried. This classic border perennial is a stiff-stemmed plant and has gamboge-yellow domed discs up to 15cm/6in across in summer. A shorter alternative is *Achillea* 'Coronation Gold' with rich yellow flowerheads. Preferable to these for subtle colour schemes is 'Taygetea', with a combination of silver-grey feathery foliage and cool yellow flowerheads standing about 60cm/2ft high.

There is a broader range of colours in the domed heads of the Galaxy Hybrids, all ferny-leaved perennials growing to 45–90cm/18–36in high and flowering in summer. 'Hoffnung' is biscuit-cream, 'Lachsschönheit' soft salmon pink and 'Wesersandstein' red and pink shading to cream.

Allium 'Globemaster'
Bulb H 90cm/3ft, S 20cm/8in Z4
Full sun Well-drained soil

Allium 'Globemaster' is one of the most consistent and dramatic performers among the many ornamental onions that produce spherical heads packed with many starry flowers. The sphere, supported by a stout purplish red stem, can be up to 25cm/10in across and the flowers, which are produced in early summer before the strap-shaped leaves wither, are rich violet-purple. The dried brown heads are excellent for winter arrangements.

Many other alliums that flower in early summer do well in sunny well-drained beds. The spectacularly tall *A. giganteum* can be more than 1.5m/5ft tall and its heads of purple-pink flowers are about 10cm/4in across. The globes of *A. hollandicum* 'Purple Sensation', intermediate in height between these two, are of similar size but the flowers are of an intense violet-purple. See also *A. cristophii*, p.20.

▲ *Echinops ritro*

▲ *Hydrangea aspera* Villosa Group

Echinops ritro

Perennial H 1.2m/4ft, S 60cm/2ft Z3

Full sun Well-drained soil

The typical globe thistle has grey-backed and jagged prickly leaves, through which rise stiff-stemmed drumsticks, the spherical heads packed with nectar-rich flowers that attract bees and moths to the garden. The drumsticks make dramatic accents in borders during late summer, are good for cutting and can be dried. The heads of *Echinops ritro* are prickly and metallic blue at first, richer blue when the flowers open.

Slightly taller are 'Veitch's Blue', a strong-coloured cultivar, and subsp. *ruthenicus*, bright blue with the stems and undersides of leaves conspicuously white. Slightly larger again is *E. bannaticus* 'Taplow Blue'.

The grey-stemmed *E. sphaerocephalus* is a coarser and larger plant with grey stems carrying grey-white spherical heads to a height of 1.8m/6ft or more.

Hydrangea aspera Villosa Group

Deciduous shrub H and S4m/13ft Z7

Partial shade or sun Humus-rich, moist but well-drained soil

Hydrangeas with flattened heads consisting of a centre packed with small fertile flowers surrounded by larger sterile florets are described as lacecaps. This wide-spreading shrub is an exceptional example, producing its lacecap heads in late summer. It has velvety leaves and the domed flowerheads, as much as 25cm/10in across, have purplish blue or blue fertile flowers in the centre surrounded by pale mauve or mauve-pink sterile florets.

Like the mophead hydrangeas (see below), the flower colour of the lacecap forms of *H. macrophylla* is influenced by the acid/alkaline balance of the soil. On a suitable acid soil, preferably in dappled shade, the vigorous 'Mariesii Perfecta' is one of the best, and a good clear blue, the sterile florets making a paler circlet around the richly coloured dome of fertile flowers. 'Mariesii Lilacina' is a tougher cultivar, accepting sun or shade, with flowerheads varying from rich mauve-pink to blue, the paler ray florets with prettily toothed edges. 'White Wave' has blue to pink fertile flowers and white florets. All these grow to about 1.8m/6ft.

Outstanding among lacecaps of compact growth is *H. serrata* 'Bluebird', a deciduous shrub that grows to about 1.2m/4ft. The blue dome of the fertile flowers is surrounded by large sterile florets that are blue-green on acid soils and red-purple where the soil is alkaline.

Hydrangea macrophylla 'Générale Vicomtesse de Vibraye'

Deciduous shrub H 1.5m/5ft, S 2.5m/8ft Z6

Partial shade or sun Humus-rich, moist but well-drained soil; in containers

soil-based compost (John Innes No. 3)

The Hortensias or mopheaded hydrangeas come into their own in the second half of summer, when dome-shaped or spherical flowerheads of large sterile florets make blobs on the rounded bushes. The colours are white, pink, red and blue and sometimes a combination of these colours, soil chemistry determining the blue or pink bias. In autumn, particularly if the weather is dry, the florets often develop metallic lustres and complex shades that can be retained if the heads are dried.

There are many cultivars to chose from. *H. macrophylla* 'Générale Vicomtesse de Vibraye' is clear blue on acid soils but purplish to pink in soils that are more alkaline. 'Altona', which can be a good deep pink, is a compact cultivar in a similar colour range. 'Soeur Thérèse', with flatter heads than most, is white.

Similar in style to these is the dark-stemmed hybrid *H.* 'Preziosa', which has purple-tinted young foliage. The pale ray florets pass through several shades of pink or mauve to deep red or purple-blue according to the soil.

A more extravagant plant than any of these is *H. arborescens* 'Annabelle'. It grows to about 2.5m/8ft and in summer carries corpulent greenish white flowerheads that are up to 30cm/1ft across.

Sedum 'Herbstfreude'

Perennial H and S 60cm/2ft Z4

Full sun Well-drained soil

This stonecrop gives value over many months, starting early with rosettes of fleshy grey-green leaves. The flat heads of tightly packed starry flowers open pink from green waxy buds and in autumn work through shades of copper-pink and bronze-red before giving way to brown seedheads.

The ice plant (*Sedum spectabile*) is in the same mould, with some cultivars such as the deep red-pink 'Septemberglut' having richly coloured flowerheads. Those of 'Iceberg' are greenish white.

S. 'Vera Jameson', a much shorter plant for the front of a border or rock garden, has fleshy purple leaves and loose domed heads of purplish pink flowers. 'Ruby Glow' is a similar hybrid with wine-red flowers.

Rhododendron 'Hydon Dawn'

Evergreen shrub H 1.5m/5ft, S 2.5m/8ft Z6

Sun or partial shade Humus-rich, moist, neutral to acid soil

Many evergreen rhododendrons have their flowers arranged in domed clusters, the trusses often packed densely among the dark leaves. 'Hydon Dawn' is a popular dwarf hybrid with leaves covered with creamy hairs when young. From mid-spring to early summer the bushes are covered by frilled funnel-shaped flowers, tightly gathered in trusses. They open pink, fading to near white.

A parent of this and many other compact hybrids is *R. yakushimanum*. The clone 'Koichiro Wada' is itself one of the finest small rhododendrons. The leaves are dark green with, on the underside, a white felt that darkens to buff. The pink buds, held in upright clusters, open in mid-spring to form a domed truss of bell-shaped flowers that fade from pink to white.

Among large rhododendrons flowering in early summer 'Loderi King George' is one of the most impressive when covered by trusses of white ruffled trumpets, which open from pink buds. The flowers are fragrant. 'Polar Bear', another large shrub or small tree, is one of the last hybrids to flower, often not until late summer. It too carries large trusses of fragrant white trumpets, which are pale green in the throat.

See also *R.* 'Sappho', p.129.

Viburnum opulus 'Roseum'
Snowball tree

Deciduous shrub H and S 4m/13ft Z3

Sun or partial shade Moist but well-drained soil

The guelder rose, of which this is a sterile form, is an easily pleased shrub with maple-like leaves that colour well in autumn. Its flowerheads are like scaled-down versions of lacecap hydrangeas and are followed by eye-catching red fruit. By contrast the sterile form has spherical heads as much as 15cm/6in across of white or green-tinted flowers, which often become pink with age. It is noted for the rich colours of the leaves in autumn.

OTHER GOOD PLANTS

Acacia dealbata
Mimosa, silver wattle
Evergreen tree or large shrub with grey-green to silvery leaves and sprays of small spherical flowerheads that are yellow and scented.

Agapanthus hybrids: see p.32.

Buddleja globosa **Orange ball tree**
Large semi-evergreen shrub. In early summer numerous orange-yellow ball-like flowerheads contrast with the deep green foliage. The flowers are scented.

Gomphrena globosa
Globe amaranth
Bushy annual producing colourful egg-shaped flowerheads throughout summer. The colour is in the bracts and the flowerheads dry well.

Heliotropium arborescens: see p.145.

Hydrangea anomala
subsp. *petiolaris*
Self-clinging deciduous climber easily capable of exceeding 10m/30ft. It is summer-flowering, with flattened domes of white fertile and sterile florets.

Kalmia latifolia: see p.25.

Pelargonium **Maverick Series**
Seed strain of Zonal pelargoniums grown as annuals. The domed heads of single flowers are white or in shades of pink and red. Many other pelargoniums bear flowers in domed heads.

Primula denticulata
Drumstick primula
Perennial making a rosette of pale green leaves from which rise lightly powdered stems carrying globular heads packed with small mauve flowers, white in var. *alba*. Good spring plant for a moist corner in a rockery or the edge of a pool.

P. Gold-laced Group: see p.133.

Verbena bonariensis
Tall and angular perennial, best as a colony, with wiry branching stems supporting small domes of scented purple flowers. Seeds itself freely in sunny gardens with well-drained soil.

Viburnum carlesii: see p.145.

CLOCKWISE FROM TOP LEFT ▶
Hydrangea macrophylla 'Générale Vicomtesse de Vibraye'
Rhododendron 'Hydon Dawn'
Viburnum opulus 'Roseum'
Sedum 'Herbstfreude'

INDEX References in **bold** are to illustrations

ZONES

Zone	Celsius°	Farenheit°
1	below -45	below -50
2	-45 to -40	-50 to -40
3	-40 to -35	-40 to -30
4	-35 to -29	-30 to -20
5	-29 to -23	-20 to -10
6	-23 to -18	-10 to 0
7	-18 to -12	0 to 10
8	-12 to -6	10 to 20
9	-6 to -1	20 to 30
10	-1 to 5	30 to 40

HARDINESS ZONES

The hardiness zone ratings allocated to plants are based on the zones of average annual minimum temperature devised by the United States Department of Agriculture, and suggest the approximate minimum temperature the plant will tolerate in winter. However, this can only be a rough guide, as hardiness depends on many factors, including the depth of a plant's roots, the duration of cold weather, the force of wind and the temperatures encountered during the preceding summer. Good or bad soil drainage is also important.

ACKNOWLEDGMENTS

AUTHOR'S ACKNOWLEDGMENTS

I gratefully acknowledge that in writing this book I am heavily indebted to many gardeners and writers on gardening for information on plants. I also owe thanks to those responsible for the inspired plantings of the many gardens I have been fortunate enough to see. My selection of plants has been much influenced by these gardens. Of the people at Frances Lincoln who have played a role in the production of this book I would like to express my special thanks to the following: Anne Askwith, Jo Christian, Becky Clarke and Anne Fraser. I am also grateful to my agents at Limelight Management, to Dr Tony Lord and to Penny David.

PHOTOGRAPHIC ACKNOWLEDGMENTS

a = above, b = below, c = centre, l = left, r = right

Val Bourne 34r
Jonathan Buckley 87, 139c
Garden Picture Library/John Glover 22cl; Christopher Fairweather 24, 69c, 102r–103l;
 Howard Rice 27b, 33c, 53c, 103r, 110l, 115, 160c; J.S. Sira 37cr, 54r, 70l, 86l;
 Clive Nichols 39l; Mark Bolton 49ar; David Askham 50l; Brian Carter 62al;
 Densey Clyne 63; A.I. Lord 71; Neil Holmes 75a, 161; Chris Burrows 114br, 122l, 126r;
 Mel Watson 116c; Sunniva Harte 122r, 132al, 142r; Linda Burgess 123b;
 Didier Willery 128l; David Cavagnaro 130c; Ron Evans 144l; Rowan Isaac 163
John Glover 18a, 19a, 22l, 25c, 28l, 30br, 37br, 44l, 46l, 58, 59a, 72l, 86r, 89al, 96ar, 97,
 99br, 101l, 124, 125l, 126c, 134–5, 139l, 146c, 152b, 156, 166l, 169al, 169ar
Andrew Lawson 1, 2, 4, 5, 6–7 (garden), 11 (garden), 12–13 (garden), 14–15, 18b, 19b,
 20, 21, 22cr, 22r, 23, 25l, 25r, 26, 27a, 28c, 28r, 29, 30l, 30ar, 32, 33a, 33b, 34l, 35, 37l,
 37ar, 38, 39c, 39r, 40–1, 44r, 45, 46c, 46r, 47, 48, 49al, 49b, 50c, 50r, 51, 52, 53l, 53r,
 54l, 55, 56, 57, 59b, 61al, 61cl, 61r, 62c, 62b, 68, 69a, 69b, 70c, 70r, 72r, 73, 74, 75c,
 75b, 76, 77, 82, 83, 84, 85, 86c, 89bl, 89ar, 89bl, 90, 91, 92–3, 96l, 96br, 98, 99ar, 100,
 101c, 101r, 102l, 104l, 104c, 105, 106, 107l, 108, 109, 110c, 110r, 111, 112, 113, 114a,
 114br, 116l, 116r, 117, 118–9, 123a, 125r, 126l, 127, 128c, 128r, 129, 130l, 130r, 131,
 132br, 133, 138, 139r, 140, 141, 142l, 143, 144r, 145, 146l, 146r, 147, 148–9, 152a, 153,
 154, 157, 158, 159, 160l, 160r, 162, 164, 165c, 165r, 166r, 167, 169bl, 169br
Marianne Majerus 61bl, 104r, 107r, 132bl, 165l